To Angela / Tina
Great to be
God bless in
marriage!. Eel.

AUGUSTINE

as

MENTOR

A Model for Preparing

Spiritual Leaders

EDWARD L. SMITHER

B&H
ACADEMIC
Nashville, Tennessee

Printed in the United States of America

ISBN: 978-0-8054-4707-1

Published by B&H Publishing Group
Nashville, Tennessee

Dewey Decimal Classification: 303.3
Subject Heading: LEADERSHIP, MENTORING,
SPIRITUAL LIFE

Unless otherwise indicated, all Scripture passages are taken from the New American Standard Bible, © the Lockman Foundation, 1960, 1962, 1963, 1968, 1971, 1972, 1973, 1975, 1977; used by permission.

1 2 3 4 5 6 7 8 9 10 11 12 • 17 16 15 14 13 12 11 10 09
VP

Contents

Preface

ow could a fifth-century African bishop be relevant to the twenty-first century? Judging by the amount of scholarship generated each year in English alone, Augustine of Hippo (354–430) continues to pique the curiosity of professors and students of philosophy, theology, and history. While the vast majority of Augustinian studies are in those disciplines, my reading and study of Augustine has impressed me with the quality of his pastoral ministry and theology, an area largely missed by many fine scholars. After all, pastoring the church of Hippo was his "day job" for some 40 years! Even more, Augustine was also a pastor to spiritual leaders in his day—bishops, presbyters, deacons, and others who occupied clerical offices in the African church and beyond.

This study is concerned with mentoring spiritual leaders, that is, shepherding those who shepherd the Lord's flock. After laying the foundation for mentoring in the New Testament and interacting with exemplary models in the early church period, most of this book will analyze and articulate Augustine's approach to mentoring church leaders. While carefully considering Augustine's own journey as a disciple and the contributions of those who mentored him, I will show his most prevalent methods or forms of mentoring. From this evidence I will make an argument for his principles and convictions for mentoring spiritual leaders.

Many pastors today, especially in the West, are struggling in isolation without a pastor to nurture their souls. Sadly many of these, unless they encounter a radical change, will not finish the race. Augustine might just convince them that they, too, need a shepherd as they shepherd others. In the same vein may other pastors learn from Augustine and reach out to other pastors, especially those who are just starting out in ministry. Augustine's approach to mentoring will surely provide a practical model for how to mentor others. Finally, for students of church history and followers of Jesus, Augustine's early church model for mentoring ought to give some inspiration and direction for what it means to be a disciple of Jesus and an active participant in his body.

Because of the mentoring focus in this book, the reader should beware that at times I employ some rather unorthodox "verbage" to make my point. Most notably this includes terms such as "resourcing" (to serve as a spiritual and practice resource) and "releasing" (consecrating or setting apart leaders to ministry).

Finally, let me offer a word on the limitations of this work. In dealing with Augustine's pastoral theology, I interact with his thought and development in a number of practical, philosophical, and theological areas. However, this book does not attempt to evaluate the appropriateness of his views on theological issues such as predestination, sacramental grace, baptismal regeneration, church polity, papal authority, clerical celibacy, monasticism, relics, miracles, and the Donatist controversy.

It would have been impossible to complete this project without the help of some key people in my life. I am indebted to Thomas O'Loughlin, my doctoral supervisor at the University of Wales-Lampeter, who mentored me through my doctoral thesis on Augustine with both rigor and encouragement. Jim Blunk, my former graduate assistant at Liberty Baptist Theological Seminary, provided a fresh set of eyes and helpful feedback on the manuscript. I am grateful for the opportunity to publish with B&H and to work with fine editors like John Landers and Ray Clendenen. As I work best in the anonymous yet public coffee shop context, I am also thankful for coffee shop owners in Tunis, Paris, London, Oxford, Lampeter, and Lynchburg who served great coffee and allowed me to office on their premises. Finally, I wish to thank my wife Shawn, who encouraged me to pursue this dream and allowed me protected time to write and do research.

Edward L. Smither

Abbreviations

ACW	Ancient Christian Writers
ATTA	*Augustine Through the Ages: An Encyclopedia.* Alan Fitzgerald, ed. Grand Rapids, MI: Wm. B. Eerdmans, 1999.
ep. (epp.)	*Epistulae,* Augustine
FC	Fathers of the Church
JBL	*Journal of Biblical Literature*
JECS	*Journal of Early Christian Studies*
JTS	*Journal of Theological Studies*
NBD	*New Bible Dictionary*, 2nd edition. J. D. Douglas and N. Hillyer, eds. Downers Grove, IL 1982.
TU	Texte und Untersuchungen
WSA	*Works of Saint Augustine: A Translation for the 21st Century*

Chapter One

MENTORING IN THE
FIRST CENTURY

urelius Augustinus (354–430) lived well, and his legacy
lives on today. His thought—carefully preserved in books,
sermons, and letters—has impacted theologians such as
John Calvin (1509–1564), the Arab historian Ibn Khaldoun (1332–
1406), and virtually every amateur and professional philosopher of
the last 1,500 years. His contribution continues to stimulate scholarship today in those fields of study. He was a prolific writer who
authored more than 100 books, most of which were composed after
a long day at work as the bishop of the church of Hippo Regius
(present-day Annaba, Algeria).[1] His genius is even more significant because he grew up in a family of modest resources in Tagaste
(Souk Ahras, Algeria), a rather insignificant town in Roman Africa
far from the cultivated learning centers of the Roman Empire.[2]

Although his thought and eloquence are well lauded, I find his
person, character, and ministry even more remarkable. He had a
sincere faith that remained consistent and passionate from the time
of his conversion in Italy in 386 until his death in Hippo some 44

---

[1] Possidius, *Life of Augustine* 27; all English translations are from John E. Rotelle, ed.,
Life of Saint Augustine (Villanova, PA: Augustinian, 1988).
[2] *Sermon* 356.13.

years later.[3] Yet, unlike the eremitic monks who fled the world for the solitude of the desert, this African pastor was always in the company of friends. He made his profession of faith, something regarded in the present day as highly personal, in the presence of a close friend.[4] At the monastery in Hippo, where he and other clergy and laymen lived, he deliberately left his door open to visitors, and his table was set with extra places.[5] In short, his life was characterized by friendship.

My particular interest relates to the impact Augustine had on other spiritual leaders of his day. Robert Clinton defines a spiritual leader as "a person with a God-given capacity and a God-given responsibility to influence a specific group of God's people toward His purposes for the group."[6] In Augustine's day spiritual leaders included bishops, priests, and deacons as well as subdeacons, acolytes, and readers.[7] As leaders they were men set apart to serve the people of God and carry out the responsibilities of the church. The present inquiry will consider how Augustine influenced these leaders in their training and preparation for ministry. My contention is that Augustine effectively mentored spiritual leaders and set them apart for needed ministries in the church and that many aspects of his mentoring will serve as instructive for the modern mentor. While he did not leave behind a particular manual for how to be a spiritual leader, his example and writings provide significant evidence toward understanding his principles of mentoring.

I am primarily writing for modern-day pastors and spiritual leaders who want to mentor and equip others. In evangelical Christian circles, where I tend most to frequent, mentoring and training has gained increased importance in recent years.[8] The large number of books, seminars, stadium events, prayer breakfasts, and fishing

---

3 *Confessions* 1.1; *Soliloquies* 1.1.5; also George Lawless, *Augustine of Hippo and His Monastic Rule* (New York: Oxford University Press, 1989), 34–35.

4 *Confessions* 8.8.19; 11.27; 12.30.

5 *Sermon* 355.2; *Letter* 38.2; Possidius, *Life of Augustine* 22.2, 6; also Frederick van der Meer, *Augustine the Bishop*, trans. B. Battershaw and G. R. Lamb (London: Sheed & Ward, 1961), 239.

6 Robert Clinton, *The Making of a Leader* (Colorado Springs: NavPress, 1988), 245.

7 See Lee Bacchi, *The Theology of the Ordained Ministry in the Letters of Augustine of Hippo* (San Francisco: International Scholars, 1998), 68.

8 See Robert Clinton and P. Stanley, *Connections: The Mentoring Relationships You Need to Succeed in Life* (Colorado Springs: NavPress, 1992), 18.

trips testify to an increased emphasis on mentoring. The present generation of pastors seems to be more interested in matters of the heart like integrity, humility, faithfulness, personal holiness, spiritual hunger, and service than the skills normally associated with ministry—preaching, evangelizing, teaching, administrating, and visiting. As a vast store of wisdom and insight lies preserved in the story of the early Christian movement, I believe that Augustine has something to offer modern ministers pursuing authenticity and longing to practice what they preach. Through his thought, practice, success, and even failures, my hope is that today's mentors will find hope, inspiration, and practical suggestions for how to mentor an emerging generation of spiritual leaders.

I should note what I will and will not address. First, I only intend to focus on Augustine's spiritual formation of men who were spiritual leaders occupying a clerical office. This does not mean that he did not have an edifying impact on women, particularly the nuns and virgins. Though women who serve as spiritual leaders will find points of relevant application, the case studies will be limited to Augustine's relationship with men.

A second limit is that this study will not address how Augustine discipled the general congregation in Hippo—a ministry that is clear through his recorded sermons, catechisms, letters, legal judgments, and advice. Besides his congregation Augustine also influenced other laymen through his correspondence, including letters to "servants of God"—religious men and women who had abandoned the secular world to become servants of God.[9]

The evidence surrounding Augustine's life reveals a deeply personal and passionate man who was committed to people and friendship. As a servant of the church, his thoughts, which were dictated into books and letters and formulated into sermons, served to edify the church in Hippo, Africa, and beyond. In light of what we already know about Augustine, a focused study on his approach to mentoring spiritual leaders is a valuable contribution to the study of mentoring, discipleship, and spiritual formation in the early church that has

---

[9] See Daniel Doyle, *The Bishop as Disciplinarian in the Letters of St. Augustine* (New York: Lang, 2002), 368.

much relevance for today. So let us begin to consider the life of one we should "emulate and imitate in this world."[10]

What Is Mentoring?

Though the term itself has only come into vogue in North America in recent years, the concept of mentoring is an ancient one. In certain African cultures, mentoring has referred to a boy becoming a man, a young man learning a skill like playing a drum, or a novice apprenticing under a master in a trade like carpentry. Milavec cites examples in Greek culture of novices being mentored in basket weaving, hunting with a bow, or pottery making.[11] Today in America mentoring has become synonymous with counseling, advising, training, coaching, and apprenticeship while some contexts include trades, sports, education, and the fine arts. Though the contexts and the cultures may vary, mentoring in essence means that a master, expert, or someone with significant experience is imparting knowledge and skill to a novice in an atmosphere of discipline, commitment, and accountability.

In light of the inherent need for mentoring or discipleship in Christianity, it seems best to work toward a model of mentoring by focusing on early texts, mostly from the New Testament, that largely show Jesus and Paul mentoring men at the outset of the Christian movement.[12] The remainder of this chapter will be concerned with offering an early Christian model for mentoring that will also provide a historical background for mentoring in the church prior to Augustine's ministry.

Mentoring in Early Christian Writings

Although no exact equivalent for the term *mentoring* exists in the New Testament and early Christian texts, there are, however, some

---

[10] Possidius, *Life of Augustine* 31.11.

[11] See Aaron Milavec, *The Didache: Text, Translation, Analysis and Commentary* (Collegeville, MN: Liturgical, 2003), 47; and Michael Wilkins, *The Concept of a Disciple in Matthew's Gospel: As Reflected in the Use of the Term Mathētēs* (Leiden: Brill, 1988), 34.

[12] Some reflection on early Christian mentoring will be gleaned from the *Didache*.

associated words that work together to express the concept. For example, we find verbs like "make disciples" (*mathēteuō*), "teach" (*didaskō*), "train" (*didaxō*), "be sound" (*hugiainō*), and "follow" (*akaloutheō*), as well as nouns like "disciple" (*mathētēs*), "teacher" (*didaskalos*), "imitator" (*mimētēs*), and "training" (*didachē*). With a primary emphasis on the notion of "disciple" (*mathētēs*), let us consider the key mentoring-related words that specifically tell us about a disciple's belief and conduct.

Mathētēs

Though "make disciples" (*mathēteuō*) is found only a few times in the New Testament, the most significant occurrence seems to be in Matthew's account of Jesus' final commission to the Twelve: "Go therefore and make disciples of all the nations."[13] On the contrary, the noun *mathētēs* is found 264 times in the four Gospel accounts and Acts and occurs in its plural form (*mathētai*) in 239 of these instances.[14] Hence, its significant repetition in only five books strongly suggests that "disciple" was an important concept for the early Christian writers as they accounted for the origins and spread of the Jesus movement.

The concept of a disciple was not limited to the ministry of Jesus. Mark and John recorded the Pharisees having disciples, and the Jews generally regarded themselves as disciples of Moses.[15] Each Gospel account also showed John the Baptist with disciples, while John portrayed John the Baptist as essentially giving away his disciples and orienting them toward Jesus.[16] When "disciples" was used in Acts, it referred once to Paul and Barnabas in their missionary efforts, but the rest of the time it was synonymous with Christians in general. Luke reinforced this by writing that the "disciples were first

---

[13] Matt 28:19; also Acts 14:21; Matt 13:52; 27:57; see Wilkins, *Concept of a Disciple*, 160–62.

[14] John Meier, *A Marginal Jew: Rethinking the Historical Jesus*, Anchor Bible Reference Library (New York: Doubleday, 2001), 3:41–45; see Wilkins, *Concept of a Disciple*, 11–125.

[15] Mark 2:18; John 9:28; see Wilkins, *Concept of a Disciple*, 131.

[16] Matt 9:14; 11:2; Mark 2:18; Luke 5:33; 7:18–19; John 1:35–41; 3:25.

called Christians in Antioch," rendering these believers disciples of Jesus in a general sense.[17]

The remaining references to "disciple" in its plural form (*mathētai*) in the Gospel accounts refer exclusively to those who were personally with Jesus. Three of the Gospel writers depicted a larger group of disciples, including some who parted company with Jesus after a while because they could no longer accept His teaching.[18] Luke recounted Jesus' interaction with a band of 70 followers whom He sent ahead of Him to cities where He would be preaching.[19] Yet the greatest significance given in the Gospels to Jesus and His disciples pertains to His relationship with the Twelve.[20] John Meier writes: "We imagine the followers of Jesus in terms of concentric circles: the 'crowds' form the outer circle, the 'disciples' the intermediate or middle circle, and the 'Twelve' the inner circle."[21]

In light of the significant and repeated usage of *mathētēs* in the passages cited, it seems best to approach an understanding of mentoring by observing what was going on around the disciple or group of disciples on the journey toward the "fullness of Christ." What did a disciple receive from a mentor in this process?

A Disciple's Belief

Marshall broadly defines a *disciple* as "the pupil of a teacher," indicating that learning is a key occupation.[22] In one sense this means that teaching of a cognitive nature was given for a disciple to apprehend and believe.[23] Jesus is called "teacher" (*didaskalos*),[24]

---

[17] Acts 13:52; 6:1,2,7; 9:1,19,25,27,38; 11:26,29; 14:20,22,28; 15:10; 18:23,27; 19:1,9,30; 20:1; 21:4,6; Acts 11:26.

[18] Matt 8:21; Luke 6:17; 19:37; John 6:60,66.

[19] Luke 10:1–17.

[20] Matt 10:1,2,5; 11:1; 4:12,15,19,22,26; 20:17; 26:14,20,47; Mark 3:14,16; 4:10; 6:7; 9:35; 10:32; 11:11; 14:10,17,20,43; Luke 6:13; 8:1; 9:1,12; 18:31; 22:33,47; John 6:67,70–71; 20:24; see Wilkins, *Concept of a Disciple*, 166–67.

[21] Meier, *Marginal Jew*, 3.21.

[22] I. Howard Marshall, "Disciple," in *NBD*, 285; also Matt 10:24–25; Luke 6:40.

[23] "Learn" in a mere cognitive manner seems to be reflected in the rarely used term *manthanō* that occurs only seven times in the Gospels and Acts (Matt 9:13; 11:29; 24:32; Mark 13:28; John 6:45; 7:15; Acts 23:27); see Wilkins, *Concept of a Disciple*, 158–60.

[24] Matt 8:19; 9:11; 12:38; 17:24; 19:16; 22:16,24,36; 26:18; Mark 4:38; 5:35; 9:17,38; 10:17,20,35; 12:14,19,32; 13:1; 14:14; Luke 3:12; 7:40; 8:39; 9:38; 10:25; 11:45; 12:13;

rabbi,[25] or "master" (*kyrios*)[26] 151 times in the Gospels and is depicted in the act of teaching (*didaskō*)[27] another 42 times.

Jesus is the Christ. What did His followers believe that made them disciples? Though the Gospel accounts portrayed Him teaching on subjects such as ethics and prayer, it seems that a conviction about Jesus' identity as the Christ—one who would atone for sins through His death, burial, and resurrection—was the most important qualifying attribute of a disciple.[28] This conviction was most succinctly communicated in Peter's famous confession that Jesus was "the Christ, the Son of the living God."[29] Though some of the Twelve were slow to grasp this point and many from the larger group rejected it completely, ultimately the identity of Jesus was the focal point of the good news preached by Jesus in the Gospels and what was proclaimed by the apostles in Acts.[30]

The Scriptures. Besides Jesus' identity, what other teaching contributed to a disciple's belief? Matthew recorded Jesus saying, "Do not think that I came to abolish the Law or the Prophets; I did not come to abolish but to fulfill."[31] As His discourse unfolded, He made

---

18:18; 19:39; 20:21,28,39; 21:7; 22:11; John 1:38; 3:2; 8:4; 11:28; 13:13–14; 20:16; see Milavec, *Didache*, 73.

[25] Matt 26:25,49; Mark 9:5; 11:21; 14:45; John 1:29,38; 3:2; 4:31; 6:25; 9:2; 11:8. Luke also used "master" (*epistata*) in the same sense another six times (Luke 5:5; 8:24,45; 9:33,49; 17:13).

[26] *Kyrios* is essentially the Greek rendering of "rabbi." Matt 7:21–22; 8:2,6,8,21,25; 9:28; 12:8; 14:28,30; 15:22,25,27; 16:22; 17:4,15; 18:21; 20:30–31,33; 21:3,30; 24:42; 26:22; Mark 2:28; 5:19; 7:28; 11:3; 16:19; Luke 2:11; 5:8,12; 6:5,46; 7:6,13; 9:54,59,61; 10:1,17,40–41; 11:1,39; 12:41; 13:15,23; 17:6,37; 18:6,41; 19:8,31,34; 22:33,38,49,61; 24:3; John 4:11,15,19,49; 5:7; 6:34,68, 8:11; 9:36,38; 11:3,12,21,27,32,34,39; 13:6,9,13–14,25,36–37; 14:5,8,22; 15:15; 20:28; 21:7,12,15–17,20–21; see Aaron Milavec, *To Empower as Jesus Did: Acquiring Spiritual Power Through Apprenticeship* (New York and Toronto: Edwin Mellen, 1982), 98.

[27] Matt 4:23; 5:2; 7:29; 9:35; 11:11; 13:54; 21:23; 22:16; 26:55; Mark 1:21–22; 2:13; 4:1,2; 6:2,6,34; 8:31; 9:31; 10:1; 11:1,7; 12:14,35; 14:49; Luke 4:15,31; 5:3,17; 6:6; 13:10,22; 19:47; 20:1,21; 21:37; John 6:59; 7:14,28; 8:2,20; 18:20.

[28] Matt 5–7; Luke 11:1–13; John 13–17; see Meier, *Marginal Jew*, 3.2.

[29] Matt 16:16; "the Christ" (*ho christos*) literally means "anointed one" and is the Greek equivalent of the Hebrew *mashiah*. That the Messiah would suffer and die is recounted in Dan 9:25; Matt 16:13–21; Mark 8:27–33; 9:31; Luke 9:18; John 3:16; 4:39,41; 6:69; 7:31; 8:24,30; 11:25,27; 13:17; 16:30; 20:31.

[30] Matt 16:22–23; Mark 8:32–33; John 6:60–66; Matt 16:21; 17:12; Mark 1:1; 8:31; 9:21; 14:9; Luke 9:22; 17:25; 24:26–46; Acts 2:38; 3:12–26; 4:2; 5:42.

[31] Matt 5:17.

Entry to the ancient city of Hippo Regis where Augustine served as a presbyter (391–395) and then bishop (395–430).

several references to the Mosaic Law followed by commentary and updated teaching on each subject.[32] The fact that Jesus would fulfill the law or prophets implies that His teaching stemmed from the Hebrew Scriptures. Throughout the Gospels Jesus is regularly observed teaching in the temple or synagogues where, as an unofficial rabbi, He would have read and taught from these Scriptures.[33] So, in addition to believing that Jesus was the Christ, a disciple would also have accepted the moral and ethical teachings of the Hebrew Scriptures, as well as His updated teaching like that contained in the Sermon on the Mount.

---

[32] Matt 5:21,27,31,33,35,38,43.

[33] Matt 4:23; 9:35; 13:54; 21:23; 26:55; Mark 1:21; 6:2; 11:7; 12:35; 14:49; Luke 4:15; 6:6; 13:10; 19:47; 20:1; 21:37; John 6:59; 7:14,28; 8:2,20; 18:20; see Marshall, "Disciple," 285; most of Jesus' references to Scripture (*graphē*) also make some connection to His identity as the Christ; see Matt 21:42; 22:29; 26:54,56; Mark 12:10,24; 14:49; Luke 4:21; 24:27,32,45; John 2:22; 5:39; 7:38,42; 10:35; 13:18; 17:12; 19:24,28,36–37; 20:9.

The apostles and evangelists who came after Jesus also seemed to follow this pattern of teaching. Luke wrote that Philip, Paul, and Apollos used the Hebrew Scriptures to present Jesus as the Christ.[34] The teaching apostles of the Jerusalem church in Acts—particularly those who had been with Jesus—probably also passed on what they had learned from the Lord in the three previous years.[35] This teaching seems to have been quickly handed down to disciples beyond the Jerusalem community; this explains how Barnabas, a native of Cyprus who was apparently living in Jerusalem around the time of Pentecost, and Priscilla and Aquila, who were from Rome, were educated enough in the faith to teach emerging leaders like Paul and Apollos.[36]

Sound teaching. As the community of faith grew, one challenge that Luke and Paul highlighted was the battle against heresy infiltrating the young churches.[37] Two young pastors, Timothy and Titus, received letters from Paul in which they were exhorted to maintain "sound teaching" (*hugiainousē didaskalia*) in the face of certain ascetic and Jewish teachings.[38]

What was sound teaching? The clearest response comes in 1 Timothy, where unsound teaching was described as "a different doctrine and does not agree with sound words, those of our Lord Jesus Christ."[39] So it was the teachings of Jesus, "the things which you have heard from me in the presence of many witnesses" and apparently familiar to all church leaders and teachers, that were the standard for sound teaching.[40]

In 2 Tim 3:14–17, Paul added that sound teaching was essentially what was taught in the Scriptures:

> You, however, continue in the things you have learned
> and become convinced of, knowing from whom you

---

[34] Acts 8:35; 17:22; 18:28.
[35] Acts 2:42; 6:2; 11:26; 15:22; 18:11; 20:20; 28:31; Matt 5–7; 9:37; 11:11; 16:5,13,20–21,24; 17:19; 19:23; 20:17; 26:1,26; Mark 4:34; 8:27,33–34; 9:28,31; 10:23–24; 12:43; Luke 6:20; 9:18,40,43; 10:23; 11:1; 12:22; 16:1; 17:1,22; 20:45; 22:11; John 6:61; 13:5,35; 15:18; 16:29; see Wilkins, *Concept of a Disciple*, 144.
[36] Acts 4:36; 18:2; 11:25–26; 18:26.
[37] Acts 15:1ff; Rom 16:17–18; Gal 1:6–7; Col 2:8; 1 Tim 4:1ff; 2 Tim 4:3–4.
[38] 1 Tim 1:10; 4:6; 6:3; 2 Tim 1:13; 4:3; Titus 1:9; 2:1.
[39] 1 Tim 6:3.
[40] 2 Tim 2:2; also *Didache* 11:2.

have learned them, and that from childhood you have known the sacred writings which are able to give you the wisdom that leads to salvation through faith which is in Christ Jesus. All Scripture is inspired by God and profitable for teaching, for reproof, for correction, for training in righteousness; so that the man of God may be adequate, equipped for every good work.[41]

The "sacred writings" (*hiera grammata*), familiar to Timothy since his early education in a Jewish home, and "all Scripture" (*pasa graphē*) both refer to the Hebrew Scriptures.[42] Yet, in 1 Tim 5:18, Paul had written: "For the Scripture says, 'You shall not muzzle the ox while he is threshing,' and 'The laborer is worthy of his wages.'" Here Paul quoted Deut 25:4 and Luke 10:7 and referred to them both as "the Scripture" (*he graphē*). Hence, sound teaching for the early Christians meant teaching that conformed to the Hebrew Scriptures, the teachings of Jesus that were transmitted by the apostles, and the eventual New Testament writings, of which Luke is included.

Why was the notion of the Scriptures important in promoting sound doctrine and ultimately a key for mentoring and disciple-ship in early Christianity? The message of Christianity as well as Judaism was conveyed through revelation. The Jews believed that God spoke to them through their prophets and leaders like Moses who received the law. Though this revelation was initiated by an intimate divine-human encounter, the message was ultimately written down and preserved for members of the covenant community to learn and even memorize. While accepting the authority of the Hebrew Scriptures, the early church believed that ongoing revelation in the form of Scripture accompanied the rise and expansion of the Christian movement. John wrote that Jesus was not merely a means of revelation but that He was the Word of God incarnate (*ho logos*).[43] As noted, Paul considered Luke's writings to be Scripture, while Peter communicated the same about Paul's writings.[44]

---

[41] 2 Tim 3:14–17.

[42] 2 Tim 1:5.

[43] John 1:1–14.

[44] 2 Pet 3:16.

Written Scriptures brought unity and continuity to the Jews and the early church as they served as a reference point for teaching and preserving the faith. At the same time they provided a means of discerning counterfeit teaching. As noted, Paul held up the Scriptures as well as the teachings of Jesus as the test for sound teaching, which safeguarded a disciple's doctrinal belief.

A Disciple's Conduct

According to the Gospel writers, one became a disciple by believing that Jesus was the Christ and through accepting His teachings—the moral and ethical teachings of the Hebrew Scriptures and His teachings that fulfilled the law. But was being Jesus' disciple limited to belief? On the contrary the Gospel writers showed that it was quite impossible to separate belief about Jesus' person and teachings from obeying those teachings.[45] In light of this inseparable link, Milavec argues that *didaskolos* ought to be rendered "master" instead of "teacher" and *didaskō* should be translated "to apprentice" instead of "to teach." He comments on *didaskō*, "it could only refer to that apprenticing which consumed the whole life and purpose of every Jew—that of assimilating the way of *YHWH*."[46] In his commentary on the *Didache*, Milavec adds that the word *didachē*, most often translated as "teaching" should be rendered "training" because of the practical nature of the teaching.[47]

The practical manner of obeying Jesus' teachings was clearly expressed by the active way in which Jesus called His disciples—"follow me" (*akolouthei moi*).[48] Meier writes, "In the case of people specifically called disciples, especially the particular group called the Twelve, the physical act of following usually expresses an inner adherence to the person and message of Jesus."[49] Matthew emphasized practical obedience in his account of Jesus' Sermon on the

---

[45] The idea of "hearing" (*akouō*) is used nearly synonymously with obeying in texts like Matt 7:24,26; Luke 6:47; John 12:47.

[46] See Milavec, *To Empower as Jesus Did*, 85.

[47] See Milavec, *Didache*, 44; *Didache*, 2:1; 6:1.

[48] Matt 8:22; 9:19; 10:38; 16:24; 19:21,28; Mark 2:14; 8:34; 10:21; Luke 5:27; 9:23,59; 18:22; John 1:43; 8:12; 10:27; 12:26; 13:36; 21:19,22.

[49] Meier, *Marginal Jew*, 3:20.

11

Mount, an ethical discourse characterized by practical commands for living summarized by the command to "be perfect, as your heavenly Father is perfect."[50] As noted, John portrayed Jesus in the role of a master not only commanding obedience but also demonstrating it by washing the feet of His disciples before teaching them in the upper room.[51]

While Jesus presented a model for the Twelve, Paul called the Corinthian believers to be "imitators" (*mimētēs*) of him, emulating his "ways which are in Christ."[52] Paul's "ways" (*hodous*) referred to his own morally upright conduct that conformed to the conduct and teachings of Jesus, whom John referred to as "the way" (*hē hodos*).[53] With no separation in His conduct and teachings, Jesus was the embodiment of moral perfection and all that pleased the Father. So the Corinthian believers were challenged to a higher level of conduct by imitating Paul, who imitated Christ. In the early epistles Christians were also encouraged to imitate the good example of hardworking and honest people, the faith of the saints of the Hebrew Scriptures, the example of teachers who have taught the Word of God and demonstrated a holy life, as well as God and Christ.[54]

Summary

An early Christian disciple believed in the identity of Jesus as the Christ and cognitively accepted and sought to obey the moral and ethical teachings of Jesus, which stem from the Scriptures. In addition, the disciple imitated the conduct of Christ and others in the community of faith whose conduct conformed to that of Christ.

Mentoring or discipleship, as observed in the New Testament and early Christian writings, was the work of one Christian helping another disciple or group of disciples grow in their knowledge and application of the teachings of Jesus and the Scriptures. Put another way, the mentor coached his disciples toward realizing the fullness

---

[50] Matt 5:48.
[51] John 13:3–17.
[52] 1 Cor 4:16–17; 11:1.
[53] John 4:16.
[54] 1 Thess 1:6; 2 Thess 3:7,9; Heb 6:12; 13:7; *Didache* 4:1–2; Eph 5:1–4.

of their salvation.[55] A mentoring relationship was a personal and caring relationship between disciples committed to this common goal.[56] The mentor probably had been a disciple longer than his disciples and had a more profound understanding of the teachings of Jesus and the Scriptures. With that he was a winsome model whose conduct was continually being conformed to the way of Christ. His teaching and conduct were coherent with each other, meaning that he practiced what he preached. Finally, the atmosphere of the mentoring relationship was both gracious and rigorous and characterized by encouragement and exhortation.

Mentoring Spiritual Leaders

On one level mentoring or discipleship was possible for all Christians. The word *disciples*, as we have noted, could refer to the broader group of those who followed Jesus or even members of the early Christian movement as recorded in Acts. Yet because our inquiry is concerned with the mentoring of spiritual leaders, it seems most helpful to concentrate on how Jesus mentored the Twelve and how Paul mentored his coworkers in mission. Meier makes the important point that Jesus called disciples not merely for their own salvation and benefit but to join Him in His purpose—promoting the kingdom of God.[57] Also, Paul clearly selected men and mentored them in the context of the missionary enterprise. To complete our model of early Christian mentoring of spiritual leaders, I propose the following eight characteristics of mentoring drawn from the evidence already presented.

1. The Group

The first apparent reality of mentoring spiritual leaders in early Christianity is that mentoring happened in the context of a group. As noted, *mathētēs* is repeated 239 times in the plural form in the Gospels and Acts compared to only 25 times in the singular form. Twenty of the 25 occurrences referred to the "disciple that Jesus

---

[55] Eph 2:8; 4:13; Col 1:28.
[56] See Milavec, *Didache*, 88.
[57] Meier, *Marginal Jew*, 3:157.

loved" in John's Gospel or to the hypothetical notion of a disciple.[58] In fact, the only individual disciple named in the Gospels was Joseph of Arimathea.[59] Hence, disciple was almost exclusively a group concept in the Gospels and Acts. The Lord is simply never observed mentoring any of the Twelve or members of the broader group on an individual basis.[60] Meier correctly asserts, "As presented in the Gospels, discipleship involves not just an individualistic relation of a single pupil to his teacher but the formation of a group around the teacher who has called the group into existence."[61]

Though Paul was not initiated into the community as the other apostles were, he also mentored spiritual leaders in a group context. His key mentoring contexts were the missionary journeys recorded in Acts, where emerging leaders like John Mark, Titus, Timothy, Silas, Judas, and Luke accompanied him as disciples and coworkers.[62]

Why did early Christian mentoring happen in a group context more than on an individual basis? Some may reasonably make the cultural argument that first-century Palestine was more communal than modern Europe or North America, where individualism is more highly valued; but I suggest that the more compelling reason, which is above culture, is that Jesus and Paul and other early Christian mentors were mentoring leaders in the context of their goal—the establishment of the church.[63] As the church was to be a body of believers living together in faith, hope, and love, its leaders needed to be trained in the context of a community. Wilkins rightly adds, "The church as a whole can identify with the group of disciples."[64]

Ultimately, mentoring in a group context seems to be more effective because it takes into account the relational makeup and needs

---

[58] John 18:15–16; 19:26–27; 20:2–4,8; 21:7,20,23–24; Matt 10:24–25,42; Luke 6:10; 14:26–27,33.

[59] John 19:38; the remaining singular usages of disciple are in Acts 9:10,26,36; 16:1.

[60] There are a few instances where only Peter, James, and John accompany Jesus, though this does not diminish the group context of His teaching; see Matt 17:1; Mark 5:37; 9:2; Luke 8:51; 9:28.

[61] Meier, *Marginal Jew*, 3:51–52; also Wilkins, *Concept of a Disciple*, 169.

[62] John Mark (Acts 13:13; Col 4:10; Phlm 1:24); Titus (Gal 2:1; 2 Cor 8:23); see Luke's "we" statements (Acts 16:10–13,16; 20:6–8,13–15; 21:1–8,10,12,14–17; 27:1–8,15–16,18,27,29; 28:1,10–14,16).

[63] Matt 16:18; Acts 11:26; 14:23–27.

[64] Wilkins, *Concept of a Disciple*, 170.

of human beings. Milavec highlights the vital role of the family, particularly parents, in forming children in their basic belief system and serving as an ideal nurturing community.[65] Aside from the family, the expression "no man is an island" signifies that humans do not flourish or develop well in isolation. Theologians explain the relational makeup of humans by pointing to their creation in the image of a triune God, One who by necessity is in relationship with the Godhead.[66] Humans who already demonstrate a need for others are in even greater need of relationships as they pursue relationship with God. Hence, we begin to understand a bit of the theological speculation between the mystery of the Trinity and the doctrine of the body of Christ. In summary, mentoring in the context of a group, as demonstrated by Jesus and Paul, is most effective because it meets the inherent relational needs of the disciple.

2. The Mentor as Disciple

Paul wrote to the Philippians, "Not that I have already obtained it or have already become perfect, but I press on so that I may lay hold of that for which also I was laid hold of by Christ Jesus."[67] Though far from having "arrived" spiritually, the mentor was still growing, his conduct becoming more and more Christlike. The mentor was still a disciple.

The New Testament also depicted Jesus in human form living by faith and dependence on God, though his divine nature was never compromised. Such dependence, characterized by prayer, demonstrated that he also took the posture of a disciple. The writer of Hebrews described it this way: "In the days of His flesh, He offered up both prayers and supplications with loud crying and tears to the One able to save Him from death, and He was heard because of His piety. Although He was a Son, He learned obedience from the things which He suffered."[68]

---

[65] Milavec, *To Empower as Jesus Did*, 8,11.
[66] Gen 1:26–27.
[67] Phil 3:12.
[68] Heb 5:7–8.

This attitude and way of life qualified a mentor to be imitated by his disciples. The mentor's continual posture of learning demonstrated authenticity and humility for his disciples, making his mentoring more attractive and effective. Augustine aptly communicated this point in *Sermon* 340: "For you I am a bishop, with you I am a Christian."[69]

Practically speaking, the mentor continued to meditate on the teachings of Jesus as transmitted by the apostles as well as the Scriptures. Milavec, describing Jesus' commitment to knowing the Scriptures, writes, "Employing the time-honored methods of his day, Jesus was the master who sensitively immersed himself in God's Torah with his disciples."[70] With this teaching in mind, the mentor continually pursued behavioral change essentially working out his salvation with "fear and trembling."[71] Also, he probably had been or continued to be mentored by another spiritual leader. In the case of Paul, Barnabas initially served as his mentor, though later they seem to have more of a peer-mentoring relationship.[72]

3. Selection

In each mentoring context surveyed, there was a definite point of selection in which the mentor called a disciple or group of disciples to join him in spiritual growth and serving the community. Although Jesus invited disciples to follow Him, at some distinct point He specifically set apart the Twelve to be with Him, learn from Him, and minister with Him.[73] Meier summarizes, "Jesus' initiative in summoning a person to discipleship is a necessary condition for becoming his disciple."[74] Similarly, Barnabas traveled to Tarsus in search of Paul to recruit him for the important work of teaching the recently converted Greeks in Antioch.[75] Later Paul, upon receiving

---

[69] Augustine *Sermon* 340.1; all English translations of Augustine's sermons are from John E. Rotelle, ed., *Works of Saint Augustine: A Translation for the 21st Century*, pt. III, vol. 1–11 (Hyde Park, NY: New City, 2001).
[70] Milavec, *To Empower as Jesus Did*, 134, 317.
[71] Phil 2:12.
[72] Acts 9:27; 11:25–26.
[73] Mark 3:13–19; Luke 6:13–16.
[74] Meier, *Marginal Jew*, 3:54; see 3:21,45,50–54.
[75] Acts 11:19–26.

the good recommendation of the church at Lystra, chose Timothy to travel and minister with him.[76]

Milavec writes that "Jesus' choice of collaborators was one of the most critical of his career," meaning that this stage of selection involved risk.[77] First, there was risk that the disciple would not hold up over time, causing potential damage to the ministry or friction within the mentoring community. Though having received good references from the Lystra church about Timothy, Paul surely had not forgotten the incident of another disciple, John Mark, who had abandoned him and Barnabas after their preaching campaign in Cyprus. John Mark's departure had resulted in conflict and a parting of ways between Paul and Barnabas.[78] Second, the mentor potentially risked his own reputation as a spiritual leader if the disciple did not hold up. Barnabas modeled this when he vouched for the recently converted Paul before the apostles at Jerusalem.[79] Though the element of risk in selecting disciples was unavoidable, a mitigating factor was the mentor's ability to identify potential in a person.[80] The mentor was aided in making this decision if he had already observed faithfulness in a disciple, as in the case of Jesus and the Twelve, or if he had a good report from a reliable source as Paul had with Timothy.

4. The Mentor-Disciple Relationship

The mentor invited a disciple or group of disciples into a caring personal relationship characterized by both discipline and grace. Because the mentor wanted to see the potential of the disciple fulfilled, the training program was rigorous. When the Twelve wanted to send the crowds away because the hour was getting late, Jesus challenged His men to feed them.[81] Coleman suggests that it was the objective of the Twelve's training, to be prepared to lead the church when Jesus was gone, that caused Him to demand total

---

[76] Acts 16:1–3.
[77] Milavec, *To Empower as Jesus Did*, 110.
[78] Acts 12:25–13:13; 15:36–40.
[79] Acts 9:27.
[80] See Clinton and Stanley, *Connections*, 38; Milavec, *To Empower as Jesus Did*, 110.
[81] Mark 8:35–37.

obedience and to train them in such an atmosphere of discipline.[82] Perhaps it was a similar conviction that led Paul to reject John Mark as a companion on the next missionary journey.

The mentoring relationship was also marked by grace. That is, the mentor was patient and forbearing with his disciples in the growth process. In John's Gospel, Jesus was depicted as a shepherd: "My sheep hear My voice, and I know them, and they follow Me."[83] Paul repeatedly referred to Timothy as "my child."[84] One way that grace was demonstrated was through the mentor's patient manner in dealing with his disciples in their immaturity. The Twelve argued among themselves over who would be the greatest in the kingdom, they offered to call down fire from heaven against those who disagreed with them, and they were irritated with parents who brought their children to Jesus.[85] Yet, as Coleman writes, "Jesus patiently endured these human failings of His chosen disciples because in spite of all their shortcomings they were willing to follow him."[86] Similarly, a mentor demonstrated grace in how he responded to a disciple's failure. According to John, Jesus tenderly restored Peter, who had denied Jesus and then returned to the comfortable confines of fishing. As the text records, Jesus renewed the call for Peter to follow Him and continue in the ministry.[87]

Because of the mentor's stature of spiritual maturity and ministry experience, there was clearly a spiritual hierarchy that existed in the relationship.[88] While the mentor's spiritual authority over his disciples was clear, it was an authority realized through caring influence more than by title or rank. Mentoring required servant leadership. As noted, before beginning His upper room discourse, Jesus dem-

---

[82] Robert Coleman, *The Master Plan of Evangelism* (Old Tappan, NJ: Revell, 1987), 58–59.

[83] John 10:27.

[84] 1 Cor 4:17; Phil 2:22; 1 Tim 2:2; 2 Tim 1:2; Titus 1:4; also *Didache* 3:1–8; 4:1; Milavec, *The Didache: Faith, Hope & Love*, 147–48.

[85] Matt 18:1–5; Mark 9:33–37; 10:13; Luke 9:46–48,51–54.

[86] Coleman, *Master Plan*, 55; also Clinton and Stanley, *Connections*, 38.

[87] John 21:3,15–19.

[88] See *Didache* 4:1; and Milavec, *Didache*, 13, 49.

onstrated the humble servitude of a mentor by washing the feet of His disciples.[89]

Despite being their rabbi and master, Jesus also referred to the Twelve as His friends.[90] The fraternal and friendly nature of their relationship was evidenced by the significant time and the various contexts that they were together. Apart from spending time together in teaching and ministry, they ate and rested together, even attending a wedding together.[91] More than a group of students studying under a teacher, the Twelve were more like a family or group of friends living together.

Paul also seemed to have a fraternal mind-set with His disciples. In a letter to the Corinthians, he called Titus "my partner and fellow worker among you."[92] In the salutations of eight of Paul's epistles, the recipients were greeted not only by Paul but also by disciples like Silas and Timothy who were referred to as "brothers."[93] That Paul would include the names of these friends in what was generally regarded as his writings also reflected his humility and fraternal mind-set.

5. Sound Teaching

As teaching that conformed to the words of Jesus, a mentor drew from the Hebrew Scriptures, the teachings of Jesus, and the early writings that circulated throughout the churches that were later confirmed as Scripture. As noted, written Scriptures, a hallmark of the Christian movement, provided a point of reference not only for teaching sound doctrine but also for guarding against unsound teaching. (See 1 Tim 6:20; 2 Tim 1:14.)

---

[89] John 13:4–5; also Matt 20:28; Mark 10:45; and Brian Patrick McGuire, *Friendship and Community: The Monastic Experience 350–1250, Cistercian Studies* 95 (Kalamazoo, MI: Cistercian Publications, 1988), xxvii.

[90] John 15:15.

[91] Matt 5:1; 8:23; 9:10,19,37; 11:1; 14:22; 16:5; 17:19; Mark 3:7; 4:34; 6:45; 8:34; 10:13,46; 13:1; 2:15–16; Luke 5:30; 6:20; 7:11; 9:40; 10:23; 12:22; 16:1; 17:1,22; John 2:2,11–12; 3:22; 11:7–12.

[92] 2 Cor 8:23.

[93] 1 Cor 1:1; 2 Cor 1:1,19; Gal 1:1; Phil 1:1; Col 1:1; 1 Thess 1:1; 2 Thess 1:1; Phlm 1:1; see Harry Gamble, *Books and Readers in the Early Church: A History of Early Christian Texts* (New Haven and London: Yale University Press, 1995), 99.

Jesus insisted that the apostles uphold sound teaching. The final command given to the Twelve, to make disciples of all nations, was to be accomplished through teaching what Jesus had taught them.[94] Timothy was commanded to teach "the things which you have heard from me in the presence of many witnesses" (2 Tim 2:2) and to "retain the standard of sound words which you have heard from me, in the faith and love which are in Christ Jesus" (2 Tim 1:13).[95] The follower of the resurrected Jesus, and even more an emerging spiritual leader in the church, was one who believed in the person of Jesus as the Christ as well as what Jesus taught.

A clear necessity for the spiritual leader committed to maintaining sound doctrine was the ability to read the Scriptures. Although first-century Palestine could be characterized as an oral culture, and although it was possible for a Jew to hear Torah in the synagogue, the spiritual leader entrusted with teaching had to be literate. Milavec writes, "The Pharasaic masters customarily required that their disciples be able to read the text of the Scriptures before undertaking to train them in its proper interpretation."[96] It would be unlikely that Jesus, who emerged from the rabbinic tradition, would have required any less of His disciples.

6. Modeling and Involving in Ministry

A mentor was not only a growing disciple and a winsome model for imitation; he also demonstrated faithfulness and skill in the work of ministry. The Twelve watched Jesus confound the Jewish leaders, attempting to trap Him by their questions. They observed how He drew in the crowds and amazed them with His teaching in the Sermon on the Mount. They also learned how to rest and pray after a long day of ministering to the crowds.[97] Paul surely learned much about teaching new believers from Barnabas during the year they spent together in Antioch before the missionary journeys to the Gentiles.[98] Clinton writes that emerging leaders learn through "imi-

---

[94] Matt 28:19; see Wilkins, *Concept of a Disciple*, 144.
[95] See *Didache* 11:2.
[96] See Milavec, *To Empower as Jesus Did*, 109.
[97] Matt 7:29; 14:22; 21:23–27; Mark 3:7; 6:45; Luke 20:1–8.
[98] Clinton, *Making of a Leader*, 83 (see Acts 11:25–26).

tation modeling" and that ministry skills are acquired in large part through observation.[99] Milavec similarly suggests that skill begins to be grasped intuitively by disciples over time.[100]

The mentor not only modeled ministry, but he deliberately involved his disciples in the work as well. Clinton adds that ministry skills are developed through "informal apprenticeships" and "experience."[101] Though the initial tasks may not have been overly spiritual, responsibility was increased with time and faithfulness on the part of the disciples.[102] As noted, the Twelve were involved in distributing food and cleaning up after Jesus' miraculous feedings as well as in securing the colt for His triumphal entry into Jerusalem. They were also entrusted with tasks like baptizing, preaching, and casting out demons.[103] Finally, after a few years of traveling and serving with Jesus, they were promoted to the greater assignment of making disciples of all nations.

Timothy began traveling with Paul and his team on the second missionary journey. Later he was sent on a few occasions to minister in place of Paul. Paul's letters to Timothy indicate that Timothy was entrusted with a greater responsibility of serving as pastor of the church in Ephesus.[104]

An important quality of mentoring at this stage was debriefing. A group of disciples was entrusted with a task, executed it successfully or unsuccessfully, then returned to discuss the experience with their mentor. Luke recorded that Jesus assigned the 70 to go and preach in towns and cities where He would later preach.[105] In this case they returned elated at their success. Jesus responded by encouraging them to be humble, and He openly praised the Father for their success.[106] Matthew recorded an instance when some of the

---

[99] Ibid., 31, 89.

[100] See Milavec, *To Empower as Jesus Did*, 19.

[101] Clinton, *Making of a Leader*, 31, 89.

[102] Ibid., 35, 81; Milavec, *To Empower as Jesus Did*, 133.

[103] Matt 14:19; 15:36; 21:1,6; Mark 6:7–12,41; 8:6; 11:1; Luke 9:14,16; 19:29; John 4:1–2; 6:3,12; see Wilkins, *Concept of a Disciple*, 166.

[104] Acts 16:1–3; 17:14–15; 18:5; 19:22; 20:24; Rom 16:21; 1 Cor 4:17; 16:10; Phil 2:19; 1 Thess 3:2,6; 1 Tim 1:3; 2 Tim 4:19; see Donald Guthrie, "Timothy," *NBD*, 1201.

[105] Luke 10:1–24; also Mark 6:7–13.

[106] Luke 10:20–24.

Twelve unsuccessfully attempted to cast out a demon. Jesus arrived, cast out the demon, and later used it as an object lesson to teach them about faith.[107] In summary, the Mentor effectively mentored His disciples at this stage through modeling ministry, involving the disciples in ministry, and debriefing successes and failures in preparation for future ministry.

7. Releasing to Ministry

Releasing a leader logically flowed from the previous stage of increased involvement and responsibility in ministry. Jesus had taught and trained the Twelve, entrusted them with the commission to make disciples, and then purposefully departed, leaving them on their own to succeed or fail in the task. Paul used this same method with Timothy. After years of observing Paul and receiving assignments of increasing responsibility, Timothy was entrusted with the authority and responsibility to pastor the church at Ephesus, where some of his tasks included teaching sound doctrine, leading the church, raising up other leaders, and caring for widows.[108] These tasks could not be delegated back to Paul when they became difficult. This stage was a veritable weaning for the disciples and was probably painful for both mentor and disciples alike. Yet given the proper training and timing, this stage was crucial and necessary to keep the disciples from developing an unhealthy dependency on the mentor and ultimately depriving the church of needed ministers.

8. Resourcing Leaders

Though the disciples were released with authority and responsibility, a mentor could still be available as a resource or consultant, providing encouragement and perhaps practical advice. Because distance could make personal contact or visits difficult, the forms of mentoring probably needed to change. Paul resourced both Timothy and Titus with letters, affirming their ministries while addressing specific issues they were facing. Though the role of the mentor

---

[107] Matt 17:19–20.
[108] 1 Tim 1:10; 3:1–13; 4:6; 5:3–22; 6:3,20; 2 Tim 1:13; 2:24–26; 4:3.

changed at this point, the caring relationship between mentor and disciples remained the same.

Outcomes of Mentoring

The impact of the mentor continued through his disciples as they mentored other groups of disciples. This influence continued in a multiplying fashion. Timothy was to take the teachings he had learned and "entrust these to faithful men who will be able to teach others also."[109] In short, the mentor left a legacy.

The testimony of early Christianity was that the disciples of Jesus and Paul did become mature disciples and leaders in the church in most of the known world.[110] That the Jesus movement, born among Galilean fishermen, has continued to the present and taken root worldwide is as remarkable as it is undeniable. And although mentoring and discipling leaders has played an important role in the church's ongoing mission, the mentor's legacy is largely out of his control. Nothing functions automatically. What would have happened, for instance, if the Twelve had changed their minds after Jesus left and gone back to fishing? We should also note that the legacy or influence of a person will differ according to the gifting and contribution of the mentor. Some mentors write and have their books preserved; others preach and have their sermons recorded, while others simply serve and their nameless example lives on. Each mentor's legacy will look different, but it is difficult if not wrong to judge or rate a person's legacy. A mentor's legacy may lie dormant for a while, only to resurface in a later generation. (Van Gogh never sold a painting in his lifetime!) We can at least say that a spiritual leader, ministering in the community of faith, generally has left some lasting influence to the next generation of spiritual leaders.

---

[109] 2 Tim 2:2.
[110] See Milavec, *To Empower as Jesus Did*, 149.

Chapter Two

THE MENTORING MATRIX

The goal of this chapter is to set the stage for Augustine's mentoring of spiritual leaders by examining some examples of mentoring that took place in the church in the third and fourth centuries. Our inquiry will begin in the mid-third century and extend to the beginning of Augustine's ministry, focusing on areas such as North Africa, Egypt, Asia Minor, and Italy. We will survey four key characters: Cyprian of Carthage (195–258), the Egyptian monk Pachomius (290–346), Basil of Caesarea (329–379), and Ambrose of Milan (340–397). Each leader except Pachomius was a metropolitan bishop, that is, with authority over a certain region, its bishops, and parishes. Pachomius, however, has been included because of his significant work as a mentor in the context of cenobitic or communal monasticism (as opposed to eremitic or hermit monasticism), which has great relevance to Augustine's mentoring. These leaders have been chosen because of their significant contribution as leaders and mentors to the Christian movement of the third and fourth centuries—the backdrop to Augustine's life and ministry.

Cyprian of Carthage

Cyprian came from a prominent family in Carthage, was educated in both classical and religious literature, and probably initially worked as a teacher of rhetoric.[1] He converted to Christianity in 246 and was ordained bishop of Carthage just two years later. His tenure as bishop was dominated by the imperial persecutions of the church under the Emperors Decius (249–50) and Valerian (257–58), when Christians were ordered to deny their faith by sacrificing to the Roman deities. During the Decian persecution, Cyprian chose to go into hiding—a decision that drew mixed reactions from his clergy. Though physically absent, he endeavored to lead the church and clergy of Carthage by means of messengers and letters.[2] During Valerian's oppression of the church, Cyprian was first banished to exile for a year before returning to Carthage, where he was put to death in 258 for refusing to comply with an imperial edict to sacrifice to the Roman gods.

Following the Decian persecution, the church wrestled with and at times became divided over issues that arose out of the persecution. The first issue was the restoration of the lapsed—those who gave in to the order to sacrifice. Cyprian sought to implement a consistent policy of penance for the fallen. Meanwhile, Novatian, a rigorist living in Rome, opposed Bishop Cornelius and brought schism to the church, which prompted significant correspondence, treatises, and councils from the bishop of Carthage. Finally, Cyprian tangled with Bishop Stephen of Rome, over the issue of rebaptizing heretics—specifically those entering the catholic church from the Novatian party. Hence, the political situation put pressure on the church and provoked at least a few battles inside the church that occupied Cyprian for much of his career as bishop. This was the terrain in which Cyprian led and mentored his clergy.

Clarke notes that Cyprian's style of leadership and particularly his view of the authority of a bishop resembled that of a Roman proconsul.[3] Undoubtedly, his background and familiarity with Roman administration influenced his philosophy of church leader-

---

[1] See Maureen Tilley, "Cyprian of Carthage," *ATTA*, 262; and Richard Seagraves, *Pascentes Cum Disciplina: A Lexical Study of the Clergy in the Cyprianic Correspondence* (Fribourg: Editions Universitaires, 1993), 1.

[2] *Letter* 20.12; see J. Patout Burns, *Cyprian the Bishop* (London: Routledge, 2002), 2.

[3] See G. W. Clarke's commentary in *Letters of St. Cyprian*, ACW (New York: Paulist, 1986), 43:19.

ship. For Cyprian, the church was composed of bishops, clergy, and faithful members, and she was made complete because of the unity of bishop and church.[4]

Cyprian as Bishop

What was the role of a bishop for Cyprian? As a priest (Lat. *sacerdos*) in the legacy of Melchizedek and the Levites of the Hebrew Scriptures, Cyprian presided over all liturgical assemblies including the Eucharist and baptisms.[5] As a pastor, he listened to confession and restored the lapsed. As a teacher (Lat. *doctor*), it was his duty to preach the Scriptures, which he articulated to the clergy in *Letter* 73: "Our duty is clear: we must hold fast to the faith and truth of the catholic church, we must continue to teach it, and by the means of all the commandments of the Gospels and the apostles we must set forth the nature of the order and unity ordained by God."[6] As a metropolitan bishop, he convened and participated in councils with the council (Lat. *collegium*) of bishops. Finally, as our present study will show, he not only set apart clergy for service but also oversaw the ministry of the clergy at Carthage, providing instruction, exhortation, rebuke, encouragement, and opportunities for service and development.[7]

Cyprian's Clergy in Carthage

Although he was a young Christian at the time of his consecration, Cyprian seemed to have had a mature understanding of the offices and roles of church leadership. Aside from the bishop, the clerical offices in Cyprian's day included presbyters, deacons, subdeacons, readers, exorcists, and acolytes. Only the bishop and presbyters were consecrated by the laying on of hands; while the other

---

[4] *Letters* 33; 66; *On the Unity of the Church* 5; also Victor Saxer, *Vie Liturgique et Quotidienne à Carthage Vers Le Milieu Du IIIè Siècle: Le Témoignage de Saint Cyprien et des Ses Contemporains D'Afrique* (2nd ed., Citta del Vaticano: Pontificio Instituto di Archeologia Cristiana, 1984), 72; Jan Joncas, "Clergy, North African," *ATTA*, 213; and Seagraves, *Pascentes*, 49.

[5] *Letter* 63.4.1; also Seagraves, *Pascentes*, 26; G. S. M. Walker, *The Churchmanship of St. Cyprian* (Richmond, VA: John Knox, 1969), 40; and Saxer, *Vie Liturgique*, 88.

[6] *Letter* 73.20.2; English translation from Seagraves, *Pascentes*, 69; also ibid., 66–70, 174; and Joncas, "Clergy, North African," *ATTA*, 213.

[7] See Joncas, "Clergy, North African," *ATTA*, 213.

clergy were simply appointed by the bishop. Since Cyprian's letters alone reveal no less than 39 clergy serving with him in Carthage, the structure of the church leadership in that city was quite developed. Let us briefly consider the role of each clerical office in Carthage during Cyprian's ministry.[8]

In general, the *presbyter* served, assisted, and advised the bishop. In the bishop's absence he presided over the Eucharist and in some cases heard confession from the lapsed and offered reconciliation.[9] Presbyters were entrusted with teaching, especially of catechumens—those preparing for baptism. They also visited the sick, ministered to Christians in prison, and dispensed material aid to the poor. Some presbyters performed administrative tasks such as carrying letters and money on behalf of the bishop. Finally, they participated with the bishop in church councils.[10]

Cyprian's *deacons* also largely existed to serve the bishop.[11] Their tasks included visiting the sick and imprisoned, ministering to the needs of the poor, handling church finances, assisting in the liturgy and baptisms, and distributing the cup during the Eucharist.[12] In the absence of the bishop, some deacons were allowed to hear the dying confession of the lapsed and offer them reconciliation.[13] Subdeacons assisted the deacons in their ministry, primarily by delivering letters and dispensing money.[14]

Cyprian highly regarded readers for their ministry of reading the Scriptures in the worship assembly.[15] Some readers assisted the presbyters in reading the Scriptures to the catechumens during their instruction, and others delivered letters for Cyprian.[16] This

[8] See Seagraves, *Pascentes*, 278, 173, 318.
[9] *Letter* 29; see Joncas, "Clergy, North African," *ATTA*, 214.
[10] *Letters* 14.3.1; 16.1.2; 1; 4; 29; 38; also Joncas, "Clergy, North African," *ATTA*, 214; Seagraves, *Pascentes*, 97–98; and Saxer, *Vie Liturgique*, 82–84.
[11] *Letters* 3.3.1; 52.2.3; see Seagraves, *Pascentes*, 110; and Saxer, *Vie Liturgique*, 80.
[12] *Letters* 5.1.2; 5.2.1; 12.1.1; 13.7; *On the Lapsed*, 25; also Joncas, "Clergy, North African," *ATTA*, 214; ACW, 43:168; and Burns, *Cyprian the Bishop*, 19.
[13] *Letter* 18.1.2; also Joncas, "Clergy, North African," *ATTA*, 214; and Seagraves, *Pascentes*, 113.
[14] *Letters* 9.1.1; 9.2.1; 20.3.2; 35.1.1; 36; 45.4.3; 47.1.2; 77–9; ACW, 43:206; also Seagraves, *Pascentes*, 139.
[15] *Letters* 38–39; also Seagraves, *Pascentes*, 150; and Saxer, *Vie Liturgique*, 78.
[16] *Letters* 24; 29; 32; also Saxer, *Vie Liturgique*, 78; and Seagraves, *Pascentes*, 151.

office was generally occupied by youth with clear reading voices. It served as a stepping stone to the higher ranks of the clergy as the individual increased in age and spiritual maturity.[17]

Cyprian also included *exorcists* among the clergy in Carthage. Their ministry included leading catechumens through a renunciation of the evil one and the flesh prior to baptism as well as caring for others who were apparently oppressed by demons. They also accompanied the bishop and presbyters on visits to the sick.[18] The remaining clerical office noted by Cyprian was the acolyte, who generally served the presbyters, deacons, and subdeacons while carrying letters and distributing money to prisoners.[19]

How Did Cyprian Mentor?

Readers of Cyprian's letters, *On the Unity of the Church* and *On the Lapsed*, as well as Pontius's *Life of Cyprian*, gain a sense of Cyprian's mentoring relationship to the clergy in Carthage and in other parts of Africa. Four key approaches to mentoring emerge from his repeated behavior: participation in church councils, resourcing them with letters, resourcing them with books, and disciplining the clergy.

Church councils. Following in the footsteps of his predecessor, Agrippinus of Carthage (c. 220), Cyprian greatly valued convening councils of African bishops to deal with church matters. Arguably, Cyprian's greatest lasting influence on the structure of the North African church was advancing and developing this forum.

Cyprian participated in seven councils during his time as bishop. The first four, convened in 251, 252, 253 and 254, largely dealt with the question of the lapsed.[20] The council of 254 in particular chastised clergy who had prematurely restored the lapsed without proper penance. The other three councils—held in 255, the spring

---

[17] See Saxer, *Vie Liturgique*, 80; Joncas, "Clergy, North African," *ATTA*, 214; and *Letters* 24; 39.

[18] *Letters* 69.15.2; 75.10.4; *An Address to Demetrianus*, 5, 15; *On the Vanity of Idols*, 7; ACW, 43:343; also Seagraves, *Pascentes*, 162, 164.

[19] *Letters* 45.4.3; 52.1; 59.1; 77.3.2; 78.1; ACW, 43:202; also Seagraves, *Pascentes*, 168.

[20] *Letters* 42; 45; 49; 57; 64; 67; also Saxer, *Vie Liturgique*, 13–14; and Burns, *Cyprian the Bishop*, 5, 8.

of 256, and in September 256—addressed the question of whether heretics requesting membership in the catholic church needed to be rebaptized.[21] The council of 255 as well as the one in the spring of 256 essentially reaffirmed the decision of the council of 220 under Agrippinus in which those coming out of heresy were ordered to be rebaptized. Finally, the September 256 council was an outright condemnation of Bishop Stephen of Rome, who opposed rebaptism.[22]

How did Cyprian mentor the clergy through church councils? As metropolitan bishop, he took the initiative to convene the bishops for the first time in more than 30 years, and they responded to his call.[23] This was especially significant in the initial years when Cyprian endeavored to establish these meetings as a regular practice. Cyprian's opinion on doctrinal matters, as in the case of rebaptizing heretics, also seemed to carry more weight than that of his colleagues. In the second council of 256, Cyprian's correspondence with Jubianus on rebaptism was read aloud followed by a decision that remained consistent with Cyprian's opinions.[24] Cyprian's influence over the council extended further as he customarily drafted the letters that articulated the proceedings and decisions of the council.[25] Hence, he influenced the clergy through initiating the gathering, through his actual participation in the council, as well as in the period following the council.

Though he led the councils with authority, Cyprian also led with a great deal of humility. In the midst of one council, he made the famous remark that "no one is a bishop of bishops."[26] Though some are skeptical of Cyprian's declaration of humility, some of his actions ought to be taken into consideration. During one council, he humbly postured himself by being the last to sign the council's

---

[21] *Letter* 70; 72; see Saxer, *Vie Liturgique*, 14–15; and Burns, *Cyprian the Bishop*, 106.

[22] See Burns, *Cyprian the Bishop*, 9, 106.

[23] *Letters* 3–4; 56; 58; 62–64; 70; 72; also Burns, *Cyprian the Bishop*, 15.

[24] *Letters* 70; 73; see *Seventh Council of Carthage* at http://www.newadvent.org/fathers/0508.htm; and Burns, *Cyprian the Bishop*, 106.

[25] *Letters* 57; 64; 67; 70; and 72 comprise the conciliar letters; also *Letter* 48.2.2.

[26] See *Opinion of the Bishops* (*Sententiae episcoporum*, 87), in J. P. Migne, *Patrologiae Cursus Completus*, Series Latina (Paris: Garnier Frères, 1844, 1958–1974), 3.1054; also Saxer, *Vie Liturgique*, 17.

proceedings.[27] He went to great lengths to assemble the council, which demonstrated his desire for the African bishops' involvement and a value for collective decision-making. Requiring much patience, he endeavored to model the unity of the church through the unity of its bishops.[28] During some councils he humbly solicited the input of presbyters, deacons, and sometimes even the laity, especially regarding decisions pertaining to the lapsed.[29] If Cyprian had not been a humble leader, he surely would not have gone to the trouble to unify the bishops and involve the clergy.

Letters. Cyprian attached great importance to messages and written correspondence. Clarke asserts that Cyprian's letters were intended to be read publicly and that copies were generally made before they were sent so that they would also serve as a resource to others.[30] Fifty-seven of Cyprian's 67 surviving letters were written to members of the clergy.[31] Nineteen were addressed to his own clergy in Carthage, while another 38 were intended for other clergy in Africa and beyond.[32] He used letters to resource the clergy by answering questions on practical church matters, giving practical instructions for ministry, exhorting the clergy to faithfulness and ministry, at times disciplining the clergy, encouraging them, dealing with doctrinal issues, or simply communicating church-related information. He wrote five additional letters to communicate the decisions of church councils in Africa.

In at least 12 of Cyprian's letters, he responded to questions regarding practical church matters. In five of these letters, he gave instructions for dealing with the lapsed.[33] Four letters included affirmation and instruction to clergy for carrying out church dis-

---

[27] See Saxer, *Vie Liturgique,* 17.

[28] *Letters* 26.1.2; 55.6.1–2; also Burns, *Cyprian the Bishop,* 87–88; Jane Merdinger, *Rome and the African Church* (New Haven: Yale University Press, 1997), 37.

[29] *Letters* 11.7.3; 16.4.2; 19.2.2; 26.1.2; also Burns, *Cyprian the Bishop,* 21.

[30] See G. W. Clarke's commentary in *Letters of St. Cyprian,* ACW, 43:9.

[31] Cyprian's total body of correspondence numbers 82, but this includes 15 letters that were addressed to him.

[32] *Letters* 5–7; 11–14; 16; 18–19; 26; 29; 32; 34; 38–40; 43; 81 were letters written to Carthaginian clergy; *Letters* 1–4; 25; 27–28; 35; 37; 41; 44–48; 51–52; 55–57; 59–74; 76; 80 were written to clergy outside of Carthage.

[33] *Letters* 19; 25–27; 56.

cipline in the case of both clergy and laypeople.[34] In one letter he responded to clergy who were trying to rectify the situation of a presbyter who was improperly installed as acting bishop after the death of the previous bishop.[35] In another letter he gave instructions on how to deal with a former actor who joined the church but was earning a living by teaching his former profession to youth.[36] Finally, Cyprian replied to one bishop on how to prepare the wine for the Eucharist.[37]

Three letters written in 250 contained instructions for specific ministry assignments for clergy in Carthage while Cyprian was in hiding. Some tasks included distributing money to the poor, visiting the confessors in prison, and properly honoring and burying those confessors who died in prison.[38]

Cyprian sent five letters of exhortation to the clergy. In one letter, he urged them to get along with one another, to be steadfast in prayer, to stand firm in their faith, and to be careful about what they ate and drank.[39] In two other letters the clergy were strongly reminded to continue in the work of ministry by dispensing money to the poor, ministering to the confessors in prison, and rebuking any confessors for inappropriate behavior.[40] In a fourth letter Cyprian wrote exhorting Bishop Stephen of Rome to use his influence to have a schismatic bishop in Gaul removed.[41] Finally, Cyprian wrote to some clergy at Rome who had supported Novatian's election as bishop and urged them to break with the schism.[42]

Three of Cyprian's letters were specifically intended to discipline the clergy. In two letters, written to his Carthaginian clergy from hiding in 250, he chastised them for taking matters into their own hands by prematurely readmitting the lapsed to communion.[43] In

---

[34] *Letters* 3–4; 34; 41; also *Letter* 64.

[35] *Letter* 1.

[36] *Letter* 2.

[37] *Letter* 63.

[38] *Letters* 5.1.2; 5.2.1; 7.2; 12.1.2; 12.2.1.

[39] *Letter* 11.3.2; 11.5.1; 11.7.3; 11.5.3; 11.6.2.

[40] *Letters* 13.7; 14.2.1–2; 14.3.2.

[41] *Letter* 68.

[42] *Letter* 46.

[43] *Letters* 16; 18. Though grouped with the letters of exhortation, *Letter* 11 has a disciplinary tone to it as well.

another letter he severely rebuked a certain Puppianus for living an immoral lifestyle.[44]

Cyprian wrote 16 letters of encouragement to his clergy in Carthage as well as to leaders serving elsewhere. In two letters he encouraged the clergy for their role in providing spiritual counsel to those who were suffering.[45] One letter affirmed and encouraged a bishop whose position was being challenged by a fallen bishop.[46] Cyprian addressed six letters to Cornelius of Rome, encouraging him in his role as bishop in the face of the Novatian schism.[47] Another four were written to encourage clergy who were either in prison or sentenced to hard labor because of their refusal to offer sacrifices to the Roman deities.[48] Cyprian also sent a letter of encouragement to one bishop and his colleagues who had just returned from exile.[49] In another letter he responded with practical encouragement to a group of Numidian bishops who had had some of their flock kidnapped by a band of thieves. He provided verbal encouragement but also sent a monetary gift to help ransom the believers.[50] Finally, Cyprian's last letter contained a message of hope and encouragement to the clergy as well as the laity in light of his imminent martyrdom. He encouraged them to accept his suffering with courage and calm.[51]

Five of Cyprian's letters were replies to doctrinal questions. The first was a persuasive work written to a certain Bishop Antonianus to keep him from being swayed by Novatian's teaching.[52] The other four letters dealt with the importance of rebaptizing heretics who desired membership in the church.[53] In one of the four letters, Cyprian responded to a certain Pompeius who had asked Cyprian to give him Stephen's argument for refusing to rebaptize heretics.

---

[44] *Letter* 66.
[45] *Letters* 19; 43.
[46] *Letter* 65.
[47] *Letters* 44–45; 47–48; 51; 60.
[48] *Letter* 6; 28; 37; 76.
[49] *Letter* 61.
[50] *Letter* 62.4.1; 62.3.2.
[51] *Letter* 81.
[52] *Letter* 55.
[53] *Letters* 69; 71; 73–74; also *Letters* 70; 72.

Cyprian not only sent Stephen's letter but also attached a significant note refuting Stephen's thinking.[54]

Cyprian wrote nine letters to the clergy to update them on church business. In one letter he was merely "copying" his clergy on official correspondence with Rome, information that they were free to pass on to others who were in need of it.[55] In another letter Cyprian updated some Roman clergy on a case of church discipline.[56] Cyprian sent two letters to Cornelius, informing him about what he was doing with schismatic clergy in Africa while discussing the Novatian schism in general.[57] In a letter addressed to a certain Bishop Successus, Cyprian informed him of the persecution that had happened under Valerian and encouraged the bishop to prepare for it.[58] In the final four letters, Cyprian made the clergy aware of some clerical appointments he had made.[59]

Cyprian's final five letters were written to communicate decisions made by the council of bishops. The first letter, addressed to Cornelius, communicated the decision of the council on the situation of the lapsed.[60] A second letter, written to a certain Fidus, dealt with the doctrinal issue of baptizing children as well as the practical issue of a fallen presbyter who had been restored too hastily.[61] A third letter, addressed to Spanish clergy Felix and Aelius, was rather disciplinary in tone as Cyprian affirmed high standards of holiness required for a bishop. It should be noted that this letter was written as a response to the moral failure of two Spanish clergy.[62] The final two letters were both doctrinal and practical, written to clarify the need for rebaptism of those who had come into the church from heresy.[63]

---

[54] *Letter* 74.
[55] *Letter* 32.
[56] *Letter* 35.
[57] *Letters* 52; 59.
[58] *Letter* 80.
[59] *Letters* 29; 38–40.
[60] *Letter* 57.
[61] *Letter* 64.
[62] *Letter* 67.
[63] *Letters* 70; 72.

Hence, Cyprian made great use of letters to mentor both his Carthaginian clergy as well as to influence other clergy. During times of hiding, exile, peace, and following church councils, Cyprian used letters to give practical instruction, to exhort, to discipline, to encourage, and to give information that would equip the clergy in carrying out their ministry.

Books. Aside from his correspondence, Cyprian sent small books as a means of resourcing the clergy. In 251, following his return from hiding, he wrote two significant treatises addressed primarily to the clergy—*On the Lapsed* and *On the Unity of the Church.*

On the Lapsed explained how to reconcile those who had given in to the order to sacrifice.[64] As many clergy had responded to the crisis of the lapsed and Cyprian's self-imposed exile by doing what was right in their own eyes, Cyprian used this treatise to solidify once again the authority of the bishop while correcting the thinking of the church on the issue. Burns writes, "It reveals a shrewd program through which he moved the church to affirm its protective boundary and to realign its system of offices and roles which had been distorted by the martyrs, confessors, and laxist clergy."[65] Burns adds that prior to its publication, Cyprian probably delivered *On the Lapsed* in the form of a speech to the clergy at Carthage following his return from hiding.[66]

The practical purpose of *On the Unity of the Church* was to defend the authority of the office of bishop and specifically that of Cornelius of Rome, who was opposed by Novatian.[67] Yet the circumstances of schism in Rome following the Decian persecution also afforded Cyprian the opportunity to enlighten the clergy on the nature of the church. Cyprian winsomely argued in this treatise for the necessity of the unity of the church against all attempts at factions and schisms.[68]

The clergy at Carthage, it seems clear, were intimately aware of Cyprian's thought on restoring the lapsed and the unity of the

---

[64] See Tilley, "Cyprian of Carthage," *ATTA*, 263.
[65] See Burns, *Cyprian the Bishop*, 37.
[66] See ibid., 85.
[67] See Tilley, "Cyprian of Carthage," *ATTA*, 263.
[68] See Merdinger, *Rome and the African Church*, 37–38.

church. Yet, by publishing the books through the hands of careful copyists, the bishop of Carthage enjoyed a mentoring influence on the clergy outside of Carthage as well as on future generations.

Discipline. A final mentoring form observed in Cyprian was disciplining the clergy. Though not the rigorist that Novatian was, Cyprian held high moral standards for the clergy since he believed that their impropriety could thwart God's blessing on the church. For this reason it was necessary that Cyprian confront and even dismiss clergy who were immoral.

Cyprian's letters and writings are filled with instances of clergy being disciplined or dismissed.[69] Some were disciplined for improperly dealing with the lapsed, for rebellion, for greed or fraud, or for lapsing in the faith.[70] Though Cyprian was severe with immoral clergy, he hoped that they would repent and be restored to communion with the church. However, the more significant value of discipline as a mentoring tool was that the clergy in good moral standing were indirectly warned when the immoral were disciplined.[71]

Discipline does not have to be simply regarded as penal. As shown in Cyprian's correspondence, he wrote disciplinary letters to exhort and rebuke the clergy toward fulfilling their duties.[72] These clergy apparently continued in their ministries following their receipt of Cyprian's letter.

Because of his view of the priesthood, Cyprian maintained high standards of holiness for the clergy. It was this conviction that compelled him to discipline and remove unworthy clergy while rebuking and exhorting to good deeds those who remained faithful.

Cyprian's Thought on Mentoring

Given the four approaches to mentoring observed in Cyprian's ministry, what were his convictions for mentoring spiritual leaders?

---

[69] *Letters* 1.2.1; 3.3.1–3; 4.4.1; 9.1; 16.4.2; 34.1, 34.4.1–2; 45.4.1; 52.3; 59.1; 64.1.1–2; 65.4.2; 66.10.1; 67.3.1–5.2; 68.2.1–4.3; 72.2; *On the Lapsed*, 10–11; also Burns, *Cyprian the Bishop*, 15.

[70] *Letters* 3; 16.4.2; 34.1; 34.3.2; 34.4.1; 41.2.2; 52.1.2; 55.4.3; 59; also Seagraves, *Pascentes*, 105, 110, 125, 169.

[71] *Letters* 54; 67.

[72] *Letters* 11; 14; 16; 18.

His thought on mentoring generally follows the New Testament model proposed in the first chapter.

The group. Cyprian valued the group as essential for mentoring for several reasons. First, the mere fact that he supervised nearly 40 clergy in the work of the Carthage church created a group context for mentoring. Second, because Cyprian's clerical correspondence was characteristically addressed to groups of clergy serving together, his direction, exhortation, or encouragement was probably meant to be received by the group. Third, his letters, which contained ministry instruction or assignments, were also often directed to groups of clergy. Hence, he probably believed that the group would provide both support and accountability toward completing the task. Fourth, on at least one occasion, Cyprian set apart spiritual leaders together—Celerinus and Aurelius who were appointed to the office of reader.[73] Cyprian's intention was that they would advance in the ranks of the clergy, eventually becoming presbyters. Hence, it is plausible that they could support and encourage one another along the way. Finally, Cyprian influenced church councils and had a mentoring influence on the African bishops. Cyprian had insisted on these gatherings because he believed that church matters of great importance should be settled by a body of clergy. Joncas asserts that Cyprian probably coined the word *collegium* to refer to the group of bishops.[74]

A mentor is a disciple. Pontius, in the *Life* of his mentor Cyprian, mentioned Caecilian, the Carthaginian presbyter who discipled Cyprian when he was a new believer. Pontius referred to Caecilian as a teacher ("doctor"), perhaps indicating that he was responsible for instructing catechumens.[75] It is significant that Pontius recognized that their highly regarded bishop, a teacher himself, had also spent time being mentored in doctrine.

In *Letter* 74, Cyprian wrote to his clergy, "It is thus a bishop's duty not only to teach; he must also learn. For he becomes a better teacher if he makes daily progress and advancement in learning

---

[73] *Letters* 38–39.
[74] See Joncas, "Clergy, North African," *ATTA*, 213; and *Letters* 55; 68.
[75] Pontius, *Life of Cyprian*, 4; also Seagraves, *Pascentes*, 102.

what is better."[76] Cyprian was not only taught as a new believer but he valued continual, lifelong learning realized through daily study and interaction with the Scriptures.[77]

Cyprian showed that he was a continual disciple and learner by humbly looking to his clergy for advice in important areas like restoring the lapsed and appointing clergy. Though he was a metropolitan bishop, his humility in gathering the council of bishops and seeking the input from subordinate clergy also reflects a learner's posture.

Mentor-disciple relationship. Cyprian exercised significant authority over his clergy.[78] This authority was clear in his correspondence through the posture he took in assigning ministry tasks, in exhorting the clergy to ministry, and in disciplining wayward clergy. Although some clergy ignored his directives during his time in hiding in 250, he never lost his grip on the leadership of the Carthaginian church. Burns comments, "Cyprian had managed to meet the threats which might have resulted in the dissolution of the community or his own isolation. . . . He had asserted the rights of his office within the context of its service to the whole church."[79] Seagraves summarizes the purpose of Cyprian's authority: "To preserve this dignity of the church, the bishop (in this case, Cyprian) needs and has his God-given authority. The sole possession of authority, however, is not sufficient: the bishop must exercise it in the various facets of his direction and guidance of his subordinates."[80] Though Cyprian did manage to maintain and exercise authority over the clergy, this characterization alone is far from complete. As shown, Cyprian demonstrated great confidence in the clergy during his times of exile by entrusting them with significant ministry responsibility. He showed much humility in seeking the advice of the clergy in important church decisions and in including them in church councils. In these senses Cyprian allowed the clergy to be

---

[76] *Letter* 74.10.1; English translation from Seagraves, *Pascentes*, 69.

[77] Andre Hamman, *Etudes Patristiques: méthodologie, liturgie, histoire, théologie* (Paris: Beachesne, 1991), 285.

[78] *Letters* 16.3.2; 16.4.2; 43.5.2; 59.7.3; 70.3.1; 73.11.1; also Burns, *Cyprian the Bishop*, 96.

[79] See ibid., 84.

[80] See Seagraves, *Pacentes*, 273.

his peers. The fact that he referred to other bishops and presbyters as "our fellow presbyters" *(conpresbyteri nostri)* and that younger clergy were called "brothers" also illustrates the peer aspect of their relationship.[81] Though leading with authority, Cyprian also believed that the bishop must teach and lead through his example.[82] In summary, Cyprian's relationship to the clergy was a delicate balance of authority and cooperation.

Sound teaching. Nemesianus of Numidia, in his eulogy of Cyprian, praised him for being a "good and true teacher" *(bonus et uerus doctor).*[83] Aside from his regular duties of preaching, the situation of the lapsed and the question of rebaptizing heretics provoked a thorough doctrinal response from Cyprian. This often came in the form of books and letters addressed to the clergy. In addition, his convening of church councils allowed him to influence the clergy and involve them in the process of upholding sound doctrine. The importance Cyprian placed on sound teaching was perhaps most strongly reflected in how he stood up to the recognized church hierarchy, particularly in his opposition to Bishop Stephen of Rome over the issue of rebaptizing heretics. Cyprian underscored this value in a previously cited letter where he urged the clergy to "hold fast to the faith and truth of the catholic church," which must be taught "by the means of all the commandments of the Gospels and the apostles."[84]

Modeling and involvement in ministry. Though regarded as a Roman pro-consul type bishop, possessing authority and a certain power in the church, it would be fallacious to think that Cyprian took all the church responsibilities on himself—something already evident from the brief survey on the clergy's roles. Moreover, I argue that he was active in involving his clergy in ministries where responsibility and authority were delegated and where the spiritual leader had the opportunity to grow and develop as a leader.

How did Cyprian involve his clergy in ministry? First, virtually every member of the clergy, including presbyters, was at some point

---

[81] See Walker, *Churchmanship of Cyprian*, 44.
[82] *Letter* 4.3.3; also Seagraves, *Pacentes*, 69.
[83] *Letter* 77.2.1; also Seagraves, *Pacentes*, 267.
[84] *Letter* 73.20.2.

involved in carrying letters for Cyprian.[85] Though this administrative task does not seem to have tremendous importance, Cyprian believed it did. The minister was not simply a postman but one entrusted with official church documents; one who needed to ensure that the true and accurate message of the bishop reached its destination. This ministry was so important to Cyprian that he demanded that his couriers be men of irreproachable character.[86] Furthermore, he often sent his correspondence with a group of clergy traveling together, which perhaps provided some sort of accountability. What seems most significant is that Cyprian would entrust such an important ministry to lower members of the clergy.

Second, deacons along with presbyters were entrusted with providing financial help for the confessors in prison, celebrating the Eucharist with them, and caring for their needs in general.[87] He must have placed great confidence in these deacons to manage and disperse finances, yet their responsibilities extended beyond mere administration to pastoral care and serving at the altar.

Third, Cyprian involved presbyters and deacons in ministry through seeking their advice. He sought their input on how to proceed in the question of the lapsed and welcomed their thoughts as he was setting apart men for ministry.[88] As noted, he welcomed their presence in decision making by involving them in the African church councils.[89] Thus, it is clear that Cyprian did not merely employ yes-men as advisors but seriously solicited their input for leading the church. As a result, they received training in real-life decision making that contributed to their development as spiritual leaders.

Fourth, Cyprian delegated significant responsibility to his presbyters. While maintaining the authority of bishop, he gave much responsibility to the presbyters, particularly during his time in hiding and exile. In fact, the main roles of the bishop—presiding over worship, hearing confession and restoring the lapsed, preaching and

---

[85] *Letters* 29.1.1; 34.4.1; 44.2.2; 45.4.3; 47.1.2; 49.3.1; also Seagraves, *Pacentes*, 19.
[86] *Letters* 9.2.2; 49.3.1; 59.9.4; 20.1.1; also Seagraves, *Pacentes*, 115, 140.
[87] *Letters* 5.1.2; 13.7; 5.2.2; 12.1.1; 5.2.1; also Burns, *Cyprian the Bishop*, 19.
[88] *Letters* 17.3.2; 19.2.2; 26.1.2; 38.1.1; also Seagraves, *Pacentes*, 107–8.
[89] *Letters* 14.4; 19.1; 19.2.2; 26.1.2; 43.3.2; also Seagraves, *Pacentes*, 118.

teaching, and participating in councils—were at some point fulfilled by the presbyters.

Did Cyprian's time in hiding and exile accelerate the clergy's involvement in ministry and delegation of responsibility? Judging from the content of his correspondence during this period, Cyprian seemed to be encouraging the clergy to do more than they would actually be doing if he were present.[90] In *Letter* 5, he provided a specific list of duties to be carried out in his absence; in *Letter* 14, he directed the clergy to do his job of caring for the poor and ministering to the confessors in prison.[91] Finally, the departure of a strong leader who nevertheless provides direction and encouragement to continue the ministry in his absence would challenge some developing leaders to realize their potential.[92] Though the circumstances of Cyprian's time in hiding and exile did seem to accelerate his clergy's involvement in ministry and increased responsibility, this did not occur against his will. Rather, as his correspondence indicates, he was encouraging that development with the unselfish heart of a pastor who longed to see the flock cared for whether he was present or not.

Cyprian communicated well his desire to involve clergy in ministry in *Letter* 41: "I desire to be informed about them all and to advance everyone who is suitable, humble and meek to the duties of the ecclesiastical office."[93] Though he exercised a high level of scrutiny in appointing even the lower orders of clergy, Cyprian still seemed willing to take a risk in setting apart leaders to be raised up for the work of the church.[94] It is apparent that Cyprian saw the lower levels of clergy as reasonable entry points into the ministry after which faithful clergy could be promoted to the higher offices

---

[90] *Letters* 5–7 and 14 were written while he was in hiding in 250, and *Letters* 76 and 81 were written from exile in 257–58.

[91] *Letters* 5.1.1; 14.2.1–2.

[92] Cyprian's absence did of course have the opposite effect on some clergy who took the matter of the lapsed into their own hands and began prematurely restoring the fallen. This scandal is the subject of *Letters* 16 and 18. Burns (*Cyprian the Bishop*, 21, 80) argues that these were clergy unfavorable to electing a bishop who was such a young Christian. Also *Letters* 5.2; 16.4.2; 34.1; 59.12.1–2; Pontius, *Life of Cyprian*, 5.

[93] *Letter* 41.1.2; English translation from Seagraves, *Pacentes*, 101.

[94] *Letter* 29.1.2; also Seagraves, *Pacentes*, 93.

of increased responsibility. This was most evident in his nomination of Celerinus and Aurelius to the office of reader in anticipation of their promotion to presbyter.[95] Though Cyprian himself was elected directly to the office of bishop, he praised Cornelius of Rome for having gone through all the orders of the clergy, which made him more qualified to serve as bishop.[96]

Resourcing. Although Cyprian delegated virtually all the ministry to his clergy during his time in hiding and exile, he did arm them with letters of instruction, encouragement, exhortation, and even discipline. Also, as noted, he sent resourceful letters to clergy outside of Carthage, while his books provided some clarity in doctrinal and practical church matters. There is even evidence that he may have resourced some clergy outside of Carthage through personal visits.[97]

Pachomius

Nearly a half century after Cyprian's death, Pachomius was born into a pagan family in Upper Egypt. While serving in the Roman army as a young man, he was deeply impacted by the kindness of a Christian who cared for him during a time of difficulty.[98] Upon his release from the army, Pachomius returned to Upper Egypt, converted to Christianity, and became part of the church. Later he sought out the hermit Palamon and spent seven years pursuing an ascetic lifestyle in his company.[99] While learning from Palamon, he reportedly heard a voice calling him to begin a monastery in the deserted village of Tabennesi. Because Pachomius's vision differed from Palamon's monasticism, it became necessary that he leave his mentor, though the two covenanted to remain in contact.[100] Pachomius is generally recognized as the father of cenobitic

---

[95] *Letters* 38–39.

[96] *Letter* 55.8.2; also Seagraves, *Pacentes*, 57.

[97] *Letters* 48.2.2; 58.1.1.

[98] See J. McGuckin, "Pachomius, St.," in William M. Johnston, ed., *Encyclopedia of Monasticism* (Chicago and London: Fitzroy Dearborn, 2000), 985–86.

[99] *Life of Pachomius*, 6–11; also Phillip Rousseau, *Pachomius: The Making of a Community in Fourth-Century Egypt* (Berkeley: University of California Press, 1985), 59.

[100] See McGuckin, "Pachomius, St.," *Encyclopedia of Monasticism*, 985–86; and William Harmless, *Desert Christians: An Introduction to the Literature of Early Monasticism* (Oxford: Oxford University Press, 2004), 119.

(community) monasticism, while Antony (251–356) is the recognized pioneer of eremitic living.[101] Although the history of the two movements did not unfold so neatly, it is still valuable that we consider the work of Pachomius as innovative and representative of Egyptian cenobitic monasticism.

Beginning at Tabenessi, Pachomius attracted disciples who came to abandon the world.[102] The community later expanded to include other settlements down the Nile in Upper Egypt. According to the historian Palladius, Pachomius's movement grew to 3,000 monks during his lifetime, though others have speculated that the number was as high as 5,000.[103]

As monastic communities grew in Egypt, conflict arose between the monasteries and the organized church because, in some areas, the monastic communities rivaled the purpose of the church. For instance, the duties of monks, which included ministering to physical needs, performing liturgical functions, and teaching, tended to mirror those of the clergy.[104] While church leaders could feel threatened by the monasteries, the monastic superiors (Gk. *abba,* "father") also feared the church would conscript their monks into the ranks of the clergy. Though Pachomius refused ordination for himself and his monks, the ordination of monks did increase during his lifetime. Two Egyptian bishops, in particular, began as monks with Pachomius.[105]

Despite the potential conflict between church and monastery, Pachomius enjoyed good relations with the organized church and particularly with Athanasius of Alexandria (296–373). Athanasius, who authored the *Life of Antony,* highly esteemed the monastic movement and made personal visits to strengthen ties with each

---

[101] The English "coenobite" is derived from the Latin *coenobium,* which is transliterated from the Greek *konobiam,* which emphasizes that they held things in common and thus acted like a community. The eremitic monks, on the other hand, pursued more of an isolated experience. See Harmless, *Desert Christians,* 115.

[102] *Life of Pachomius,* 23; also Rousseau, *Pachomius,* 61.

[103] See McGuckin, "Pachomius, St.," *Encyclopedia of Monasticism,* 985; and Harmless, *Desert Christians,* 124.

[104] See Andrea Sterk, *Renouncing the World yet Leading the Church: The Monk-Bishop in Late Antiquity* (Cambridge, MA: Harvard University Press, 2004), 15, 19–20.

[105] See ibid., 18–20; and Phillip Rousseau, "The Spiritual Authority of a 'Monk-Bishop,'" *JTS* 23 (1971): 398.

abba.[106] He led a movement of clergy interested in incorporating aspects of monasticism into the life and work of the clergy, which culminated in the notion of the monk-bishop—a way of life that would later be observed as far away as Cappadocia and Hippo.[107] At the same time, he was not opposed to recruiting clergy from the monastery as he considered it an excellent training center for ministers.[108]

How Did Pachomius Mentor?

Though Pachomius was not mentoring men in the context of church ministry, his monastic values certainly began to catch on and influence the training of clergy. Let us for the moment, however, consider Pachomius's forms of mentoring in the context of the monastery. Three key forms include the monastery itself, dialogue between master and disciple, and his writings.

The monastery. The monastic movement under Pachomius was organized by houses, monasteries, and an overall *koinōnia* that consisted of a network of monasteries in different locations. Each monk lived in a house that was directed by a "housemaster" *(oikiakos)* who was assisted by a "second" *(deuteros)*.[109] The housemaster was responsible for teaching the monks and assigning tasks of manual labor; he was generally responsible for the actions of his monks. Harmless writes: "For the average monk, the housemaster was at once supervisor and superior, teacher, and spiritual father."[110] About 40 monks lived in a house, and each one had his own cell where he prayed and slept.

An individual monastery was comprised of 30 or 40 houses and was led by a superior known as a "steward" *(oikonomos)* who was also assisted by a second. Pachomius referred to the network of monasteries in various locations along the Nile as the *koinōnia*. It developed and expanded because of the increased enrollment of monks as well as adherence of previously existing monasteries that

---

[106] See Harmless, *Desert Christians*, 34.
[107] See Rousseau, *Pachomius*, 153.
[108] See Sterk, *Renouncing the World*, 16–17, 34.
[109] See Harmless, *Desert Christians*, 126.
[110] Ibid.

Probably the location of Augustine's clerical monastery inside the bishop's house next to the basilica of peace.

began to affiliate with the Pachomian network. Pachomius served as the *abba* or father and exercised authority over the entire *koinōnia*. Though he personally lived at the monastery at Pboou (Faw Qibli, on the Nile in Egypt), he regularly traveled to visit and resource the stewards of the individual monasteries.[111]

What did the daily routine consist of in the monastery? After waking up, the monks walked to an assembly reciting Scripture along the way. During the assembly the monks prayed and listened to Scripture readings while weaving baskets. Following the gathering, they returned to their houses and waited for the housemaster to assign them manual labor for the day. The work, which included working in the fields, making crafts, or preparing food, was carried out in silence. The monks ate two meals a day in silence but fasted on Wednesdays and Fridays.[112] Following the meal, they returned

---

[111] See ibid., 122, 125.
[112] See ibid., 128; and Rousseau, *Pachomius*, 84.

to their houses for evening prayers. On days of fasting, the house-master gave an evening teaching in the house that was followed by a discussion. On the weekends Pachomius or the steward of a particular monastery would also teach, and the Eucharist was celebrated on Saturdays and Sundays. Finally, the monks retired at night to a seat in their individual cells where they kept vigil or slept only lightly.[113]

The hierarchical structure meant that the *abba* mentored the stewards, the stewards mentored the housemasters, and the housemasters mentored the individual monks. The monks were discipled in an ascetic manner that incorporated the physical disciplines of manual labor, fasting, and keeping vigil, as well as spiritual disciplines like prayer, Scripture memory, teaching, and dialogue. The monastic context assured that this mentoring happened in a community.

Dialogue. Within the monastery Pachomius employed an interesting form of mentoring—dialogue. Though much of the day, including work and meals, was carried out in silence, the post-teaching times of dialogue gave the monks the chance to speak up. While most of the physical and spiritual disciplines were directed in a rather authoritative manner, the dialogue sessions with their housemaster allowed monks to express opinions and even disagree with their teacher.[114] Pachomius commented on the importance of this time by saying: "Everything that is taught them in the assembly of the brothers they must absolutely talk over among themselves, especially on the days of fast, when they receive instruction from their masters."[115] In dialogue Pachomius or a housemaster could open up about his spiritual life or understanding and impart it to the disciple, even as the monk contemplated and wrestled with spiritual instruction.

Dialogue as a mentoring tool gained increased importance in the monastic movement following Pachomius. The *Conferences* of John Cassian (360–435) summarized Egyptian monasticism. According to Steward, "The format [was] generally that of the classical dialogue

---

[113] See Rousseau, *Pachomius*, 85; and Harmless, *Desert Christians*, 129.
[114] *Life of Pachomius*, 61, 88, 125; also Rousseau, *Pachomius*, 81.
[115] *Praecepta*, 138 in Harmless, *Desert Christians*, 129.

or *erotapokriseis* (question and answer session)."[116] O'Loughlin adds, "One of the preferred literary conventions in early monastic theology is that of master-pupil dialogue. The disciple questions and craves knowledge, and the master replies and dispenses it. Such question-and-answer texts cover the liberal arts, theology, scriptural exegesis, monastic training . . . and even the history of the monastery."[117]

Writings. Although Pachomius was not a prolific writer, he did write his *Rule* and some letters, which were intended as a resource for stewards and housemasters. Harmless comments, "Pachomius not only dictated 'ordinances' and 'talks' but also sent cryptic letters to the heads of the various monasteries."[118] Indeed some of the letters were written in a code of Greek letters and have yet to be deciphered. Nevertheless, in one portion of an otherwise encrypted letter, Pachomius communicated his mentoring intent: "I have written to you with images and parables so that you would search them with wisdom, following the footsteps of the saints."[119]

Pachomius was indeed an innovator in that he developed the first monastic rule, which was filled with resources for the monastic leader.[120] It consists of four books: two devoted to spiritual leaders, one to housemasters, and one explaining how to deal with deviant monks.[121]

Pachomius's Thought on Mentoring

From our short survey of Pachomius's life and writings, it is also evident that spiritual mentoring was an important component of his monastic theology. At least seven principles can be identified that follow the New Testament model of mentoring.

---

[116] See Columba Steward, *Cassian the Monk* (Oxford: Oxford University Press, 1998), 30.
[117] See Thomas O'Loughlin, "Master and Pupil: Christian Perspectives," *Encyclopedia of Monasticism*, 836.
[118] See Harmless, *Desert Christians*, 131.
[119] Pachomius, *Letter* 4.6 in Harmless, *Desert Christians*, 131.
[120] See Harmless, *Desert Christians*, 124; and Rousseau, "The Spiritual Authority of a 'Monk-Bishop,'" 403.
[121] See Harmless, *Desert Christians*, 124.

The group context. The element of community distinguished his work from that of his mentor Palamon and from Antony. In his monastery the men lived, ate, worked, and performed spiritual disciplines together under the direction of a housemaster, steward, and *abba*. Leaders were responsible for the monks, but the monks also took responsibility for one another, which contributed to accountability and supported their common ascetic goal.[122] According to Rousseau, the Pachomian monks recognized "human weaknesses and individual need, and the sense that growth was necessary and possible. Those were the convictions that governed community life above all else."[123] Pachomius told his monks, "It is better for you to live with a thousand in all humility than alone with pride in a hyena's den," and he urged them to "join another who is living according to the gospel of Christ, and you will make progress with him."[124]

Mentor as disciple. Pachomius, as noted, sought out the hermit Palamon as a mentor in ascetic living and stayed with him for seven years. After his departure and a promise to stay in touch, Pachomius apparently stayed in contact with Palamon until the latter's death shortly thereafter.[125] While passing to his own disciples a conviction for prayer as well as the tendency to keep vigil, which he learned from Palamon, he took a more moderate approach to diet and embraced spiritual growth in the context of a community of monks.[126]

Though Pachomius had spent seven years with a master and probably even longer receiving helpful input from Palamon, he continued to demonstrate the heart of a disciple. Perhaps the clearest example of this is that, though serving as the *abba* over the entire *koinōnia*, Pachomius still lived in a house and "remained subject to a housemaster's authority for his everyday needs."[127]

---

[122] See Rousseau, *Pachomius*, 66, 98.

[123] See ibid., 100.

[124] *Instruction*, 1.17 in Harmless, *Desert Christians*, 130.

[125] See Harmless, *Desert Christians*, 119.

[126] *Life of Pachomius*, 14, 60; also Rousseau, *Pachomius*, 68; and Harmless, *Desert Christians*, 128–29.

[127] *Life of Pachomius*, 110; also Harmless, *Desert Christians*, 126.

That Pachomius was still a growing disciple provided a model for the stewards, housemasters, and monks to imitate. Rousseau writes:

> It was Pachomius himself who was the 'rule' in the fullest sense. The personal example of his service, the fruit of his own experience, above all his insight into Scripture, conveyed in frequent catechesis: those were the indispensable keys to his enduring influence. . . . The formative quality of his own character lay at the root of his own ascetic experiments and persisted in its effect throughout his lifetime, molding also the conduct of successors and subordinates in every community of the federation.[128]

Hence, Pachomius mentored by personal example and passed on this practice to Theodore, his eventual successor, by teaching him that a leader should be the first to keep the *Rule* and thus lead and disciple by example.[129] Later, Theodore, impacted by Pachomius's model, referred to his mentor as "an imitator of the saints" and encouraged the monks to "follow after him for he follows the saints. . . . Let us die with this man and we shall also live with him for he guides us straight to God."[130] After Pachomius's death, Theodore continued to refer to the example of Pachomius by urging the monks to imitate this spiritual father, which became a mentoring tool in itself. This naturally led Theodore to write his *Life of Pachomius,* which served a mimetic purpose for Pachomius's generation and succeeding generations as versions appeared in Coptic, Greek, Latin, and Arabic.[131]

Selection. A clearly observed tendency in the monastic movement is that the potential monk took most of the initiative to seek out a holy man as a mentor or to join a monastery. This was the case with Pachomius as he sought out Palamon. It was also true of Pachomius's monastery since his new recruits were generally

---

[128] See Rousseau, *Pachomius,* 106.
[129] See ibid., 118.
[130] *Life of Pachomius,* 36; 35 in Rousseau, *Pachomius,* 118.
[131] See Harmless, *Desert Christians,* 117, 140.

those who took the initiative toward him. In light of this tendency, Pachomius employed a doorkeeper who initially received those who came applying to be monks.

Because of his early experience with lax monks, Pachomius did not automatically accept everyone who appeared at his door. Rather, the doorkeeper interviewed each potential monk to ascertain his motivations for joining the monastery, and he led the candidate to memorize the Lord's Prayer and some psalms.[132] Because reading was crucial to learning in the monastic context, part of the training included teaching illiterate candidates to read.[133] Once he passed the entrance exam, the candidate was invited to renounce family and possessions and was taught the rules of the monastery.[134] The only formal sign of admission was the new monk's exchange of his clothes for a monastic habit, distinguishing him from those living in the world.[135]

Mentor-disciple relationship. Pachomius was largely regarded as a father to the *koinōnia*. In fact, his title, the Coptic *apa* or Greek *abba*, meant "father." As cenobitic monasticism developed, the monastic superior took the transliterated title "abbot." Pachomius's fatherly role implied his authority and organizational leadership over the *koinōnia,* including the stewards, housemasters, and monks.[136]

His fatherly authority was also evident on an interpersonal level as he expected obedience from the monks. As he interacted with them, he admonished them and instilled in them a sense of holy fear. In some extreme cases, he invoked discipline by giving a verbal rebuke or temporarily separating the monk from the community. These measures were carried out in the hope that the disciplined monk would be healed and restored to the community. Pachomius justified his authoritative position by pointing to Elijah's authority over Elisha.[137]

---

[132] See ibid., 126; and Rousseau, *Pachomius*, 70.

[133] *Praecepta*, 139; also Harmless, *Desert Christians*, 127.

[134] *Life of Pachomius*, 35; also Rousseau, *Pachomius*, 70.

[135] See Harmless, *Desert Christians*, 126–27.

[136] See ibid., 120, 125; Marek Derwich, "Abbot: Christian," *Encyclopedia of Monasticism*, 6; and Rousseau, *Pachomius*, 67.

[137] *Life of Pachomius*, 84; 86; 118; 69; 89; also Rousseau, *Pachomius*, 90–101; *Instruction*, 1.17; and Harmless, *Desert Christians*, 130.

His role as *abba* also implied a fatherly care. Though at times he needed to discipline the monks, he also was eager to hear their confession of sins and to restore them.[138] The *Life of Pachomius* indicates that he gave a great deal of personal time to the monks, "approaching each on his own, and putting his soul to work according to his capacity."[139] This time of interaction probably included dialogue as well as pastoral counseling.

Hence, the fatherly nature of Pachomius's role as *abba*, as well as that of the stewards and housemasters toward the monks, presented a clear hierarchy in the mentor-disciple relationship. O'Loughlin summarizes: "The monastery is a school of holiness, a place of disciples/disciplines, where an elder welcomes those who seek to learn and teaches by sharing his life with them." Thus, "the relationship of master to pupil was necessarily unequal."[140]

Pachomius's initial failed experience with lax monks taught him the importance of being a strong leader. Yet he won the respect and allegiance of the monks who came after by quietly serving them. In the *Life of Pachomius,* Pachomius was recorded telling the men, "As for me, it is by serving God and you according to God's commandment that I find rest."[141] His servant leadership was also reflected in a teachable and humble attitude. We further read of an encounter that he had with a young monk in which Pachomius allowed the monk to show him a more effective way to weave a basket.[142] His humility was also reflected in how he submitted himself to his housemaster, even though he was at the same time superior to him. Rousseau asserts that Pachomius "seems to stand at times at the top of the ladder, at other times virtually at the bottom."[143] That is, he led the monastic communities with the care and authority of a father as well as the posture of a servant.

[138] See McGuire, *Friendship and Community*, 22.

[139] See Rousseau, *Pachomius*, 90.

[140] See O'Loughlin, "Master and Pupil: Christian Perspectives," *Encyclopedia of Monasticism*, 836–37.

[141] *Life of Pachomius*, 24 in Harmless, *Desert Christians*, 120.

[142] *Life of Pachomius*, 86; also Rousseau, *Pachomius*, 112.

[143] Rousseau, *Pachomius*, 118.

Sound teaching. Pachomius and Athanasius were allies in the cause of orthodoxy.[144] One of the reasons Athanasius coveted monks for ordination was their thorough training in the Scriptures.[145] The daily program in Pachomius's monastery consisted of a great deal of Scripture memorization and teaching from Scripture, as well as the opportunity for dialogue about the teaching. In addition to this rigorous daily program, Pachomius made rounds to the various monasteries in the *koinōnia* to provide additional teaching.[146]

Pachomius insisted that his monks be literate mainly so they could study and memorize the Scriptures. Yet we also learn that he used other books in training his monks, though we have no precise idea of their content.[147] These books were probably exegetical resources, in light of the overall schema of scriptural study and dialogue. They were considered property of the monastery and were lent out by the housemaster. Pachomius warned against being drawn to the outward beauty of a book as he did not want his monks to be distracted from the purpose of study—advancement in the ascetic life.[148]

Pachomius made scriptural teaching and memorization a vital part of the daily monastic program and encouraged his monks to read while following a *Rule* that had Scripture as its basis. This evidence shows the value that Pachomius placed on his monks' being grounded according to sound teaching.

Releasing. From what has been presented on the organizational structure of the *koinōnia*, monastery and houses, it is clear that Pachomius favored setting apart leaders to mentor the monks. Many of these stewards and housemasters were even listed by name in the *Life of Pachomius*.[149]

The most personal account of a leader being set apart was the case of Theodore. Pachomius appears to have brought him along in leadership by entrusting him with various tasks that included

---

[144] Ibid., 26–27.

[145] See Sterk, *Renouncing the World*, 16–18; and Derwich, "Monk-Bishops," *Encyclopedia of Monasticism*, 878.

[146] Later, Pachomius's disciples Theodore and Horsiesius also made similar visits; see Harmless, *Desert Christians*, 130.

[147] See Rousseau, *Pachomius*, 81.

[148] *Life of Pachomius*, 63; also Rousseau, *Pachomius*, 81.

[149] *Life of Pachomius*, 123; also Rousseau, *Pachomius*, 185.

dealing with personnel issues among the monks and meeting with visiting philosophers. Later Theodore was entrusted with teaching the entire monastery at Tabenessi, a role that only Pachomius had previously fulfilled. Finally he replaced Pachomius as steward over the Tabenessi monastery when Pachomius moved on to begin the monastery at Pboou.[150]

Pachomius was clearly committed to setting apart leaders who would replace him. In the case of Theodore, Pachomius entrusted him with tasks of increasing responsibility until Theodore had essentially replaced him. O'Loughlin describes this process of setting apart leaders: "Having shared the life of each of the fathers and heard them speak, the young become fit to succeed them." The result was that the disciple "becomes master in place of his teacher."[151] According to the *Life of Pachomius,* Theodore and another monk visited Antony after Pachomius's death in order to share the grief they felt at their master's passing away. Antony illustrated the monastic value of releasing leaders by responding, "Do not weep. All of you have become *Abba* Pachomius."[152]

Resourcing. As Pachomius set apart leaders, he continued to resource them. Theodore, for example, would reportedly walk two kilometers each day to hear Pachomius's teaching, then return to Tabenessi and pass on that teaching to his monks.[153] Pachomius also traveled to the different monasteries and taught. In addition, Pachomius resourced the stewards and housemasters with his monastic *Rule,* with the cryptic letters, and with teaching that had been transcribed for the purpose of circulation.

Basil of Caesarea

Basil, along with his brother Gregory of Nyssa (335–394) and his close friend Gregory of Nazianzus (329–389), made up the famed

---

[150] *Life of Pachomius,* 77; also Rousseau, *Pachomius,* 180; and Harmless, *Desert Christians,* 132.

[151] O'Loughlin, "Master and Pupil: Christian Perspectives," *Encyclopedia of Monasticism,* 836.

[152] *Life of Pachomius,* 120 in Harmless, *Desert Christians,* 135.

[153] *Life of Pachomius,* 88; also Rousseau, *Pachomius,* 181; and Harmless, *Desert Christians,* 133.

threesome known as the Cappadocian fathers. They originated from and served the church of Cappadocia in Asia Minor, which is modern central and eastern Turkey. The Cappadocians are perhaps best known for their theological works on the Trinity and for upholding the legacy of Athanasius of Alexandria and Nicene orthodoxy.[154] They were also influenced by Athanasius in that they pursued a cenobitic monastic lifestyle while serving as ordained clergy, furthering the notion of the monk-bishop that was briefly mentioned in the last section. Though Basil's work as a mentor will be the primary focus of this section, since he was the most influential of the Cappadocians in this area, we will also consider the thought of Gregory of Nazianzus and Gregory of Nyssa at various points.

Basil was born into an upper-class family known for its Christian piety. His grandmother Macrina lived an ascetic lifestyle and was influenced by Bishop Gregory Thaumaturgus of Neocaesarea (c. 213–275), who had come to faith through Origen's teaching.[155] Along with Gregory of Nazianzus, Basil studied rhetoric and philosophy in Cappadocia, Constantinople, and Athens. After an abbreviated career teaching rhetoric, Basil went East in 356 to Egypt, Palestine, and Syria in pursuit of the renowned ascetic Bishop Eustathius of Sebaste.[156] In 357, he was baptized and retired to a family estate in Pontus where Gregory of Nazianzus and a group of others joined him to form a type of monastery. Having been influenced by the ascetic bishops Eustathius and Gregory Thaumaturgus, Basil did not reject ordination to the ministry and was appointed as a reader by Bishop Dianius of Caesarea (in Asia Minor) in 360. He was promoted to presbyter in 364 and finally ordained bishop of Caesarea in 370.[157]

Basil ministered amid the ongoing Christological controversy in Asia Minor. As a metropolitan bishop responsible for some 50

---

[154] See Phillip Rousseau, *Basil of Caesarea* (Berkeley: University of California Press, 1994), 2; and Lewis Ayres, "The Cappadocians," *ATTA*, 122.

[155] See Ayres, "The Cappadocians," *ATTA*, 121; Sterk, *Renouncing the World*, 35; and H. Leclercq, "St. Gregory of Neocaesarea," www.newadvent.org/cathen/07015a.htm.

[156] See Rousseau, *Basil*, 27; Ayres, "The Cappadocians," *ATTA*, 121; and Sterk, *Renouncing the World*, 39–40.

[157] Basil, *Letters* 207.2; 223.5; Gregory of Nazianzus, *Letter* 6.37; also Rousseau, *Basil*, 2, 68–69; 84–85; and Sterk, *Renouncing the World*, 43.

bishops and even more clergy, he was forced into messy church politics and theological battles. Despite regular contact with theological allies and enemies as well as secular leaders who often became involved, Basil seemed to balance his roles as an urban-dwelling monk and a metropolitan bishop.[158]

Basil also ministered amid a crisis of leadership in the church. As Sterk points out, there was a "lack of suitable candidates for the episcopate," which made it difficult to set apart leaders.[159] Perhaps an even greater problem was the lack of suitable clergy already in positions of leadership. Some church leaders were marred by immorality and greed, and not a few had actually paid for their ordination.[160] Hence Basil's monastic ideals—reflected in his writings, letters, and influence—would fly in the face of these existing tendencies. His influence in setting apart leaders would further demonstrate his determination to purify the leadership of the church.

Basil the Bishop and His Clergy

Compared to Cyprian, it is much more difficult to describe Basil's role as bishop, to list the clergy around him in Caesarea, or to give much detail about their roles. Because Basil seemed to dislike the existing hierarchical structure of the clergy, he was "imprecise in his vocabulary regarding positions of authority in the church."[161] His lack of attention to specific offices and roles seemed to flow from the monastic influence on his ideas about the ordained ministry.

As bishop of Caesarea, Basil was first involved in preaching. Employing a more literal hermeneutic following the Antiochene school of interpretation, Basil's surviving work includes homilies on the books of Moses and the Psalms, as well as moral and doctrinal discourses.[162] Second, Basil was responsible for convening and conducting church councils. Third, he strongly believed that a bishop should care for the physical needs of the poor in his city. Following the example of his mentor Eustathius of Sebaste, Basil

---

[158] See Sterk, *Renouncing the World*, 44–46, 73.
[159] See ibid., 47.
[160] Basil, *Letters* 53–54; also Sterk, *Renouncing the World*, 47.
[161] Sterk, *Renouncing the World*, 48.
[162] See Joseph McSorley, "St. Basil the Great," www.newadvent.org/cathen/02330b.htm.

founded the *Basileiados*, a hospice for the poor located on the outskirts of Caesarea. Fourth, as a monk-bishop, he oversaw the monasteries in his province.[163] Fifth, Basil presided over the worship assembly, celebrating the Eucharist and performing baptisms. Finally, he served as a mentor to those clergy serving with him in Caesarea and to the 50 bishops and their clergy in his province.

Basil's presbyters probably assisted him with preaching, presiding over the Eucharist, and in pastoral ministry, which would have included the work of the hospice.[164] Most fourth-century presbyters also presided over the liturgical assembly in the absence of the bishop. Basil's correspondence reveals that at least one presbyter, Sanctissimus, was involved in delivering some of his letters.[165]

Basil's deacons probably assisted him in his duties as bishop, including involvement in some preaching and baptizing.[166] Basil's letters also show that a deacon named Dorotheus, who later became a presbyter, was responsible for delivering some of Basil's correspondence.[167] The remaining clergy serving with Basil probably included subdeacons, who assisted the deacons in their work, and readers, who of course read the Scriptures in worship.

How Did Basil Mentor?

Basil responded to the church leadership crisis in Asia Minor by mentoring men for ministry. His correspondence, moral and doctrinal writings, as well as some of Gregory of Nazianzus's *Orations* provide evidence to support the claim that he was mentoring clergy in Asia Minor and sometimes beyond. His main strategies included monastic living, books and writings, letters, and church councils.

Monastic living. Before his ordination Basil had gone east to pursue the ascetic life and later invited others to join him in a monastic retreat *(aprogmon)* on his family's estate in Pontus. Yet even after his ordination to ministry and eventually to the office of bishop, he

---

[163] See Sterk, *Renouncing the World*, 70, 74.
[164] *Letters* 150; 176; also Phillip Schaff, *History of the Christian Church*, vol. 3 (Peabody, MA: Hendrickson, 1996), 258.
[165] *Letters* 120; 132; 221; 225; 253–54.
[166] See Schaff, *History*, 3.259.
[167] *Letters* 47; 50; 52; 61–62; 243; 273.

continued to live as a monk—a lifestyle that included regular retreats to the estate in Pontus.[168] Sterk writes, "Basil saw all the more need to hold monastic life and ecclesiastical authority in tandem."[169]

How did Basil mentor spiritual leaders through the monastery? Essentially, the monastery served as an indirect training center for monks who would eventually be ordained. In light of the weak spiritual state of the clergy that Basil and Gregory of Nazianzus decried, Basil's program was a great spiritual foundation for future clergy and included daily Psalm singing and Scripture reading, mealtime reading, memorizing Scripture, training against heresy, and ascetic discipline. Some monks ended up being set apart to serve as Bible teachers for other monks. His monastic rule—both the *Short Rules* and *Long Rules*—provided written direction for common life, especially in how monks and superiors ought to relate to one another.

Though it has been asserted that Basil's monastery was an indirect training center for clergy, it would be difficult to argue that that was what he purposed. However, in considering Basil's standards and qualifications for the clergy, especially those quoted in Gregory Nazianzus's *Orations*, it becomes clear that those qualities were also important for a monk. Hence, in light of the great need of the church for holy and trained leaders and the strategic recruiting pool that the monastery presented, Basil, Gregory of Nazianzus, Gregory of Nyssa, and John Chrysostom all followed the example of Athanasius and chose to ordain monks to the clergy.[170]

Finally, there is evidence that clergy came to Caesarea for the purpose of living and serving in the hospice. Though the primary focus of this institution was to care for the poor, it also became a community where monks and clergy could grow together in a common existence of serving and living out the precepts of their faith.[171]

Books and writings. Basil was a prolific writer who used books to speak to his fellow clergy about the key issues of his day, the crisis

---

[168] The Greek *aprogmon* is rendered *otium* in Latin, meaning "leisure"—a notion that will be significant in our study of Augustine; see Rousseau, *Basil*, 71, 85; Sterk, *Renouncing the World*, 43, and *Letter* 43.

[169] See Sterk, *Renouncing the World*, 43.

[170] Gregory of Nazianzus, *Oration*, 2.49; 43.60–66; also Sterk, *Renouncing the World*, 136, 147–50.

[171] *Letters* 150; 176; also Sterk, *Renouncing the World*, 27; and Rousseau, *Basil*, 142.

of doctrine and lack of holy leadership in the church. In 375, he wrote *On the Holy Spirit* in which he dealt with both issues. Though addressed to his disciple Amphilochius, Basil was clearly writing to a much larger audience of clergy as he assailed the orthodox bishops for spending more energy fighting among themselves and jockeying for positions of power than dealing with the Arian struggle.[172] After affirming Amphilochius for his desire for truth over mere speculation and inviting him to an in-depth investigation of the Scriptures, Basil gave a clear defense of the divinity of the Holy Spirit in response to charges of heresy that had been made against him.[173]

Among his ascetic works Basil wrote *Morals*, a treatise on spiritual leadership for those in church leadership. Though his audience included monastic overseers, his primary readers were the clergy. In the introduction he wrote of his desire to pass on what he had learned from the Scriptures to "recipients who should fulfill the word of the apostle: 'Entrust these things to faithful men who will be able to teach others.'" He also indicated that he was writing to "those who preside in the teaching of the word of God."[174]

The work's main goal was to impress upon leaders the holy character required of a priest of God as well as the value of ascetic discipline. With holiness as his key theme, he treated numerous supporting themes such as repentance, good works, focusing on the call and work of ministry, holiness, the fear of God, being bold witnesses in the faith, trusting God, constantly being a disciple, believing and obeying the Word of God, maintaining sound doctrine, benefiting from the influence of a godly community, imitating God and the saints of Scripture, being a godly example, serving God, showing hospitality, remaining steadfast in the faith, and exercising spiritual disciplines such as prayer and thanksgiving. He also commended holy character in avoiding lying, quarreling, and scandal, in showing humility, generosity, and simplicity, as well as working, forgiving, and mortifying the flesh.

---

[172] *On the Holy Spirit*, 30.76–79; also Sterk, *Renouncing the World*, 46; and McSorley, "St. Basil the Great," www.newadvent.org/fathers/cathen/02330b.htm.

[173] *On the Holy Spirit*, 1; also Rousseau, *Basil*, 122, 265.

[174] Introduction to *Morals* in Sterk, *Renouncing the World*, 53.

In chapter 70 of *Morals*, Basil continued to discuss the character of spiritual leaders while giving some instruction on their roles. First, he urged that leaders be set apart carefully, and he provided a set of qualifications for bishops, presbyters, and deacons, similar to the Pastoral Epistles. Second, a spiritual leader must not deny his call to the ministry. Third, a leader must practice what he preaches, never asking more of his disciples than he himself is doing. Fourth, a leader must encourage his flock through preaching as well as visiting them. Fifth, he should demonstrate mercy and care for the physical needs of those in the church. Sixth, a leader should avoid becoming entangled in worldly affairs and pursue simplicity. Finally, Basil gave some direction on the act of preaching itself. He urged (1) that the gospel message should not be compromised nor ears tickled by preaching, (2) that the preacher should prioritize his teaching according to the most important needs of the church, (3) that he should demonstrate humility, (4) that style should not supercede content in a message, (5) that the goal of teaching should be sanctification, (6) that the preacher should confront gently, and (7) that those who continue to be unresponsive to teaching should ultimately be abandoned.[175]

While *On the Holy Spirit* contained some pastoral exhortation, it was largely a treatise on the doctrine of the Holy Spirit. Though *Morals* included some encouragement to maintain sound teaching, it was primarily a handbook for holy conduct in a spiritual leader's personal life and ministry.

Letters. Basil made extensive use of letters as at least two-thirds of his 366 surviving letters were written while he was bishop of Caesarea, and one-fourth of them were addressed to fellow clergy.[176] Sterk asserts, "The large number of extant letters to bishops throughout the Roman Empire suggests that he consistently attempted to influence ideas and decisions both within and beyond

---

[175] *Morals*, 1.1–4; 13.1–2; 2.1; 30.1; 11; 6.1; 8; 9; 12.2; 17.1; 18.1–6; 26.1–2; 28; 41; 44; 16.1; 48.5; 52.1; 27; 72.1; 34.1; 37.1; 38–39; 55–56; 24.1; 25.1–2; 54.1–2; 33.1–4; 45; 48; 57; 59; 47; 48.3, 6; 49.2; 53; 69; 70.1–2; 71.1–2; 70.3; 70.8–9; 70.11, 17; 70.19–20; 70.27–28; 70.12, 22, 29; 70.21; 70.23; 70.25; 70.30; 70.31–32, 34.

[176] See McSorley, "St. Basil the Great," www.newadvent.org/cathen/02330b.htm.

his diocesan frontiers."[177] Although Basil indeed wrote letters to influence church leadership in Asia Minor, this influence should not be merely construed as political or manipulative; rather, he used letters to mentor clergy. Basil's clerical correspondence can largely be categorized as letters in which Basil himself was being mentored, those that involved peer mentoring, invitation or selection for mentoring, encouragement, exhortation, discipline, theological resourcing, doctrinal influence, practical ministry instruction, and church business.

Basil as the disciple. In four letters Basil himself took the posture of the disciple and sought the help of mentors. Two of these were addressed to Eustathius of Sebaste, Basil's personal mentor at the outset of his ascetic journey. In the first letter Basil shared with Eustathius some of his struggles in leading the church, and in the second he humbly recounted his spiritual journey and continual need for prayer.[178] Basil also wrote two letters to Athanasius, whom he never personally met. In the first letter he confided in him about the difficulty of leading the church and asked for prayer and wisdom. In the second he requested that Athanasius prepare a circular letter for the bishops of Asia Minor to offer wisdom for their ministries.[179]

Peer mentoring. In 18 letters Basil exchanged friendly correspondence with eight different clergy that reveals an element of peer mentoring. While still a presbyter, he wrote two letters to Gregory of Nazianzus describing where he lived while also communicating the value of friendship.[180] Similarly, Basil rejoiced in the friendship and fellowship experienced through correspondence with clergy such as Arcadius, Innocent, Theodorus, Peter, and Paeonius.[181] For instance, he wrote to Paeonius: "I am always eager to receive news from your Perfection, but, when I took your letter into my hands and read it, I was not more pleased with what you had written than I

---

[177] See Sterk, *Renouncing the World*, 91.
[178] *Letters* 79, 119. Unless otherwise indicated, all English translations of Basil's letters are from FC.
[179] *Letters* 80, 82.
[180] *Letters* 14; 19.
[181] *Letters* 49–50, 124, 133–34.

was grieved at considering how great a loss had befallen me during your period of silence."[182]

In two letters to Ascholius of Thessalonica, the two carried on a bit of a dialogue about the state of the church, and Basil admitted that he was "nourished by frequent letters" from Ascholius.[183] Basil's key peer mentoring relationship seemed to be with Bishop Eusebius of Samosata since he sent Eusebius nine letters. Basil did not hesitate to open his heart to Eusebius, sharing about his illnesses, the death of his mother, the challenges of church ministry including the threat of heresy, and his need for prayer. Basil further affirmed Eusebius's work and ministry and sought his advice about ordaining clergy outside of his diocese. Finally, as shown in other peer mentoring letters, Basil expressed a deep sense of friendship and his longing to see Eusebius. Though a personal visit was preferable, Basil nevertheless acknowledged that "letters are not a trifling matter" and were a valuable means of mutual encouragement and mentoring.[184]

Four of Basil's letters reveal him initiating a *mentoring relationship*. In two letters Basil invited Amphilochius of Iconium to join him in the work at the hospice in Caesarea.[185] In another letter he invited Theodotus to dialogue in a relationship of mutual encouragement.[186] In a final letter he replied positively to Ascholius's initiative toward Basil for mentoring and communicated that he looked forward to a relationship through correspondence.[187]

Twenty letters show Basil mentoring clergy through *encouragement or comfort*. Two such letters were sent to clergy who had experienced death in their families, another five were written to those experiencing persecution, while eight letters were addressed to spiritual leaders who had been exiled.[188] Basil wrote two letters affirming leaders for their orthodoxy, one of which was written to the presbyters of Nicopolis who were serving under a bishop who

---

[182] *Letter* 134.
[183] *Letters* 164–65.
[184] *Letters* 30; 136; 141; 162; 31; 138; 239; 241; 145.
[185] *Letters* 150; 176.
[186] *Letter* 185.
[187] *Letter* 154.
[188] *Letters* 5; 206; 184; 219; 246–47; 256; 57; 89; 168; 182; 198; 264; 267–68.

was doctrinally unsound.[189] Finally Basil wrote letters encouraging Diodorus of Antioch to exercise his gift as a writer while also affirming Amphilochius of Iconium and Ambrose of Milan on the occasion of their ordinations.[190] Regarding Amphilochius, Basil made himself available to the young bishop and exhorted him to "be a man . . . and be strong and go before the people whom the Most High has entrusted to your right hand."[191]

Exhortation was the theme of six of Basil's letters. He exhorted Abramius of Batnae to faith, love, and fellowship and challenged the newly appointed Bishop Peter of Alexandria to carry on the legacy of his predecessor Athanasius.[192] In more of a rebuke, Basil confronted the young Bishop Artabius of Neocaesarea for working in isolation and exhorted him to work with other church leaders in the region.[193] Similarly, Basil made an appeal to unity to the bishops of Pontus and exhorted Evagrius of Antioch to avoid schism in the church.[194] Finally, Basil confronted the bishops of Neocaesarea for slandering him and also exhorted them to unity.[195]

Discipline was the theme of seven letters. Three were addressed to the body of bishops entrusted with ordaining new clergy. Basil condemned them for accepting money in exchange for ordination; for ordaining friends, family, and unqualified clergy; and for mixing worldly pursuits with the call to ministry.[196] Two letters were sent to rebuke immoral clergy including a priest named Paregorius who was living with a woman.[197] In another letter Basil confronted a bishop for resisting the council of bishops and invited him to meet personally.[198] Finally, Basil did not hesitate to write and condemn his own brother, Gregory of Nyssa, for sending a forged letter in the name of their uncle![199] Basil's disciplinary correspondence gives

---

[189] *Letters* 172; 240.
[190] *Letters* 135; 161; 197.
[191] *Letter* 161.
[192] *Letters* 132–33.
[193] *Letter* 65. Artabius was also a distant relative of Basil.
[194] *Letters* 203, 156.
[195] *Letter* 204.
[196] *Letters* 53–54; 291.
[197] *Letters* 55, 170.
[198] *Letter* 282.
[199] *Letter* 58.

us an idea of some of the excesses and immorality present among church leaders as well as his need to mentor at times through rebuke and discipline.

Nine of Basil's letters served as a *theological resource* to other clergy. In one letter, addressed to an unknown recipient, he laid out his theology of the monastic life.[200] He wrote another letter to Gregory of Nyssa in the midst of the ongoing Arian struggle, explaining the difference between Christ's substance *(ousia)* and person *(hyposta-sis)*. Basil wrote a third letter to a certain Cyriacus giving some corrective teaching on the person of the Holy Spirit.[201] In a fourth letter Basil responded to a letter supposedly from Diodorus of Antioch answering theological questions about marriage.[202] Basil wrote another letter to Optimus of Pisidia providing exegetical help on the meaning of Gen 4:15.[203] Finally, Basil resourced Amphilochius with five theological letters dealing with themes such as instruction on heresy, animals in the Scripture, interpreting Scripture, the nature of the mind, the substance of God, the relationship between faith and knowledge, and the relationship between the Father and the Son.[204]

Basil used 18 letters to exert *doctrinal influence* on his fellow clergy. In two letters he defended himself against heresy and wrote another to clear the name of two other clergy who had been similarly accused.[205] Basil wrote three letters encouraging the clergy to maintain orthodoxy.[206] Five letters show Basil exerting a doctrinal influence by collaborating with his theological allies. In three of these letters, he specifically discussed the orthodoxy of three bishops who were about to be ordained while in the other two he emphasized the importance of separating from heretics and maintaining sound doctrine in the churches.[207]

---

[200] *Letter* 22.
[201] *Letter* 114.
[202] *Letter* 160. Some have alleged that the letter from Diodorus was spurious.
[203] *Letter* 260.
[204] *Letters* 188; 233–36.
[205] *Letters* 25; 224; 266.
[206] *Letters* 113; 129; 245.
[207] *Letters* 27; 227; 238; 128; 258.

In two other letters Basil confronted clergy who had departed from sound doctrine and urged them to repent.[208] A final five letters of doctrinal influence related to Eustathius of Sebaste, Basil's former mentor who had apparently gone into heresy. In one letter Basil drafted a declaration of faith consistent with the council of Nicea and asked Eustathius to sign it. In a follow-up letter Basil wrote to condemn Eustathius who had apparently refused to sign the initial letter.[209] In the other three letters Basil wrote to the clergy recounting the unsound doctrine of Eustathius and his reasons for breaking fellowship with him.[210] Hence Basil used the negative example of Eustathius to warn his fellow clergy against heresy.

Basil wrote four letters giving *practical instruction* on church matters. All four were addressed to Amphilochus of Iconium and are also known as the "canonical epistles."[211] While giving instruction on issues from abortion to polygamy, Basil also advised on delegating responsibility and selecting leaders for a nearby church.[212] As in the case of his theological correspondence with Amphilochius, the canonical letters were intended to resource a broader audience of clergy.

Three final letters are dedicated to *church business*. They reveal Basil in the role of a mentor seeking the input of other church leaders and involving them in church decisions. For instance, in two letters to Gregory of Nazianzus, Basil included Gregory in the discussion over how to proceed with the immoral deacon Glycerius, whom Basil eventually disciplined.[213] Finally, Basil sought the help of Poemenius of Satala over the ordination of a certain Bishop Anthimus, who was not ordained according to church canons.[214]

Church councils. According to his correspondence, Basil convened an annual council in Caesarea every September.[215] Like

---

[208] *Letters* 126; 207.
[209] *Letters* 125, 223.
[210] *Letters* 130; 244; 250.
[211] *Letters* 188; 190; 199; 217.
[212] *Letter* 190.
[213] *Letters* 169; 171.
[214] *Letter* 122.
[215] *Letter* 100; also Sterk, *Renouncing the World*, 74.

Cyprian he used this form of interaction with church leaders and in turn exercised a mentoring influence.

As in his writings Basil used church councils to address the key issues facing the church. Sterk asserts that one goal of the councils was "theological clarification."[216] In his famous appeal to the western bishops at the height of the Arian crisis in Asia Minor, Basil's main request was that they send a delegation to strengthen the orthodox cause in an impending confrontation that would probably take the form of a council.[217] Basil also used councils to address the crisis of church leadership. Sterk explains, "Through such episcopal gatherings, Basil was able to influence a wide range of decisions affecting the life of the church, not least of which was the selection and discipline of ecclesiastical leaders."[218]

As metropolitan bishop and convener of church councils in Caesarea, Basil's influence was greater than that of his fellow bishops, and he did not hesitate to exercise this influence. Yet like Cyprian, Basil was committed to the collegiality of bishops and to involving other clergy in decision making. When he invited the younger Bishop Amphilochius to participate in a council, he welcomed him to participate in the dialogue and share his "spiritual gifts."[219] Hence, as a mentor, Basil used councils to influence the clergy toward sound doctrine, to restore clerical holiness, and to allow clergy to participate in decision making.

Basil's Thought on Mentoring

As a monk-bishop leading the church in Caesarea, Basil was committed to mentoring spiritual leaders, especially as the church in Asia Minor dealt with heresy and immoral clergy. Seven aspects of mentoring that relate to the New Testament model become apparent in Basil's relationships with the clergy.

The group. Unlike the three other leaders surveyed in this chapter, Basil was mentored from his childhood in an ascetic community.

---

[216] Sterk, *Renouncing the World*, 74; *Letters* 92; 98; 204–5.
[217] *Letter* 92.
[218] Sterk, *Renouncing the World*, 74.
[219] *Letter* 176.

Hence it comes as no surprise that in his adult years he would also initiate a monastic retreat on the family estate in Pontus. After becoming the bishop of Caesarea, he continued to value the group as a means of spiritual growth by overseeing monasteries and by establishing a hospice, a ministry where monks and clergy alike could serve the poor and live in community. As a result the monasteries and probably the hospice served as an indirect training center for those who would eventually be ordained. Finally, Basil, like Cyprian, valued gathering bishops together at least once a year to strengthen the unity of the church, to set apart leaders, and to deal with heresy. The council gave Basil an opportunity to influence and encourage the bishops, rendering it a form of mentoring in a group context.

Basil's writings also reflect the value he put on mentoring in a community. In *Rules* he articulated down to the smallest detail how the monastic community should function.[220] In *Morals*, he encouraged spiritual leaders to benefit from the godly influence of a community, to consider the needs of the community, and to confront the sins of one another.[221] McGuire concludes that in Basil's writings "community is exalted as desirable in itself" and that "Basil is the first monastic writer in the East to be totally convinced that a common life provided the best way of bringing individual men to God."[222]

A mentor is a disciple. Gregory of Nazianzus, alluding to Basil's ascetic upbringing and the influence of Gregory of Thaumaturgus, concluded that Basil had been "exercised in piety."[223] When Basil headed east in 356 to know more of the ascetic life, he was also pursuing a mentor in Eustathius of Sebaste. Rousseau comments:

> His very search for models and mentors, in the period immediately following his departure from Athens, shows that he was not content merely to respond to, let alone cater for, existing forms of ascetic life. His

---

[220] See G. B. Ladner, *The Idea of Reform: Its Impact on Christian Thought and Action in the Age of the Fathers* (New York: Harper & Row, 1967), 341–42.

[221] *Morals*, 16.1; 48.5; 52.1; 27; 30–31; 33–34; 37–38; 42–46; 60; 70.

[222] McGuire, *Friendship and Community*, 25, 31.

[223] Gregory of Nazianzus, *Orations*, 43.12; English translation from Rousseau, *Basil*, 5; also *Letters* 204.6; 223.3; also Rousseau, *Basil*, 3–6; 10; 12; and Sterk, *Renouncing the World*, 36.

most characteristic inclination was to interweave the moral with the social and practical aspects of Christianity.[224]

Once ordained to the ministry as a reader, Basil was apparently mentored by Bishop Dianius, who modeled for him holy character, simplicity of life, and practical ministry skills. Though their relationship was at times marked by conflict, Basil continued to value the input and example of Dianius.[225]

When Basil became bishop of Caesarea and was responsible for other spiritual leaders, he continued to learn and grow as a disciple. By maintaining an ascetic lifestyle of simplicity in community, he showed his humility and need for further growth. As noted, Basil corresponded with Eustathius and Athanasius, seeking their mentoring input.[226] Similarly Rousseau cites Basil's regard for Athanasius of Ancyra and Musonius of Neocaesarea as mentors and models in the early days of his ministry.[227] Finally, in correspondence with other peers, Basil was equally vulnerable about his need for growth and repeatedly requested the prayers of his colleagues.[228]

Basil's writings also reveal his conviction that the spiritual leader must continue to be a disciple. In *Morals* he communicated this verbatim.[229] In *Short Rules* he cited the posture of a learner as an important quality for superiors in the monastery: "I conclude that the one entrusted with the leadership and care of the larger body ought to know and learn by heart everything that they may teach all men what God wishes, showing each one his duty."[230] Also, in light of his stress on monastic overseers, Basil encouraged monastic overseers to seek out other more experienced overseers as mentors while also taking time to discuss the main issues that they were facing with their peers.[231]

---

[224] Rousseau, *Basil*, 5.

[225] *Letter* 51.1; also Rousseau, *Basil*, 154.

[226] *Letters* 79–80; 82; 119.

[227] *Letters* 28–29; also Rousseau, *Basil*, 154–55.

[228] *Letters* 2.1; 98.1; 99.1; 119; 136.2; 204.4; 223.2; 248; 258.2; also Sterk, *Renouncing the World*, 97.

[229] *Morals*, 9.

[230] *Short Rules*, 235; English translation from Sterk, *Renouncing the World*, 50.

[231] *Short Rules*, 104; *Long Rules*, 48; also Sterk, *Renouncing the World*, 51.

Like Pachomius, Basil's ongoing commitment to spiritual growth made him an example for imitation. In Gregory of Nazianzus's funeral eulogy of Basil, he held up Basil as the standard for a worthy and upright bishop, comparing his life and ministry to Abraham, Joseph, Moses, and Elijah.[232] Basil had encouraged spiritual leaders to look to the example of the saints of Scripture that they might in turn be such examples to their flocks.[233] Finally, Basil summarized the imitative value of a mentor by writing that the spiritual leader "must make his life a clear example of every commandment of the Lord so as to leave the taught no chance of thinking that the commandment of the Lord is impossible or may be despised."[234]

Selection. Prior to his consecration as bishop of Caesarea, Basil invited Gregory of Nazianzus to join his monastic retreat in Pontus. Though initially refusing Basil's initiative, Basil and Gregory's correspondence reveals that Gregory eventually accepted the invitation and later would write about the spiritual impact Basil had on his life.[235]

As bishop, Basil continued to move toward potential disciples. We noted his initiative toward Amphilochius, whom he invited on two occasions to join him in the hospice in order to grow with him as a disciple.[236] He described a mentor as "a man who both knows much from the experience of others, as well as from his own wisdom, and can impart it to those who come to him."[237] Finally, we noted that Basil approached Theodotus for dialogue and mutual encouragement and favorably responded to Ascholius's request for mentoring.[238] Ascholius was following the example of Pachomius, Basil, and others who had initiated a relationship with a mentor.

---

[232] Gregory of Nazianzus, *Orations*, 43.2, 35–37; 71–76; also Sterk, *Renouncing the World*, 131–32.

[233] *Letters* 2.3; 150.4; also Sterk, *Renouncing the World*, 64; and Rousseau, *Basil*, 81.

[234] *Long Rules*, 43; English translation from Sterk, *Renouncing the World*, 52; also *Morals*, 70.8–9.

[235] *Letters* 2; 4; 19; Gregory of Nazianzus, *Letters* 4–6; 16.4; 58.4; *Orations*, 43; also Rousseau, *Basil*, 65–68.

[236] *Letters* 150; 176.

[237] *Letter* 150.4. English translation from Rousseau, *Basil*, 118.

[238] *Letters* 185; 154.

Mentor-disciple relationship. Rousseau indicates that the most important aspect of mentoring for Basil was the relationship between mentor and disciple.[239] Basil, throughout his writings, described the mentor's care for the disciple with pictures of parental tenderness and nurture. In a homily on Psalm 33, he said that a disciple was "formed by [a mentor] and brought into existence just as an infant is formed within a pregnant woman."[240] Within the monastery the mentoring overseer offered his disciples nourishment *(trophos)* by opening the Scriptures and his own soul to them.[241] Basil's relationship with Amphilochius was also quite paternal. Basil wrote two letters to Amphilochius as a "father to a son," and in several other letters his tone expressed paternal affection.[242] Finally Basil exhibited similar fatherly care in his letters of encouragement to those clergy who were enduring persecution and exile.

Basil also believed that there was a clear hierarchy of spiritual authority in the mentor-disciple relationship. He demonstrated this authority in his correspondence with other clergy in a persuasive, exhorting, and even disciplinary manner. His authority was also clear in convening and presiding over church councils in Caesarea. In the monastery Basil believed that monks needed the authority of a superior to help overcome the weaknesses of the flesh.[243] Basil stated that the overseer should be obeyed and that he should only be reproved by his peers. Sometimes the superior had to discipline his monks though always with mildness and patience.[244]

While the mentor-disciple relationship was a balance between fatherly tenderness and spiritual authority, Basil also valued what a disciple could learn from his peers. His 18 peer mentoring letters reveal him being vulnerable about his spiritual state and seeking practical ministry help from his peers. As shown, his most significant peer mentoring relationship was with Eusebius of Samosata.[245]

---

[239] See Rousseau, *Basil*, 213.

[240] *Homily on Psalm 33:8*; English translation from Sterk, *Renouncing the World*, 59.

[241] See Rousseau, *Basil*, 213.

[242] *Letters* 161.2; 176; 200; 202; 231; 248; also Rousseau, *Basil*, 260.

[243] See Rousseau, *Basil*, 215.

[244] *Short Rules*, 235; *Long Rules*, 25; 27; 31; 35; also Sterk, *Renouncing the World*, 49–50, 52; and Rousseau, *Basil*, 217.

[245] *Letters* 27; 30–31; 34; 127–28; 136; 138; 141; 145; 162; 198; 239; 241; 268.

Sound teaching. With the death of Athanasius in 373, the orthodox party looked to Basil to lead them in the fight against Arianism in the East. According to Gregory of Nazianzus, the battle for orthodoxy drew Basil and Gregory from their ascetic retreat in Pontus to accept ordination in the church.[246] Basil's letters to the Western church leaders provide some insight into the extent of the battles with the Arians as well as the opposition the orthodox party faced from the state.[247]

How did Basil mentor the clergy toward maintaining sound teaching? First, as noted, he made use of regular church councils to influence his fellow clergy toward orthodoxy. Second, he wrote 18 letters to influence clergy toward sound doctrine to some degree. Gregory of Nazianzus described Basil's ongoing campaign for orthodoxy among the clergy by writing:

> He drew up a sketch of pious doctrine, and by wrestling with and attacking their opposition he beat off the daring assaults of the heretics. . . . Again, since unreasoning action and unpractical reasoning are alike ineffectual, he added to his reasoning the succor which comes from action; he paid visits, sent messages, gave interviews, instructed, reproved, rebuked, threatened, reproached.[248]

Gregory's remarks about Basil drawing up "a sketch of pious doctrine" surely referred to his famous confrontation with Eustathius.[249] Yet following Eustathius's apparent refusal to comply with orthodoxy, Basil condemned him by letter and corresponded with three other clergy, effectively making an example out of Eustathius so that other leaders would not be led astray.[250] The fact that Basil would publicly denounce his own spiritual mentor strongly showed

---

[246] Gregory of Nazianzus, *Orations*, 43.30–31; *Letter* 8; also Rousseau, *Basil*, 88.

[247] *Letters* 90–92; 242–43; also Sterk, *Renouncing the World*, 44–45.

[248] Gregory of Nazianzus, *Orations*, 43.43; English translation from www.newadvent.org/fathers/3102.htm.

[249] *Letter* 125.

[250] *Letters* 130; 223; 244; 250.

his commitment to sound teaching.[251] Finally, we have shown that Basil helped the clergy maintain sound doctrine by writing letters and books that served as a theological resource. In particular, Basil's treatise *On the Holy Spirit*, as well as five thorough letters addressed to Amphilochius, provided a theological resource for Amphilochius and other clergy.

The basis of Basil's orthodoxy was a high view of the Scriptures. In *Morals* he emphasized the primacy of the Scriptures for spiritual growth and for ministry. The Scriptures were to be believed, followed, obeyed, and faithfully taught.[252] In *Long Rules*, Basil asserted that Scripture should be the basis of monastic education and that a key occupation of the overseer was teaching the Scriptures.[253] Basil's emphasis on the Scriptures reveals that he clearly regarded them as more valuable than the liberal arts. Having experienced both a sacred education at home and a secular one in Athens, Basil clearly preferred the former for himself and his disciples.

Releasing. One of Basil's roles as metropolitan bishop was influencing the process of setting apart leaders to be ordained as clergy. Overall, Basil, Gregory of Nazianzus, and Gregory of Nyssa were hesitant about ordaining new leaders in light of the lack of qualified men.[254] Basil examined candidates thoroughly through a gathered council or by writing to other leaders for their input on the candidate's worthiness.[255]

What qualities did Basil look for in a spiritual leader? His standards were perhaps most clearly expressed in a letter to Amphilochius in which he required the young leader to commit to ascetic living, to serve a community, and to teach sound doctrine. Sterk adds that a spiritual leader must also have experience in ministry and be morally above reproach.[256]

---

[251] See Rousseau, *Basil*, 101, 242.

[252] *Morals*, 8; 12.2; 17.1; 18; 26.1–2; 41; 44; 70.12.

[253] *Long Rules*, 15; 41; 47; also Rousseau, *Basil*, 326; and Sterk, *Renouncing the World*, 51.

[254] *Morals*, 70.1; Gregory of Nazianzus, *Orations*, 2.8, 49, 71; Gregory of Nyssa, *Letter* 17; also Sterk, *Renouncing the World*, 54, 113, 123–24; and Rousseau, *Basil*, 87.

[255] *Letters* 120–22; 190; also Sterk, *Renouncing the World*, 77–78.

[256] *Letters* 150; 222; also Sterk, *Renouncing the World*, 60, 85, 90.

As noted, in light of the lack of morally upright and doctrinally sound candidates, Basil at times leaned on the monastery and ordained monks to fill needed ministry positions in the church.[257] Basil seems to have also leaned on his friends a time or two as he was involved in Gregory of Nazianzus's rather forceful ordination while not opposing the same happening to Gregory of Nyssa.[258] Finally, though Basil was generally committed to the canons of Nicea, which dictated the process for ordaining clergy, he did not mind overlooking them at times when he found a suitable choice for the clergy. This was the case when Basil ordained Poemenius in Satala, a morally upright and orthodox clergy who had served with him in Caesarea.[259]

Resourcing. While releasing and setting apart spiritual leaders to their own ministries, Basil actively served as a resource to clergy in Asia Minor. As noted, Basil helped Amphilochius and other leaders by writing letters that treated theological and practical issues. In addition, through works like *On the Holy Spirit* and *Morals*, Basil resourced the clergy on matters of doctrine, spiritual leadership, and practical ministry. Gregory of Nazianzus indicated that Basil even provided him at times with material for preaching.[260] Finally, Basil served as a resource by making himself personally available. Again, in the case of Amphilochius, Basil not only promised to be available to the young bishop, but he made this more of a reality by having Amphilochius ordained in the diocese next to him.

Ambrose of Milan

The ministry was a career change for Ambrose, as it was for some of the other Latin fathers. Born in Trier (in modern Germany), Ambrose was the son of a prefect and received an education in the liberal arts at Rome, specializing in law. After climbing the ladder of government service, he was appointed governor of Aemilia-Liguria in northern Italy in 370. McLynn, referring to Ambrose's

---

[257] Gregory of Nazianzus, *Letter* 63.6; also Sterk, *Renouncing the World*, 80.
[258] See Sterk, *Renouncing the World*, 83.
[259] *Letters* 102–3; also Sterk, *Renouncing the World*, 87.
[260] Gregory of Nazianzus, *Orations*, 43.1.

career change, writes, "As governor he intervened in a disputed episcopal election at Milan and was unexpectedly appointed bishop (374)."[261] Previously unbaptized, Ambrose received this rite only eight days before his consecration as bishop and his new career was underway.[262] He served as bishop of Milan until his death in 397.

Ambrose carried out the office of bishop much as a respected governor—with benevolent authority.[263] As a metropolitan bishop, his influence was felt not only in Milan but also throughout Italy. Ambrose was no stranger to controversy even in his dealings with government officials and the emperor. Finally, as he had succeeded an Arian bishop in a region sharply divided over the Arian controversy, he would defend Nicene orthodoxy for much of his career in Milan.[264]

Ambrose the Bishop

Ambrose's duties as bishop resembled those of Cyprian and Basil with some exceptions. His first and most important role was preaching. In the opening line of *On the Duties of Ministers*, a manual for the clergy, he wrote: "A bishop's special office is to teach."[265] A second responsibility was presiding over worship, especially the Eucharist and baptism. Third, he prepared catechumens for baptism by instructing them on the Creed. Fourth, in cooperation with some of the clergy, Ambrose exorcised catechumens and baptized Christians who were experiencing demonic oppression. Fifth, he was active in combating heresy, particularly Arianism, while also

---

[261] See Neil McLynn, "Ambrose of Milan," *ATTA*, 17.

[262] See Paulinus, *Life of Ambrose*, 9; and Boniface Ramsey, *Ambrose* (London: Routledge, 1997), 20–21.

[263] See Emilien Lamirande, *Paulin de Milan et* La Vita Ambrosi: *Aspects de la religion sous le Bas Empire* (Paris: Desclée, 1983), 76.

[264] *Letters* 20; 41.27–28; also McLynn, "Ambrose of Milan," *ATTA*, 17; Henry Chadwick, "The Role of the Christian Bishop in Ancient Society," in *The Role of the Christian Bishop in Ancient Society*, ed. E. C. Hobbs and W. Wuellner (Berkeley: Center for Hermeneutical Studies in Hellenistic and Modern Culture, 1979), 11; and Ramsey *Ambrose*, 6–7.

[265] *On the Duties of Ministers*, 1.1; English translations of this work are from http://www.ewadvent.org/fathers/3401.htm; also Lamirande, *Paulin de Milan*, 80.

fighting the influence of paganism.[266] Sixth, Ambrose was involved in providing for the needs of the poor. Seventh, he rendered verdicts in civil cases, for as a bishop he was empowered by the state to serve as a judge. Finally, Ambrose was responsible for overseeing the clergy attached to his church in Milan, which will be the focus of our inquiry in this section.[267]

Ambrose's Clergy in Milan

Besides the bishop, there were six orders of clergy in Milan. They included three higher orders—presbyters, deacons, and subdeacons—that functioned primarily around the altar, whereas the three lesser orders—exorcists, readers, and doorkeepers—performed nonsacramental services.

Presbyters served the bishop, advising and assisting him in leading the church. Ambrose involved them in aspects of the worship assembly—particularly in baptism, the Eucharist, and occasionally preaching. At times the presbyter was sent in place of the bishop to minister in other churches within the diocese.[268]

Deacons aided the bishop around the altar by reading the Gospel during worship and serving the cup during the Eucharist. They also assisted the presbyters with baptisms. In addition, they were involved in attending to the physical needs of the poor in the church and community. Subdeacons served the bishop around the altar and carried out some administrative functions.[269]

The lower clerical orders began with the exorcists. This was often the first assignment for adults entering the ministry in Milan. They were responsible for casting out demons from catechumens

[266] See Lamirande, *Paulin de Milan*, 80–82; also Edward Yarnold, *The Awe Inspiring Rites of Initiation: The Origins of the R.C.I.A.* (Edinburgh: T&T Clark, 1994), 98–149; William Harmless, *Augustine and the Catechumenate* (Collegeville, MN: Liturgical, 1995), 94–98; and *Letter* 20.4.

[267] See Angelo Paredi, *Saint Ambrose: His Life and Times*, trans. Joseph M. Costelloe (Notre Dame, IN: University of Notre Dame Press, 1964), 132–36; and Chadwick, "Role of the Christian Bishop," 6.

[268] *On the Mysteries*, 6; *On the Duties of Ministers*, 1.152; 2.69; *Letter* 20.22; see F. Holmes-Dudden, *The Life and Times of St. Ambrose, Vol. I–II* (Oxford: Clarendon, 1935), 131–32.

[269] *On the Duties of Ministers*, 1.204; 252; 255; 248; 2.140; *On the Mysteries*, 6; 8; *On the Sacraments*, 1.4; also Holmes-Dudden, *Life and Times of St. Ambrose*, 130–31.

before baptism as well as from others who lived in the vicinity of the church. The exorcist generally performed his ministry by laying hands on individuals while leading them through a prayer renouncing evil and confessing Christ.[270]

Those entering the ministry as youth were most often assigned to the office of reader. They read the Scriptures in the worship assembly and led the singing of psalms—a practice made popular by Ambrose. His writings reveal that some younger readers were raised among the clergy and went on to be ordained to higher orders.[271]

Doorkeepers made up the last group of lower orders in Milan. We learn about them in Augustine's *Confessions* when Monica had an encounter with the doorkeeper of the Milan church.[272] Generally, they kept the church clean and prohibited unauthorized visitors from entering the church during the Eucharist.[273]

How Did Ambrose Mentor?

Ambrose's letters, *On the Duties of Ministers,* and *On the Mysteries,* as well as Paulinus's *Life of Ambrose* reveal an important quality of Ambrose's mentoring. Like Cyprian and Basil, Ambrose favored mentoring other spiritual leaders through participating in church councils and by writing books and letters.

Church councils. As noted, Ambrose carried out his ministry in northern Italy, an area sharply divided by the Arian controversy. Though appearing cool and aloof at times, Ambrose was fully engaged in fighting for orthodoxy and sound doctrine within his spheres of influence. The clearest form that this took was his involvement in at least six church councils during his tenure as bishop of Milan.[274]

The first council met at Sirmium sometime between 375 and 380. Ramsey writes, "Although Ambrose had only recently been elected bishop, he was the natural leader of the gathering both because of

[270] See Holmes-Dudden, *Life and Times of St. Ambrose*, 131.
[271] *Letters* 1.13; 70.25; also Holmes-Dudden, *Life and Times of St. Ambrose*, 129.
[272] Augustine, *Confessions*, 6.2; also Holmes-Dudden, *Life and Times of St. Ambrose*, 129.
[273] Holmes-Dudden, *Life and Times of St. Ambrose*, 129.
[274] *Letters* 13–14; 21.17–18; 42; 51.6; also Ramsey, *Ambrose*, 40; and Holmes-Dudden, *Life and Times of St. Ambrose*, 126.

the importance of Milan and because of his connections with the highest circles in Sirmium."[275] Ramsey continues, "The result of the synod . . . was a strengthening of the orthodox Christian position through the deposing of several Arian clerics."[276] A second council, probably held in the following year in northern Italy, also saw a bishop with Arian tendencies removed from his position. Finally, at the council of Aquileia in 381, Ambrose influenced the gathered bishops to denounce the Arians Palladius and Secundianus. The outcomes of each council show that Ambrose was successful in using his position to stamp out heretical influences on the church.[277]

To consider more precisely how Ambrose mentored the clergy through church councils, let us look more closely at his role in the council of Aquileia. The acts of the council show that Ambrose was the first and most frequent speaker.[278] Yet the atmosphere was such that the other bishops freely contributed, and at one point Ambrose specifically asked for the participation of the African delegates.[279] As Ambrose questioned Palladius, he made clear that the issue was the deity of Christ, and he refused to alter that focus despite Palladius's repeated attempts to blur the issue.[280] Though Ambrose was always diligent, he also demonstrated fairness to the accused. At one point he said to Palladius and the members of the council, "Lest it should appear that he has been unfairly treated, let him state his opinion."[281] Finally, Ambrose called on the members of the council, those responsible for the sound interpretation of Scripture, to condemn Palladius as a heretic. Paredi asserts that "Ambrose knew how to bring matters to a point."[282]

Ambrose demonstrated to the clergy present at the council a zeal for orthodoxy based on a correct interpretation of Scripture, which

---

[275] Ramsey, *Ambrose*, 40.

[276] Ibid.

[277] Ibid.

[278] *Acts of the Council of Aquileia*, 2.

[279] Ibid., 16.

[280] Ibid., 5; 9; 12; 18; 20–22; 25; 33; 39.

[281] Ibid., 71; English translations of Ambrose's letters (including *Acts of the Council of Aquileia*) are from: http://www.tertullian.org/fathers/ambrose_letters_00_intro.htm.

[282] *Acts of the Council of Aquileia*, 53; see Paredi, *St. Ambrose*, 194.

he communicated in a letter to the Emperor Theodosius after the council:

> This was why we asked for a council of bishops, that no one should be permitted to state what was false against a person in his absence, and that the truth might be cleared up by discussion in the council. We ought not then to incur any suspicion either of over-zeal or over-leniency, seeing that we made all our observations in the presence of the parties.[283]

As he pursued getting to the bottom of the matter, Ambrose demonstrated to his fellow clergy an ability to stay focused on the issue, to refrain from quarreling, to be fair to the accused, and to involve less influential members in the discussion. He also served the bishops after the council by writing a concise summary to the emperor of what transpired, which indirectly served as a record and reminder to the clergy.[284] In short, the church council was one of Ambrose's important tools for mentoring clergy.

Letters. A second way Ambrose mentored spiritual leaders was in letter writing. In his day it was common practice for a newly appointed bishop to write to the existing bishops announcing his ordination while making a declaration of orthodoxy. The bishops generally replied with words of affirmation and encouragement, as did Basil in his letter to Ambrose.[285] Of Ambrose's 91 surviving letters, at least 43 were written to the clergy. McLynn asserts, "From Milan, letters of instruction, exhortation and advice radiated outwards to the churches of Trent, Verona, Claterna, Piacenza, and Vercelli."[286]

Was mentoring the intent of Ambrose's correspondence? In *Letter* 47 written to Bishop Sabinus of Placentia, Ambrose likened his own writing to Paul's and communicated a mentoring purpose:

---

[283] *Letter* 14.5.
[284] *On the Duties of Ministers*, 1.99.
[285] Basil, *Letter* 197; also Paredi, *St. Ambrose*, 126–27.
[286] See Neil McLynn, *Ambrose of Milan: Church and Court in a Christian Capital* (Berkley: University of California Press, 1994), 282.

And why need I produce the example of our ancestors, who by their letters have instilled faith into the minds of the people, and have written to whole nations together, and have shown themselves to be present although writing from a distance, according to the words of the apostle, that he was absent in body, but present in spirit, not only in writing but also in judging.[287]

Ambrose believed that letters to fellow clergy were a means of making his presence known though he was personally distant. He used letters to mentor the clergy in at least three ways: to instruct them in practical church matters, to respond to theological and exegetical questions, and to encourage and exhort them to the work of ministry.

Six letters were devoted to practical matters related to leading the church. In *Letter* 19, Ambrose wrote to encourage Bishop Vigilius of Trent on the occasion of his ordination in 385.[288] In the letter Ambrose also warned against the dangers of intermarriage between Christians and pagans and against fraud and usury in the church, and he encouraged church members to be hospitable.[289] In *Letter* 23, he wrote to the bishops of Aemilia answering their question about the correct date of Easter. In *Letter* 5, he counseled Syagrius of Verona on how to handle a certain case brought before him for judgment.[290] In *Letters* 59 and 87, Ambrose wrote to the bishops commending certain believers who had recently come into their midst.

Most of Ambrose's 30 mentoring letters were devoted to theological questions. In *Letters* 7 and 8, written to Justus of Lyon, Ambrose treated questions related to the interpretation of Scripture as well as how the Scriptures were actually written. Eleven letters were addressed to a certain Irenaeus who had probably been trained as a cleric in Milan.[291] They included replies to exegetical questions,

---

[287] *Letter* 47.6–7.
[288] *Letter* 19.1.
[289] *Letter* 19.2–4, 6, 8–33; also Holmes-Dudden, *Life and Times of St. Ambrose*, 127.
[290] *Letter* 6 was also written to Syagrius; see Ramsey, *Ambrose*, 38.
[291] *Letter* 27; also Holmes-Dudden, *Life and Times of St. Ambrose*, 126.

why the law was given, and an exposition on Ephesians.[292] Similarly, Ambrose resourced Honorontius with eight letters treating subjects like the nature of the soul, the death of Paul, and creation.[293] Ambrose also wrote to Sabinus regarding the days of creation and the refutation of an Arian heretic in Milan.[294] He even resourced his own theological teacher, Simplicianus, with four letters of reply to exegetical questions.[295] Finally, he wrote *Letter* 72 to Constantius on the significance of circumcision for Christians.

Seven final letters focused on simple encouragement and, at times, exhortation to the ministry. In 393, Ambrose addressed *Letter* 81 to his clergy in Milan who remained behind following his departure from the city after he had excommunicated the Emperor Eugenius for reopening of the pagan temples. He sought to encourage them amid the difficult pagan influence in the city and exhorted them to carry on the work of the ministry.[296] In *Letter* 2, Ambrose wrote to Constantius at the time of his ordination exhorting him to minister and giving some specific instruction on preaching. Also, Ambrose encouraged him to look after the congregation in a neighboring city that had no bishop.[297]

Ambrose's two letters to Felix of Como testified to the friendship between the two bishops.[298] While Ambrose offered encouragement and the exhortation to "fight the good fight of faith," the tone of the letters suggests more of a peer mentoring relationship in which Ambrose asked Felix for prayer.[299] The same was true of some of his correspondence with Sabinus. In *Letter* 48 Ambrose asked for Sabinus's feedback on books that he had written, placing Sabinus in something of an editorial role. In *Letter* 49 he added that he particularly liked writing to Sabinus when he was alone because it made him feel close to his friend. Finally, in *Letter* 58 he raised the

---

[292] *Letters* 27; 32–33; 64; 69; 73–74; 76; also *Letters* 28–31.

[293] *Letters* 34–36; 43–44; 70–71; 77–78.

[294] *Letters* 45–47.

[295] *Letters* 37–38; 65; 67.

[296] See Paredi, *Saint Ambrose*, 360, 433.

[297] *Letter* 2.4–8, 27 also *Letter* 19.

[298] *Letter* 3 is a letter of thanks with some playful humor as well.

[299] *Letter* 4.3–6.

issue of Paulinus of Nola's decision to renounce the world, inviting Sabinus to a discussion on the matter.

There was also evidence that Ambrose mentored Paulinus of Nola by letter.[300] In Paulinus's *Letter* 3 he wrote, "I still consider the venerable Ambrose as my spiritual father. It was Ambrose who instructed me on the mysteries of the faith, who still gives me the advice I need to carry out my duties as a priest worthily."[301] This letter is noteworthy because, while he may have spent some time with Ambrose in Milan, Paulinus spent most of his career in ministry elsewhere. Ambrose's continual advice may have come through lost letters or perhaps personal interaction during the Italian church councils.

The fact that Ambrose wrote 43 of his 91 letters to other clergy is significant, for he deemed it important to be in contact with other clergy, especially those in northern Italy. The content of his letters—advice on practical church matters, theological questions, and encouragement and exhortation to the ministry—support the claim that Ambrose was using letters as a means of mentoring the clergy.

Books. Paulinus wrote that although Ambrose employed a stenographer, he wrote many of his books by his own hand.[302] Ramsey adds that most of Ambrose's books were initially sermons he preached in the church.[303] Further, Ambrose's books, though addressed to a specific recipient or group, were probably intended for a wider audience including the clergy. In 378 when Ambrose replied to the Emperor Gratian's request for an exposition of orthodoxy with his book *On the Faith*, the clergy probably benefited as well, for the work was largely a summary of the discussion at the council of Sirmium.[304] Likewise, *On the Mysteries* was a book of teaching on baptism and the Eucharist. Although addressed to catechumens, it refers to the clergy and their role in the sacraments at least five times.[305] While surely aware of their ministry, perhaps the clergy were reminded of the importance of their role around the altar

---

[300] See Paredi, *Saint Ambrose*, 372.

[301] Paulinus of Nola, *Letter* 3.4. English translation from Paredi, *Saint Ambrose*, 372; also Paulinus's letter to Alypius that appears in Augustine's correspondence (*Letter* 24).

[302] Ibid., 38.

[303] See Ramsey, *Ambrose*, 55.

[304] See Paredi, *Saint Ambrose*, 180.

[305] *On the Mysteries*, 2.6; 3.8, 14; 5.27; 6.29.

as well as the theological significance of the mysteries. Ambrose wrote in *Letter* 47 to Sabinus that he had sent a book along with his letter, which was intended to resource the bishop.[306] Since there is no record of any book by Ambrose being directly addressed to Sabinus, it stands to reason that this bishop benefited as a member of Ambrose's wider audience.

Holmes-Dudden writes, "Ambrose's solicitude for his clergy is shown by the trouble he took in their instruction. For their benefit he composed the important series of addresses which were afterwards gathered up in that very famous treatise [*On the Duties of Ministers*]."[307] "Solicitude" and "trouble" are appropriate descriptions for Ambrose's teaching, for he had inherited a largely Arian clerical staff from his predecessor Auxentius—a group of men in dire need of orthodox teaching.[308] Only later did these lectures take the form of a book intended for a wider clerical audience.

Structured with precepts heavily supported by scriptural exegesis and principles from the lives of the saints of Scripture, the book's stated intent was "to teach you, my children."[309] As Ambrose's main theme was the need for a minister to pursue holiness, the book may be divided into three broad categories: attributes the minister must adopt, things he must avoid, and general practical instruction.

First, Ambrose called his clergy to be men of holy character and conduct, following the models of the saints of Scripture. He exhorted them to "be humble, gentle, mild, serious, [and] patient" and to demonstrate the virtues of prudence, justice, fortitude, and temperance. He urged them to show love, mercy, kindness, goodwill, and to give freely out of pure motives. He also called them to be sexually pure and to have a good testimony before the secular authorities. He further advised them to demonstrate modesty in speech, tone of voice, in praying, and even in walking. In short, Ambrose's minister should live to please God alone.[310]

---

[306] *Letter* 47.1.
[307] See Holmes-Dudden, *Life and Times of St. Ambrose*, 125–26.
[308] See Paredi, *Saint Ambrose*, 127–28.
[309] *On the Duties of Ministers*, 1.24.
[310] Ibid., 1.11; 1.89; 1.115; 2.39; 1.38, 143, 147, 160–62; 1.265; 1.207; 1.67, 76, 235; 1.84; 1.70; 1.71–75; 2.2–3.

Second, Ambrose advised the men to put off or avoid things that would distract them from personal holiness. They were to decline invitations to banquets in order to resist the temptation of indulging in food, gossip, or drinking. Younger clergy were not allowed to visit the home of a virgin or widow unless accompanied by an older minister or the bishop. The clergy were to avoid the love of money by refraining from trade or lawsuits or from seeking inheritances. They were not allowed to marry a second time after being divorced; they were to avoid anger and lust, allowing reason to prevail over the soul's passions; and they were to abstain from quarreling. Finally, a minister should not be jealous when another minister was praised, nor should he posture himself in a manner superior to his bishop.[311]

Finally, Ambrose offered the clergy some practical instruction. They should show hospitality to visitors. They should strike a balance between laxness and severity in their clerical authority. He urged them to counsel the faithful with prudence and justice.[312] He also offered some instruction on how to preach:

> The treatment also of such subjects as the teaching of faith, instruction on self-restraint, discussion on justice, exhortation to activity, must not be taken up by us and fully gone into all at one time, but must be carried on in course, so far as we can do it, and as the subject-matter of the passage allows. Our discourse must not be too lengthy, nor too soon cut short, for fear the former should leave behind it a feeling of aversion, and the latter produce carelessness and neglect. The address should be plain and simple, clear and evident, full of dignity and weight; it should not be studied or too refined, nor yet, on the other hand, be unpleasing and rough in style.[313]

Ambrose called his preachers to be balanced in their presentation so that the listener would be able to understand fully what he was

---

[311] Ibid., 1.76, 86, 256; 1.87; 1.184; 3.58; 1.257–58; 1.237–38, 240; 1.99; 2.122–23.
[312] Ibid., 2.21.103; 2.120; 2.41.
[313] Ibid., 1.101.

saying. He wanted them to speak plainly and discouraged them from telling jokes.[314]

On the Duties of Ministers was a significant manual for spiritual leaders in Ambrose's day. With a focus on personal holiness and conduct illustrated by the lives of the saints of Scripture, it also contained some practical instruction. The evidence from this work alone indicates that Ambrose regarded a book as an important tool for mentoring the clergy—particularly those who were not present in Milan to hear his teaching. While *On the Duties of Ministers* was precisely intended for the clergy, books like *On the Faith* and *On the Mysteries* should also be regarded for their influence on spiritual leaders.

Ambrose's Thought on Mentoring

The evidence suggests that Ambrose was at work mentoring spiritual leaders on a personal level in Milan, through his influence in church councils, and through his letters. Ambrose also demonstrates seven aspects of mentoring that relate to the New Testament model presented in chapter 1.

A mentor is a disciple. Ambrose was a disciple who continued to grow spiritually and as a minister throughout his career as bishop. Simplicianus, whom Ambrose called his friend and father, taught Ambrose theology but also seems to have had an impact on his character.[315] Simplicianus certainly modeled humble, lifelong learning as he later wrote letters posing theological questions to his former students Ambrose and Augustine.[316]

In *On the Duties of Ministers,* Ambrose communicated his desire to learn continually: "A bishop's special office is to teach; he must, however, learn in order that he may teach" and "men learn before they teach, and receive from [God] what they may hand on to others."[317] In *Letter* 18 he added, "It is surely true that no age is too late to learn."[318] He further demonstrated this conviction in *Letter* 48, in which he sent Sabinus a book and asked for his feedback

---

[314] Ibid., 1.102, 104.

[315] *Letter* 37.2; see Ramsey, *Ambrose*, 43.

[316] See Ambrose, *Letters* 37–38; 65; 67; and Augustine, *Letter* 37 and *To Simplicianus*.

[317] *On the Duties of Ministers*, 1.1, 3 (translation updated by author).

[318] *Letter* 18.7; see Paredi, *Saint Ambrose*, 130.

before he published it.[319] Hence, as Ambrose went about mentoring other clergy, it seems that he had benefited from Simplicianus's example, and he remained a continual learner throughout his life.

Like Cyprian, Pachomius, and Basil, Ambrose's continual journey as a disciple rendered him an example for other leaders to imitate. Paulinus, in his *Life of Ambrose,* referred to Ambrose as holy (*sanctus*) on nine occasions.[320] Ambrose, writing to the church at Vercelli in 396 in the midst of their struggle to find a suitable bishop, expressed his convictions about the holiness of a spiritual leader: "The life of the priest ought to be pre-eminent as well as his graces, for he who obliges others by his precepts ought himself to observe the precepts of the law."[321]

In what ways did Ambrose mentor by his example? First, Ambrose's initial refusal of the office of bishop in Milan before reluctantly accepting it seems to have sharply contradicted any impure pursuit of this position.[322] Second, Paulinus recorded that upon his ordination as bishop Ambrose renounced his personal property, which distinguished him from others who sought ordination for material gain.[323] Third, Ambrose not only praised virginity but personally maintained a celibate lifestyle. Fourth, Paulinus added that Ambrose was known for his commitment to the disciplines of prayer and fasting. Finally, Paulinus highlighted the holy example of Ambrose, who guarded in confidence what confessors shared with him.[324]

While Ambrose became an example for imitation, he also made significant use of the examples of the saints of Scripture in his teaching. In *On the Duties of Ministers*, a work filled with references to the saints, he summarized his practice by writing:

> These things I have left with you, my children, that
> you may guard them in your minds—you yourselves

---

[319] *Letter* 48.1.

[320] Paulinus refers to him as "holy Ambrose" *sanctus Ambrosius* (16.3; 18.4; 52.1); "holy man" *sanctus uir* (12.1; 30.2); "holy priest" *sanctus sacerdos* (33.1; 40.1; 45.2); "holy priest of God" *sanctus Domini sacerdos* (51.1); also Lamirande, *Paulin de Milan*, 77.

[321] *Letters* 63.64.

[322] *Letters* 63.65; see Ramsey, *Ambrose*, 42.

[323] Paulinus, *Life of Ambrose*, 38; also Holmes-Dudden, *Life and Times of St. Ambrose*, 107; and Paredi, *Saint Ambrose*, 124–25.

[324] Paulinus, *Life of Ambrose*, 38–39; see Ramsey, *Ambrose*, 18.

will prove whether they will be of any advantage.
Meanwhile they offer you a large number of examples,
for almost all the examples drawn from our forefathers,
and also many a word of theirs, are included within
these three books; so that, although the language may
not be graceful, yet a succession of old-time examples
set down in such small compass may offer much
instruction.[325]

Selection. Though evidence for how Ambrose chose men for ministry is lacking, many developing leaders did join him in Milan. We know
that he invited Paulinus of Nola to serve with him and that an African
numbered among his clergy as well. Also, when Ambrose returned
to Milan in 394 following his conflict with Eugenius, he brought
with him Paulinus, who became one of his clergy and later wrote his
Life.[326] As with Cyprian, some readers came to serve with Ambrose at
a young age and were later promoted to the higher orders.[327] McLynn
summarizes, "Milan's developing position as an avenue of promotion
must have helped recruitment to the clergy there."[328]

Some of these, having heard of Ambrose's reputation, may have
taken the initiative toward Ambrose as a mentor. In *On the Duties
of Ministers*, Ambrose seemed to encourage the initiative of a disciple toward a mentor, similar to the monastic tendency of a disciple
seeking out a holy man that we observed in Pachomius and Basil.
Ambrose wrote:

It is a very good thing to unite oneself to a good man. It
is also very useful for the young to follow the guidance
of great and wise men. For he who lives in company
with wise men is wise himself; but he who clings to
the foolish is looked on as a fool too. This friendship
with the wise is a great help in teaching us, and also

---

[325] *On the Duties of Ministers*, 3.138; 2.98–100; also *On the Mysteries*, 1.1; and *Letters* 63.97; 103; 111.

[326] Paulinus of Nola, *Letter* 3.4; Paulinus, *Life of Ambrose*, 54.1; see McLynn, *Ambrose of Milan*, 284–85; and Paredi, *Saint Ambrose*, 361.

[327] *Letters* 1.13; 70.25, Paulinus, *Life of Ambrose*, 46; see Ramsey, *Ambrose*, 215.

[328] See McLynn, *Ambrose of Milan*, 284–85.

as giving a sure proof of our uprightness. Young men show very soon that they imitate those to whom they attach themselves. And this idea gains ground from the fact that in all their daily life they grow to be like those with whom they have enjoyed intercourse to the full.[329]

Mentor-disciple relationship. Ambrose's relationship to the clergy can best be described as paternal or fatherly—a delicate balance of authority and discipline as well as grace. Holmes-Dudden writes, "Towards these ministers the bishop's relation was that of a father to his sons; he was accordingly bound to keep them in good discipline, taking care to avoid the extremes of laxity and harshness."[330]

Ambrose's graceful posture was apparent in his correspondence with Irenaeus. At the conclusion of *Letter* 27, he wrote, "Farewell, my son; blush not to ask questions of your father."[331] Ambrose used similar language in at least five other instances in their correspondence.[332] In *On the Duties of Ministers*, he also addressed the clergy in a gentle and paternal manner while asserting that a bishop must serve his clergy: "The bishop should treat the clerics and attendants, who are indeed his sons, as members of himself."[333]

Ambrose's prescriptions for holiness in *On the Duties of Ministers* reveals another aspect of his fatherly posture—his disciplinary and authoritative manner. While some may argue that Ambrose's authority stemmed from his political background and that he was the bishop of an important city like Milan, Ambrose supported his understanding of the hierarchy between mentor and disciples with several examples from Scripture. He cited the relationships between Moses and Joshua; Elijah and Elisha; Barnabas and Mark; and Paul and his disciples Timothy and Titus. Essentially, the mentor's age, life experience, and personal holiness qualified him to have authority over younger disciples.[334]

---

[329] *On the Duties of Ministers*, 2.97.
[330] See Holmes-Dudden, *Life and Times of St. Ambrose*, 122.
[331] *Letter* 27.17.
[332] *Letters* 28.8; 29.24; 30.16; 32.9; 34.11.
[333] *On the Duties of Ministers*, 1.24; 2.155; 2.134.
[334] Ibid., 2.98–99; 2.100–1.

There is also evidence that Ambrose demonstrated and encouraged peer mentoring. His friendly interaction with both Felix of Como and Sabinus was apparent in his letters to these leaders.[335] While he disapproved of a minister telling jokes in a sermon, Ambrose did not refrain from humor in his interaction with Felix.[336] As noted, Ambrose recounted to Sabinus how writing letters made him feel close to his friend and that it combated loneliness.[337] Their correspondence also reveals a fraternal relationship of intellectual inquiry as Ambrose sent a book to Sabinus and asked for his feedback. In *Letter* 47, Ambrose alluded to both the affective and scholarly aspects of their friendship:

> While your judgment of my book is still in suspense, let us entertain each other by letters; the advantage whereof is that although severed from each other by distance of space we may be united in affection; for by this means the absent have the image of each other's presence reflected back upon them, and conversation by writing unites the severed. By this means also we interchange thoughts with our friend, and transpose our mind into his.[338]

In light of this friendly correspondence, it is important to remember that Ambrose was regarded as the mentor in these relationships. His posture showed that he was not only a personal, approachable mentor but that he also benefited from the interaction. Finally, he alluded to peer mentoring in *On the Duties of Ministers* when he cited the relationship between Peter and John "who were alike in virtue but unlike in years" [and] "greatly rejoiced at their union."[339]

Ambrose not only demonstrated peer mentoring, but he also prescribed it for spiritual leaders. In *On the Duties of Ministers*, he urged

---

[335] *Letters* 3–4; 47–49.

[336] *On the Duties of Ministers*, 1.102, 104; *Letter* 3.

[337] *Letters* 48–49. Ambrose expressed similar thoughts on friendship in *On the Holy Spirit*, 2.19.101–12.2.; also Joseph T. Lienhard, "Friendship in Paulinus of Nola and Augustine," *Augustiniana* 1 (1990): 283.

[338] *Letter* 47.4; also *Letters* 48–49; *On the Holy Spirit*, 2.19.101–2.2.; and Lienhard, "Friendship," 283.

[339] *On the Duties of Ministers*, 2.101.

the clergy to relate to one another as a community. Specifically, he encouraged the men to open up their hearts to one another, to bear one another's burdens, and to exercise fraternal correction when necessary. Yet, as noted, Ambrose advocated a balance between the extremes of harshness and flattery.[340]

Ambrose was like a father to his clergy, demonstrating both grace and discipline. Yet, from the evidence presented, he also demonstrated fraternal mentoring, especially in relation to Felix and Sabinus. Finally, he prescribed fraternal correction and mentoring among the clergy in Christian community.

Sound teaching. If being the bishop of Milan was simply another political appointment in ecclesiastical clothing for Ambrose, he surely would not have risked opposing Valentinian in the Portian Basilica affair.[341] Rather, the reason Ambrose stood up to the emperor in 385–386 and so vehemently fought Arianism through church councils was his commitment to sound doctrine. As we have argued, his involvement in these controversies served as a training ground for mentoring the clergy to be doctrinally sound.

For Ambrose the basis of sound doctrine was the Scriptures. In *On the Duties of Ministers,* he wrote, "The divine Scriptures are the feast of wisdom, and the single books the various dishes."[342] Throughout the work he continually argued for the supremacy of the Scriptures over philosophy.[343] The Scriptures were not only to be revered, but they also needed to be interpreted correctly. He called his fellow bishops present at the council of Aquileia to condemn the Arian Palladius based on their judgment as "interpreters of the Scriptures."[344] He sent Sabinus a book he had written and asked for his feedback, not pertaining to its eloquence but to its doctrinal accuracy and proper use of Scripture.[345]

His commitment to sound doctrine pushed him to be a diligent student of the Scriptures and to require that from his clergy as well.

---

[340] Ibid., 2.135; 3.128–29; 3.127, 134.
[341] *Letter* 20; see Ramsey, *Ambrose,* 25–29.
[342] *On the Duties of Ministers,* 1.165.
[343] Ibid., 1.30–32; 42–44; 47–50 are just a few examples.
[344] *Acts of the Council of Aquileia,* 53.
[345] *Letter* 48.3.

Though well educated in the liberal arts, training that strengthened his defense of Christianity against pagans and heretics, Ambrose did not rely on this background but remained a continual student and reader as Augustine and Monica witnessed.[346] He also encouraged a studious community of clergy around him and encouraged them to avoid idleness and to use their free time reading.[347] As noted, Ambrose's clergy in Milan had been reared in Arianism and were in need of a rigorous theological program, one that he resourced through sermons that later became books as well as the seminar version of *On the Duties of Ministers.*

Modeling and involving in ministry. Ambrose actively involved his clergy in the ministries of the church, entrusting them with various levels of responsibility. Though he had a reputation for being adept at exorcisms, he largely delegated this task to the exorcists.[348] The significant responsibility given to presbyters who were at times called upon to preach and minister in other locations on behalf of the bishop has also been observed.[349] Finally, as noted before, some young men entered at lower ranks and were later promoted.

Ambrose was committed to developing and advancing his clergy. In *On the Duties of Ministers*, he offered his thoughts on promoting and placing men in offices of spiritual leadership. A clergy could be promoted to a higher rank for merit or seniority. Hence time and faithful service were essential to moving to the next step, but negligent clerics would not be promoted. Rather, they would likely be removed from the ministry.[350] Each clergy should be placed in a ministry assignment that corresponded with his temperament and natural abilities, "since the duty which suits a man, and which is in line with his natural bent, is always discharged with greater grace."[351]

---

[346] See Agostino Trapé, *Saint Augustine: l'homme, le pasteur, le mystique* (Paris: Fayard, 1988), 69; also Paulinus, *Life of Ambrose*, 7; see Ramsey, *Ambrose*, 20; and Augustine, *Confessions*, 6.3.3.

[347] *On the Duties of Ministers*, 1.87–88; see Trapé, *Saint Augustine*, 70.

[348] See Paulinus, *Life of Ambrose*, 21, 43; and Holmes-Dudden, *Life and Times of St. Ambrose*, 130.

[349] *Letter* 20.22; also Holmes-Dudden, *Life and Times of St. Ambrose*, 132.

[350] *On the Duties of Ministers*, 2.121; 2.22–23; see Holmes-Dudden, *Life and Times of St. Ambrose*, 124.

[351] *On the Duties of Ministers*, 1.215. English translation from Holmes-Dudden, *Life and Times of St. Ambrose*, 124.

The church at Milan operated as a laboratory for training the clergy, and Ambrose was the key model and trainer. According to McLynn, "These men had imbibed the bishop's teachings at first hand, and had learned by observation the patterns of behavior that were packaged, for wider circulation in *On the Duties of Ministers*."[352]

Releasing. Once clergy had passed through Ambrose's ministry laboratory in Milan, where clergy were entrusted with assignments of increasing responsibility, they were then released to their own ministries. Paulinus tells of two clergy who had trained with Ambrose and then went on to serve as bishops in other cites—Felix, a deacon in Milan who became the bishop of Bolgna, and Theodulus, who was appointed as bishop of Modena.[353] As bishop of Milan, Ambrose also ordained these leaders to ministry. He participated in the consecration of at least three bishops—Anemius of Sirmium around 379; an unnamed bishop of Pavia in 397; and Gaudentius of Brescia in 397.[354]

Ambrose had high standards for ordained ministers, and it seems that the most important quality was personal holiness, as was noted in *On the Duties of Ministers* and in *Letter* 63. On one occasion he grieved at the death of a priest in large part because it would be hard to find a replacement "who might be considered worthy of the high priesthood."[355] He summarized his high standards for the priesthood in a letter to Ireneaus: "Nothing vulgar, nothing popular, nothing in common with the ambitions and customs and manners of the rude multitude, is expected in priests. The dignity of the priesthood demands a sober and elevated calmness, a serious life, a special gravity."[356]

Resourcing. While Ambrose was committed to releasing qualified men to places of leadership in the church, he seemed equally interested in resourcing clergy particularly in northern Italy. As noted, his letters provided answers to theological inquiries as well as practical help for leading the church. He also resourced spiritual leaders with books—most notably *On the Duties of Ministers*,

---

[352] See McLynn, *Ambrose of Milan*, 284.
[353] Paulinus, *Life of Ambrose*, 35.1; 46.1; see McLynn, *Ambrose of Milan*, 284.
[354] Paulinus, *Life of Ambrose*, 11; see Ramsey, *Ambrose*, 39–40.
[355] Paulinus, *Life of Ambrose*, 40; English translation from Ramsey, *Ambrose*, 212.
[356] *Letter* 28.2; English translation from Holmes-Dudden, *Life and Times of St. Ambrose*, 108.

which exhorted men to personal holiness while providing practical instruction for ministry.

Third- and Fourth-Century Mentoring

This chapter has considered the key approaches and thoughts on spiritual mentoring in the ministries of Cyprian, Pachomius, Basil, and Ambrose. While their cultural contexts, theological issues, and spiritual battles differed, each invested time and energy in training other leaders for ministry. Generally speaking, the New Testament model for mentoring proposed in the first chapter was adhered to by these leaders.

What were the most prevalent approaches to mentoring in this period? Perhaps surprisingly, written communication was highly important—specifically letters and books. Nearly all of Cyprian's letters, half of Ambrose's letters, and one-fourth of Basil's letters were written to spiritual leaders with some level of mentoring emphasis. Even Pachomius's cryptic letters were intended as a resource to the leaders of monasteries. The main purposes of the bishops' correspondence were encouragement, exhortation, discipline, responding to theological and exegetical questions, and practical instruction regarding church matters—much like Paul's Pastoral Epistles. Gamble comments, "The persistence of Christian epistolography through the first five centuries attests to the usefulness of this genre to the ancient church, for it was well suited to communication between widespread congregations and a valuable instrument for teaching."[357]

Each leader surveyed also mentored by writing books and treatises related to practical church matters, spiritual leadership, and doctrinal issues. Pachomius and Basil each developed a *Rule* for how the monastic community should function. As preaching was an important role for each bishop, their books were probably first delivered as sermons or discourses—as in the case of Cyprian's *On the Lapsed* and Ambrose's *On the Duties of Ministers*—before being published

---

[357] See Gamble, *Books and Readers*, 37.

for a wider audience.[358] Emerging spiritual leaders in this period, not unlike the disciples of Paul or Jesus, needed to read books and letters but mostly the Scriptures.[359] Because the Christian movement depends on a book, the clergy needed access to the Scriptures for themselves and for their congregations. To assure this, Pachomius included a literacy program as part of his initial monastic training.

A second key approach to mentoring in this period, particularly in the ministries of Cyprian, Basil, and Ambrose, was church councils. Although convening councils was one of their expected roles as metropolitan bishops, each of the three took councils seriously and valued them as a means of dealing with heresy and other issues facing the church. While all three used councils to influence the clergy toward sound doctrine, they also valued the gathering (*collegium*) of bishops that involved other leaders in a collective decision making process. Cyprian and Ambrose especially believed it important to articulate in writing the decisions of the councils that would serve as a written point of reference for the churches.

The convictions and strengths of the four leaders presented in this chapter are as diverse as their personalities and giftings and as the contexts in which they served. Because of the heretical threats faced by Cyprian, Basil, and Ambrose, it is not surprising that sound teaching was a key component in their mentoring. Yet as Basil and Pachomius pursued a monastic lifestyle, the aspects of the group and mentor-disciple relationship were most important to them. Again, despite their diversity, each was committed to mentoring spiritual leaders, and they provide a fine backdrop for the study of the mentoring ministry of Augustine.

---

[358] Some helpful studies on book publishing in the preprinting press era include William Tabbernee, "Noiseless Books and Pilfered Manuscripts: Early Christian 'Desk-Top' Publishing in Carthage," *Devotion and Dissent: The Practice of Christianity in Roman Africa,* http://ccat.sas.upenn.edu/jod/augustine.html; Gamble, *Books and Readers,* 140; and Paul Achtemeier, "*Omne Verbum Sonat*: The New Testament and the Oral Environment of Late Western Antiquity," *JBL* 109/1 (1990): 12–14.

[359] See Gamble, *Books and Readers,* 9–10; and Achtemeier, "*Omne Verbum Sonat,*" 15–17.

Chapter Three

WHO MENTORED AUGUSTINE?

odern travelers visiting the museums of Tunisia are immediately struck by the most unique art form from Roman Africa—the mosaic.[1] Constructed from tiny pieces of colored tile that combine to make a beautiful portrait or object, mosaics have survived wars, conquest, and the turnover of several civilizations to tell the story of daily life in this period. In piecing together a mosaic of Augustine's life, we must recognize that individual tiles as well as the persons who laid them contributed to the overall portrait of his life and ministry. Before we can fully consider how Augustine mentored spiritual leaders of his day, we must pose an important question: who mentored Augustine? As we will see, several people of various backgrounds and personalities influenced him at different periods of his life. In this chapter we will consider the impact of his mother, Monica, and of some close friends, Ambrose, Simplicianus, and Valerius, while also showing how these influences became apparent in Augustine's own mentoring.

---

[1] I wish to credit William Harmless for this analogy; see Harmless, *Augustine and the Catechumenate*, 39.

Monica

Monica occupies a venerated place as one of the most famous mothers in Christian history. Her presence was well recorded by Augustine in the *Confessions* as well in the Cassiciacum dialogues where it is clear that he regarded her as a model and guide for the Christian life. Like Basil of Caesarea and Gregory of Nyssa, Augustine benefited from a pious upbringing and his mother's influence. He wrote, "My mother did all she could to see that you, my God, should be more truly my father than he [Patricius] was."[2] Having surveyed the texts that show Monica's influence on her son, I suggest that she mentored him in at least four ways, mostly in the period before his conversion in 386: through her holy example, her practical faith, her commitment to sound doctrine and practice, and the early Christian education she provided at home.

Holy Example

Monica was most often characterized in the *Confessions* as a woman of prayer and tears, and the focus of her supplications was often the spiritual welfare of her wayward son.[3] Augustine often reported that his mother experienced dreams and visions confirming that her prayers would be answered.[4] He also highlighted her upright character. Among friends and acquaintances, she refrained from gossip and resolved to be a careful listener and peacemaker.[5] Despite a rocky beginning with her mother-in-law, Monica won her affections because of her character.[6] She was faithful and showed respect to an unbelieving, hot-tempered, and often unfaithful husband; and this ultimately resulted in Patricius's conversion near the

---

[2] *Confessions*, 1.11.17; all English translation of *Confessions* are from Maria Boulding in John E. Rotelle, ed., *Works of Saint Augustine: A Translation for the 21st Century* (Hyde Park, NY: New City, 2001).

[3] *Confessions*, 1.11.17; 3.4.8; 3.11.19; 3.12.21; 5.7.13; 5.9.15,17; 6.1.1; 6.2.2; 9.13.36; also André Mandouze, *Prosopographie Chrétienne du Bas-empire, Vol. I, Afrique (303–533)*, (Paris: Editions du CNRS, 1982), 759.

[4] *Confessions*, 3.11.19; 3:12.21; 8.12.30; see Margaret O'Ferrall, "Monica, the Mother of Augustine: A Reconsideration," *Recherches Augustiniennes* 10 (1975): 40–41.

[5] *Confessions*, 9.9.21.

[6] *Confessions*, 9.9.20; see John O'Meara, *The Young Augustine* (London: Longmans, 1954), 17.

end of his life.[7] As a result, Monica was a model and mentor to other women struggling with difficult marriages.

Though Augustine consistently made note of her holy life, he certainly did not "saint" her.[8] Rather, he realistically presented her as a recovering sinner not immune to struggles or weaknesses. As a young woman, Monica apparently had struggled with wine.[9] He also criticized her failure to arrange a marriage for him—a young man struggling with lust—because she and Patricius seemed to care more about his academic success than his moral purity.[10] Finally, he admitted that she could be rather controlling.[11] So, through the example of Monica, Augustine learned that Christian piety did not necessarily exclude a continual struggle with sin.

The impact of Monica's holy yet imperfect example would become evident in Augustine's later ministry as a spiritual leader and mentor. Possidius, who wrote the *Life of Augustine* "based on what I saw of him and heard from him," mentioned a pious example as Augustine's most significant tool for influencing others.[12] Augustine's example, which Possidius held up for imitation, was balanced with the transparent example of one who continued to struggle with sin. This was most apparent in his *Confessions* where Augustine spoke of his sinful past but more significantly, "what I am now."[13] The bishop of Hippo openly shared his struggle with lustful thoughts and with gluttony; his fascination with sounds, shapes, and colors; and his lust of the eyes, pride, and the praise of men.[14] Like his mother, Augustine mentored others through a personal example somewhat untainted by an ongoing struggle with sin.

Practical Faith

Monica's example instilled in her son the importance of practical faith lived out in the real world. She was concerned with prayer,

---

[7] *Confessions*, 9.19, 22.
[8] O'Ferrall, "Monica," 29–30.
[9] *Confessions*, 9.8.18.
[10] *Confessions*, 2.8.
[11] *Confessions*, 5.8.15.
[12] Possidius, *Life of Augustine*, preface.
[13] *Confessions*, 1.5.6; 1.10.16; 1.13.21–2; 1.19.30; 2.2.2; 3.1.1; 2.4.9; 10.4.6.
[14] *Confessions*, 10.30.42; 10.31.43, 45, 47; 10.33.49–50; 10.34.51; 10.35.54–57; 10.36.59; 10.37.61.

perseverance, and promoting peace in her most significant relationships.[15] Though on his spiritual journey Augustine became intrigued by philosophy and intellectual speculation, he would not escape Monica's influence of practical faith.

The most poignant example of Augustine's intellectual world and Monica's practical world converging was at the retreat at Cassiciacum. Augustine indicated that he was pleased that his mother was present in this rather philosophical community.[16] This was the same Augustine who, just a few years earlier, deceitfully left his mother behind in Carthage to continue an academic career in Italy.[17] According to the Cassiciacum dialogues, Monica was not simply present to cook and keep house, but she participated in the discussions as well.[18] Augustine wrote, "The power of her mind came home to me and I realized that it could not be more suited to true philosophizing. . . . I decided therefore, that when she was at leisure she should be present at our conversations."[19] In fact, she gained the reputation of being able to overturn a speculative conversation with a few simple thoughts. Brown writes that she was able to "dismiss a whole philosophical school in a single vulgar word."[20]

Monica's participation at Cassiciacum leads us to three conclusions. First, Augustine's intellectual world was open to his mother as he welcomed her to this community. The suggestion that this aspect of Augustine's life and faith was off-limits to his mother fails to take into consideration her presence at Cassiciacum.[21] Second, contrary to the conclusions of some scholars, Monica had the capacity to participate in philosophical discussions. Though she had not read Plato or Vergil, the fact that she could contribute to a conversation and even bring it to a grinding halt meant that she had the

---

[15] See O'Meara, *Young Augustine*, 18.

[16] *On Order*, 2.1.1.

[17] *Confessions*, 5.8.15.

[18] *On the Happy Life*, 1.6; 2.16; 3.17; 4.23; *Against the Skeptics*, 1.11.31; 2.5.13; 2.6.14; see Mandouze, *Prosopographie*, 761; and Angela Di Berardino, "Monnica," in *ATTA*, 570.

[19] *On Order*, 2.1.1; English translation from Di Berardino, "Monnica," *ATTA*, 570.

[20] *On the Happy Life*, 3.16.20; see Peter Brown, *Augustine of Hippo: a Biography*, rev. ed. (Berkeley: University of California Press, 2000), 111.

[21] O'Meara, *Young Augustine*, 16.

intellectual capacity to understand what was being said. Her lack of formal education did not keep her from being able to reason and articulate.[22] Third, her decision to contribute to the dialogues from a practical perspective of simple faith as opposed to adopting philosophical rhetoric showed that she placed greater value on the practical.[23] This value was most aptly communicated in her conclusion to the dialogue *On the Happy Life*: "Holy Trinity, hear our prayers. Here without a doubt is the happy life which is also a perfect life that includes a firm faith, a living hope and an ardent grace that guides our steps."[24]

Augustine's spiritual journey took him from the speculative to the practical. His pre-391 writings, written while at leisure in Cassiciacum or Tagaste, dealt largely with philosophical issues. Yet most of his books, letters, and sermons after his ordination in 391 were exegetical or pastoral, designed to serve the needs of the church, though he also wrote polemical works to refute the Manichees, Donatists, and Pelagians. As a presbyter and bishop, Augustine did not have the luxury of being a professional scholar, and many of his writings were composed at night after a day of dealing with the challenges of church work. His letter to a young philosopher in 410 illustrated rather bluntly his thoughts on philosophical speculation: "I wish I could snatch you away from your titillating disquisitions and ram you into the sort of cares I have to cope with."[25] As Augustine took on the cares of the ministry, his focus went from philosophical speculation to practical Christian living.

Perhaps we can also attribute to Monica Augustine's practice of communicating with less-educated audiences in a simple, understandable manner. Despite Frend's assertion that Augustine's ideas were too intellectual for rural Donatists, his famous *Psalm Against the Donatists* was a thorough apologetic in the form of a simple jingle.[26] Augustine filled his sermons with illustrations related to

---

[22] See Mandouze, *Prosopograhie*, 762; *On the Happy Life*, 2.10; *On Order*, 2.17.45.

[23] *On the Happy Life*, 2.8; 3.21; Mandouze, *Prosopograhie*, 761–62.

[24] *On the Happy Life*, 4.35; translation from Gustave Bardy, *Saint Augustin: L'homme et l'œuvre* (7ème éd., Paris: Bibliothèque Augustinienne, 1948), 117.

[25] *Letter* 118.1.1; English translation in Brown, *Augustine*, 297.

[26] The Donatists were a schismatic group that sought to establish their own church in Africa. See W. H. C. Frend, *The Donatist Church* (Oxford: Clarendon, 1952), 238; and

local life in Hippo.[27] According to van der Meer, "In the pulpit he never used language that was above his hearers' heads, but always chose his words in such a fashion that everyone would understand him."[28] Augustine's sermons addressed specific issues and sins his listeners were facing.[29]

Sound Teaching

A third way Monica mentored her son was through her commitment to sound teaching. Though simple and uneducated, her commitment to orthodoxy is recorded on at least three occasions in the *Confessions*. First, when she learned that Augustine had become a Manichean, she expelled him from her home.[30] Unwilling to tolerate heresy in her own son, only the consolation of a dream revealing that he would return to the true faith moved her to allow him back in the house again. Second, Monica's concern for sound teaching was clear in her willingness to part with the African custom of bringing offerings to the tombs of martyrs when she came to Milan. She was motivated to obey Ambrose, who had forbidden the practice, because she respected him as an "illustrious preacher and exemplar of piety," one who gave practical instruction from a sound interpretation of the Scriptures.[31] Third, Augustine noted the stand that Monica took together with Ambrose and the Milanese believers who filled the Portian Basilica in protest against the Emperor Valentian's widow Justina, who sought to give the church to the Arians.[32]

We have considered the value of sound teaching in preachers and exegetes like Paul, Cyprian, Basil, and Ambrose. In the case of Monica, we find someone who demonstrated a commitment to sound teaching not through exegesis but through practical application.

Frederick van der Meer, *Augustine the Bishop*, trans. B. Battershaw and G. R. Lamb (London: Sheed & Ward, 1961), 258.

[27] See Christine Mohrmann, "Saint Augustin Écrivain," *Recherches Augustiniennes* 1 (1958): 59–62.

[28] See Frederick van der Meer, *Augustine the Bishop*, 258.

[29] Lee Bacchi, *The Theology of the Ordained Ministry in the Letters of Augustine of Hippo* (San Francisco: International Scholars, 1998), 12–13.

[30] *Confessions*, 3.11.19.

[31] *Confessions*, 6.2.2.

[32] *Confessions*, 9.7.15; see Mandouze, *Prosopograhie*, 760.

As will be shown in the following chapters, Augustine was also committed to sound teaching based on correctly interpreted Scriptures. He wrote letters, sermons, and treatises fighting against the heresies of the Manichees, Donatists, Pelagians, and Arians while expending significant energy in church councils defending orthodoxy. Augustine was firm with heretics, but like his mother who allowed him back into the house following a dream, he also extended grace and kindness to his theological opponents.[33]

Christian Education

In the section of an article entitled "before his conversion," Madec argues that "Augustine was always a Christian."[34] If Augustine was always a Christian, then what did he become after his conversion? Augustine's own understanding was that he embraced Christian faith as an adult in a villa near Milan, that this was largely the faith his mother had taught and modeled for him for most of his life and that he had been successfully avoiding. Indeed, Monica had trained up her son in the way he should go, and he did not depart from it when he was old.[35]

Hence, a fourth way Monica mentored her son was by providing a Christian education at home.[36] Although Augustine was clear that Patricius did not oppose Monica's raising her son as a Christian, Patricius's contrary example did not seem to hinder Augustine's Christian education. Apart from registering him as a catechumen, Monica's program of education was informal.[37] As noted, she mentored her son through her example of virtue, prayer, and devotion to the church and also warned him about sin, particularly against

---

[33] See *Letter* 146 to Pelagius.

[34] Goulven Madec, "Christian Influences on Augustine," trans. Allen Fitzgerald, *ATTA*, 151.

[35] Prov 22:6.

[36] André Mandouze, *L'aventure de la Raison et la Grace* (Paris: Études Augustiniennes, 1968), 84–86.

[37] *Confessions*, 1.11.17; 3.4.8; 5.14.25; *Against the Skeptics*, 2.2.5; see Eugene Kevane, *Augustine the Educator* (Westminster, MD: Newman, 1964), 33; Harmless, *Augustine and the Catechumenate*, 80; and Mandouze, *Prosopograhie*, 759.

sexual immorality.[38] As Brown puts it, she was "the voice of God in his early life."[39]

Though he remained unconverted during his youth and early adulthood, Monica's mentoring did have an impact. Augustine rejected pagan philosophy because it lacked "the name of Christ . . . [that] my tender little heart had drunk in . . . with my mother's milk, and in my deepest heart I still held on to it."[40] Similarly, when Augustine became dissatisfied with being a Manichean and later a skeptic, he reverted to his Christian upbringing until he could find something more compelling. He wrote, "I resolved therefore to live as a catechumen in the catholic church, which was what my parents had wished for me, until some kind of certainty dawned by which I might direct my steps aright."[41] The impact of Monica's training was ultimately felt when Augustine stood before his mother in the villa near Milan converted to faith in Christ.[42]

Following Augustine's conversion, Monica continued in her role of mentor as she encouraged and affirmed him in his faith. During their time together at Ostia near Rome just before Monica's death, we witness not only a mother and a son talking about spiritual matters, but also two spiritual sojourners enjoying fellowship and offering mutual encouragement in the faith.[43]

Monica's training program was informal and largely accomplished through an example that Augustine could imitate. Yet it was obviously effective as Augustine embraced the faith of his mother and continued to live as a Christian for the rest of his life while serving the church.

Monica's legacy seems to have also impacted Augustine's philosophy of training new believers, particularly in his manual *On the Instruction of Beginners*. First, Augustine related to Deogratias, a

---

[38] *Confessions*, 2.7; 5.9.17; see Louis Bertrand, *Autour de Saint Augustin* (Paris: Fayard, 1921), 32–33; Trapé, *Saint Augustine*, 23–24; and O'Meara, *Young Augustine*, 32.

[39] See Brown, *Augustine*, 18.

[40] *Confessions*, 3.4.8; also Thomas O'Loughlin, "The *Libri Philosophorum* and Augustine's Conversions," in Thomas Finan and Vincent Twomey, eds., *The Relationship between Neoplatonism and Christianity* (Dublin: Four Courts, 1992), 119.

[41] *Confessions*, 5.14.25.

[42] Ibid., 8.12.30.

[43] Ibid., 8.12.30; 9.10.23.

deacon of Carthage, that the teacher must be experiencing the faith, hope, and love of Christ and that these qualities should be contagious to the student.[44] Augustine seemed less concerned with transferring religious propositions than with handing down a living faith as he had received from his mother. Second, Augustine believed that the teacher would be more motivated and effective if he loved the new believer as a brother, a father, or a mother.[45] Indeed, it was a mother's love that motivated Monica to train Augustine in the faith.

Friends

We have previously alluded to Augustine's natural disposition to friendship. During Augustine's youth, friends influenced him to steal pears from a tree.[46] Later he attempted to bring together a community pursuing the "happy life"—a group of friends with a common interest in philosophical pursuits.[47] After his conversion he gathered a diverse group of friends at Cassiciacum for a retreat focused on philosophical and spiritual understanding.[48] Hence for Augustine community and friendship became necessary elements for spiritual growth. Although friendship and community and their relationship to mentoring will be taken up in the coming chapters, we will consider here the mentoring impact of some of Augustine's friends leading up to his conversion and in the period immediately after.

Alypius

Alypius, the friend most often mentioned in the *Confessions*, was also a native of Tagaste who studied rhetoric under Augustine in Tagaste and Carthage and who later followed him into the Manichean sect.[49] After a period of working in Rome, Alypius joined Augustine in the villa near Milan where together they listened to Ponticianus

[44] *On the Instruction of Beginners*, 3.6.

[45] Ibid., 12.17; see George Howie, *Educational Theory and Practice in St. Augustine* (New York: Teachers College Press, 1969), 150.

[46] *Confessions*, 2.4.9.

[47] Ibid., 6.14.24; Brown, *Augustine*, 81; and Mandouze, *Prosopograhie*, 53.

[48] *Soliloquies*, 1.12.20; see Joseph Lienhard, "Friendship, Friends," *ATTA*, 372–73.

[49] *Confessions*, 6.7.11–12; see Mandouze, *Prosopograhie*, 53; and Mandouze, *L'aventure*, 188.

recount the life of Antony.[50] Augustine's famous conversion experience was paralleled by that of Alypius, who was also moved by a verse of Scripture and independently resolved in his heart to become a Christian. Alypius was also present for the retreat at Cassiciacum and was baptized alongside Augustine.[51]

How did Alypius have a mentoring impact on Augustine? Augustine referred to Alypius as "my heart's brother" (*fratrem cordis mei*); that is, he was Augustine's peer and confidant on the journey to faith.[52] While Augustine needed an intellectual sparring partner, he also needed someone for support and encouragement on this delicate and uncertain journey. The two continued as friends, providing mutual support after their conversions and were ordained to the ministry at roughly the same time. While Augustine will forever appear the genius and the strong one, he clearly needed Alypius.[53]

Nebridius

Nebridius was born in Carthage, where he made Augustine's acquaintance. Later he followed Augustine to Milan as a partner in search of the "happy life" where, along with Alypius, the three engaged in dialogue over philosophical and spiritual issues.[54] Augustine, reflecting on this time from a spiritual perspective, said that they were "looking to you [God] to give them their food in due time."[55] Though Nebridius was not present at Cassiciacum because he had returned to Carthage, he nevertheless exchanged letters with Augustine during this period in which the content resembled the discussions at Cassiciacum.[56] Augustine reported that Nebridius

---

[50] *Confessions*, 8.6.13–7.18; see Mandouze, *Prosopographie*, 53–54.

[51] *Confessions*, 8.12.30; *Against the Skeptics*; *On Order*; see Mandouze, *Prosopographie*, 54–55.

[52] *Confession*, 9.4.7; 6.7.11; also Kim Paffenroth, "Bad Habits and Bad Company: Education and Evil in the *Confessions*," in Kim Paffenroth and Kevin Hughes, *Augustine and Liberal Education* (Aldershot, UK: Ashgate, 2000), 9.

[53] Mandouze, *Prosopograhie*, 56.

[54] *Confessions*, 6.7.11; see Mandouze, *Prosopograhie*, 774.

[55] *Confessions*, 6.10.17.

[56] *Letters* 3–4; see Mandouze, *Prosopograhie*, 775.

was converted along with his family not long after his return to Africa and before his premature death around 391.[57]

How did Nebridius mentor Augustine? First, like Alypius, Nebridius was a peer and a sounding board in their quest for understanding. Second, and more significantly, Nebridius managed to play a large role in convincing Augustine to give up his involvement in the Manichean sect and his interest in astrology.[58] As a friend he exhorted Augustine to set aside frivolous thinking and ideologies, which helped to clear up Augustine's mind toward accepting Christianity. Third, once Augustine had settled back in Africa with his group of "servants of God" in Tagaste, Nebridius made a point to encourage him to take time to rest as the demands of his new life were leaving him tired.[59] Finally, it is worth mentioning that Nebridius was apparently the first recipient of any letter from Augustine—a form that Augustine would go on to employ greatly in his ministry of mentoring and encouraging spiritual leaders of his day.

Evodius

Though Evodius was also a native of Tagaste, he did not meet Augustine until 387 in Milan after Augustine's baptism and time at Cassiciacum. He was already a Christian when he met Augustine and ended up joining the group of "servants of God" who were en route to Tagaste.[60]

The main way Evodius influenced Augustine was through his participation in two dialogues with Augustine while the two were in Rome delayed for a year before their return to Africa.[61] In the first dialogue, *On the Greatness of the Soul* (c. 388), Augustine and Evodius wrestled

---

[57] *Confessions*, 9.3.6; also *Letter* 98; Brown, *Augustine*, 57; Allen Fitzgerald, "Nebridius," *ATTA*, 587–88; and Mandouze, *Prosopograhie*, 775.

[58] *Confessions*, 7.2.3; 7.6.8; 4.3.6; Mandouze, *Prosopograhie*, 774.

[59] *Letter* 5; also Roy W. Battenhouse, ed., *A Companion to the Study of St. Augustine* (New York: Oxford University Press, 1955), 57.

[60] Evodius would go on to be ordained bishop of Uzalis, a city near Carthage. See James J. O'Donnell, "Evodius of Uzalis," *ATTA*, 344; Mandouze, *Prosopograhie*, 367; and Brown, *Augustine*, 120.

[61] See Othmar Perler, *Les Voyages de Saint Augustin* (Paris: Etudes Augustiniennes, 1969), 146–47.

over issues related to the nature of the soul.[62] The second dialogue, *On Free Will* (c. 387–388), generally dealt with the tension between God's foreknowledge and human free will that became apparent as they discussed the origin of evil and the definition of sin.[63]

Evodius served as a peer mentor to Augustine through these dialogues as the two pursued truth together. Yet these works were later published, and Augustine alone is credited for the thought involved. The structure of *On Free Will* is such that it began in the form of dialogue between Augustine and Evodius before later becoming a complete discourse by Augustine.[64] Even if the work was largely the thought of Augustine, we must still recognize the presence of Evodius, whose questions and thoughts helped bring the best out of Augustine in articulating his early thought on the tension of divine foreknowledge and human freedom.

Ambrose

Not only did Ambrose mentor other leaders in the period prior to Augustine's ministry; he also had a personal impact on Augustine. In his *Confessions* Augustine introduced Ambrose as a mentor: "So I came to Milan and to Bishop Ambrose. . . . Unknowingly I was led by you to him, so that through him I might be led, knowingly, to you."[65] The main ways that Ambrose mentored Augustine were through his holy example, the primacy of properly interpreted Scriptures, the "language" of preaching, and preparing him for baptism.

Holy Example

Like Monica, it was Ambrose's holy life that profoundly touched Augustine. Augustine described him as "one of the best of men," "a devout worshipper of you [God]," and a "man of God."[66] Augustine added that Ambrose treated him like a son:

---

[62] Also *Letters* 158–64; 169; Roland Teske, *"Animae quantitate, De" ATTA*, 23; and Mandouze, *Prosopograhie*, 368.

[63] See *Letter* 162; and Teske, *"Libero arbitrio, De," ATTA*, 494.

[64] See Teske, *"Libero arbitrio, De," ATTA*, 494.

[65] *Confessions*, 5.13.23; see Mandouze, *L'aventure*, 108–9.

[66] *Confessions*, 5.13.23; also Michelle Pellegrino, *The True Priest: The Priesthood as Preached and Practiced by St. Augustine*, trans. Arthur Gibson (Langley, UK: St Paul,

> This man of God welcomed me with fatherly kindness
> and showed the charitable concern for my pilgrimage
> that befitted a bishop. I began to feel affection for
> him, not at first as a teacher of truth, for that I had
> given up hope of finding in your church, but simply
> as a man who was kind to me.[67]

Though Ambrose and Augustine are reputed for their exegesis
and thought, Augustine's heart was first touched by Ambrose before
his mind was challenged. Perhaps Ambrose was filling the void in
Augustine's life of a spiritual father figure, a role Patricius had
failed to play.

Ambrose's kindness to Monica seems to have also impacted
Augustine. Though Augustine had limited personal contact with
Ambrose, Monica apparently enjoyed more contact. Ambrose
praised the faith and example of Monica, and she was highly
impressed with her new bishop.[68] Hence, the pious examples of his
mother and Ambrose so influenced the searching Augustine that one
might speculate that the two were conspiring to bring the wayward
Augustine to faith.

Primacy of Scripture

Previously we have shown that Ambrose mentored spiritual leaders by his commitment to sound teaching based on properly interpreted Scriptures. Ambrose succeeded in opening the Scriptures for
Augustine, arousing in him a desire to discover them for himself.
Augustine wrote, "Another thing that brought me joy was that the
ancient writings of the law and the prophets were now being offered
to me under quite a different aspect from that under which they had
seemed to me absurd when I believed your holy people held such
crude opinions."[69] The "crude opinions" that led him to leave the

---

1968), 95.

[67] *Confessions*, 5.13.23.

[68] *On the Happy Life*, 1.4; *Confessions*, 6.2.2; 6.1.1; see Brown, *Augustine*, 119.

[69] *Confessions*, 6.4.6; also Maurice Jourjon, "Le Saint Évêque d'Hippone," in R. Fourrey,
ed., *La Tradition Sacerdotale* (Paris: Éditions Xavier Mappus, 1959), 133; and Brown,
Augustine, 77.

church as a young man and join the Manichean sect included the church's supposed teaching on the nature of God, the problem of evil, and the constitution of Christ.[70] Yet Ambrose, demonstrating a background in the liberal arts and Platonic thinking in particular, resolved these interpretative difficulties for Augustine by using an allegorical hermeneutic that featured Christ as the center of the Scriptures. Augustine added:

> I delighted to hear Ambrose often asserting in his sermons to the people, as a principle on which he must insist emphatically, the letter is death-dealing, but the spirit gives life. This he would tell as he drew aside the veil of mystery and opened to them the spiritual meaning of passages which, taken literally, would seem to mislead.[71]

Though Augustine would eventually develop different views on evil, the nature of Christ, and other questions, Ambrose convinced him of the divine authority of the Scriptures, which ultimately provided more satisfying answers than what the Manicheans had offered.[72]

Augustine went on to spend his career as a presbyter and bishop studying, expounding, and defending the Scriptures, never losing the conviction of their divine authority. Even toward the end of his life, as he taught younger men how to interpret the Scriptures, he held up Ambrose as one who understood the Scriptures and made them clear to others.[73]

The Language of Preaching

Augustine admitted that in his initial trips to hear Ambrose preach, he was not interested in "what Ambrose was saying, but interested

---

[70] J. Patout Burns, "Ambrose Preaching to Augustine: The Shaping of Faith," *Collectanea Augustiana*, J. C. Schnaubelt, F. Van Fleteren, eds. (New York: Peter Lang, 1990), 374.

[71] *Confessions*, 6.4.6; also Kevane, *Augustine the Educator*, 211; and Neil McLynn, "Ambrose," *ATTA*, 17.

[72] Burns, "Ambrose Preaching to Augustine," 374; and Kevane, *Augustine the Educator*, 210.

[73] *Teaching Christianity*, 4.46; 48; 50; also J. Loughlin, "St. Ambrose," *New Advent* www. newadvent.org/cathen/01383c.htm.

only in listening to how he said it."[74] At this time Augustine was earning his living teaching people how to speak eloquently, and he went to hear Ambrose to take notes from a gifted communicator. Despite his initial motives Augustine became attracted to this man who was not only kind but also demonstrated that it was possible for someone to be both an intellectual and a Christian.[75] As Ambrose's allegorical approach to the Scriptures proved to be appealing, Augustine began listening to his sermons for their content more than their eloquent packaging. As Possidius explained, "This preacher of God's word spoke very often in the church; Augustine was present in the congregation, listening with great interest and attention."[76]

As his hunger increased for the life that Ambrose described, Augustine desired to speak with him. Rousseau asserts that Augustine, following in the Egyptian monastic tradition of master-pupil dialogue, was coming to Ambrose to dialogue.[77] Yet, according to the *Confessions*, Augustine found it difficult to find a time when Ambrose was not occupied. Thus, the two ended up having very little personal contact, and when Augustine was converted he informed Ambrose of his decision by letter![78]

If Ambrose had such little personal contact with Augustine, can we really consider him Augustine's mentor? Our early Christian model of mentoring insists on the need for close, human interaction in the process of spiritual growth. Ambrose and Augustine seemed to enjoy a sense of intimacy at a distance through the form or "language" of preaching. Augustine was apparently uncomfortable speaking one-on-one with Ambrose. Yet, when Ambrose stood to preach the Scriptures, unveiling through skilled interpretation the inspiring content of their meaning in a form that was eloquent and even entertaining, this medium was a familiar "language" that Augustine the rhetor could connect with on a profound level.[79]

---

[74] *Confessions*, 5.14.24; also Mandouze, *L'aventure*, 109.

[75] See McLynn, "Ambrose of Milan," *ATTA*, 17; and O'Meara, *Young Augustine*, 111.

[76] Possidius, *Life of Augustine*, 1.3; *Confessions*, 6.3.4; also Burns, "Ambrose Preaching to Augustine," 373–74.

[77] See Phillip Rousseau, "Augustine and Ambrose: The Loyalty and Single-Mindedness of a Disciple," *Augustiniana* 27 (1977): 152.

[78] *Confessions*, 6.3.3; 4.4; 11.18; 9.5.13; see Trapé, *Saint Augustine*, 73.

[79] See Mandouze, *L'aventure*, 110–11.

Although Ambrose was the only one speaking, the sermon became a quasi-dialogue. As Augustine assimilated Ambrose's teaching, the sermon served as a catalyst for Augustine's ongoing commitment to seeking truth, a pursuit that often included dialogue with others.

Augustine the rhetor would go on to become Augustine the preacher who would deliver many more sermons than Ambrose as he greatly valued this form of teaching. Yet he would despise eloquent delivery at the expense of nourishing content in a sermon. Certainly Ambrose should be credited with helping Augustine go from a rhetor to a preacher.

Preparation for Baptism

After Augustine made his profession of faith, he wrote to Ambrose sharing the news of his conversion, submitted his name for baptism for the coming Easter, and requested advice on what he could read to grow in his new faith. Ambrose encouraged him to read Isaiah, but Augustine found it inaccessible and quickly put it aside.[80] Perhaps Ambrose overestimated the abilities of one trained in the liberal arts to understand Isaiah. Also, such advice revealed Ambrose's preference for teaching from the Hebrew Scriptures. Even so, Augustine began to prepare for baptism in the same way he had come to faith—in the company of close friends.

Besides assigning reading in Isaiah, how did Ambrose prepare Augustine for baptism? First, according to Paulinus, Ambrose was personally involved in initiating all catechumens. Though Ambrose and Augustine had little personal contact, they would have spent considerable time together during the period of Lent leading up to the Easter baptism.[81]

Second, in the context of a daily liturgical setting, Ambrose taught the catechumens a series of organized lessons.[82] The teaching consisted of a "moral education" based on principles of holy living prescribed in the Scriptures and demonstrated through the lives of

---

[80] *Confessions*, 9.5.13; 9.6.14; see Harmless, *Augustine and the Catechumenate*, 93.

[81] Paulinus, *Life of Ambrose*, 38; also Harmless, *Augustine and the Catechumenate*, 94.

[82] Harmless, *Augustine and the Catechumenate*, 100; also Edward Yarnold, *The Awe Inspiring Rites of Initiation: The Origins of the R.C.I.A.* (Edinburgh: T&T Clark, 1994), 98–149.

the saints of Scripture.[83] Ambrose's content also included a "hand-ing over" or a thorough line-by-line treatment of the Creed, which included teaching on the nature of the Trinity.[84] Finally, Ambrose's teaching also included an exhortation to take seriously the commit-ment to the Christian life.[85]

In addition to the content of Ambrose's prebaptismal teaching, it is important to note the forms in which he delivered it. Though the context was a small group of catechumens, Ambrose still communi-cated through his preferred method of the sermon, which, as we have shown, would also have been meaningful for Augustine.[86] When com-municating the creed, Ambrose employed a "chiastic rhyme scheme" that Harmless says "made his passage memorable—aptly framed to impress itself on the oral memory."[87] In a similar way, catechumens like Augustine were able to commit to memory the theological truths they were learning through hymns. Augustine wrote, "How copiously I wept at your hymns and canticles, how intensely was I moved by the lovely harmonies of your singing church! Those voices flooded my ears, and the truth was distilled into my heart until it overflowed in loving devotion."[88] Ambrose was innovative in introducing hymns into the Milan church, a controversial practice at the time.

Augustine, his friends, and fellow catechumens were baptized by Ambrose on Easter in 387. As was the custom in Milan, Ambrose, perhaps with the help of an exorcist, laid hands on each catechumen and invited them to renounce the works of Satan before baptizing them.[89]

---

[83] Ambrose, *On the Mysteries*, 1; also Harmless, *Augustine and the Catechumenate*, 94–95.

[84] While conforming in essence to the Nicene Creed, there were apparently some varia-tions in the wording of the Creed in Milan and in Augustine's later ministry. See *Ser-mons*, 212–15, and *On the Creed, to Catechumens*; and Joseph T. Lienhard, "Creed, Symbolum," *ATTA*, 254–55.

[85] *On Faith and Works*, 6.9; see Harmless, *Augustine and the Catechumenate*, 93, 96–98.

[86] *On the Mysteries*, 1; Harmless, *Augustine and the Catechumenate*, 94.

[87] Harmless, *Augustine and the Catechumenate*, 101; also Paul Achtemeier, "*Omne Verbum Sonat*: The New Testament and the Oral Environment of Late Western Antiquity," *JBL* 109 (1990): 7.

[88] *Confessions*, 9.6.14; 9.12.31; *Sermon Against Auxentius*, 34; also Harmless, *Augustine and the Catechumenate*, 99.

[89] *Confessions*, 9.6.14; *Letter* 147.52; also Yarnold, *Rites*, 102.

Ambrose had a lasting influence on Augustine. When Augustine became a presbyter in Hippo in 391, one of his first roles was preparing catechumens for baptism.[90] As bishop in 399, Augustine devoted *On the Instruction of Beginners* to training new believers for baptism. Like Ambrose, Augustine was passionate about articulating the Creed. His *On Faith and the Creed* was a commentary on the Creed that served as a revised version of the teaching he gave to the clergy at the council of Hippo in 393.[91] Toward the end of his life, Augustine authored yet another commentary *On the Creed, for Catechumens.*[92]

Simplicianus

Simplicianus was Ambrose's theological teacher and mentor and eventually succeeded Ambrose as the bishop of Milan. While Augustine was following Ambrose's sermons and going through an intense period of searching, he met Simplicianus, who was more available than Ambrose. Simplicianus mentored Augustine in three clear ways: as an intellectual resource, by emphasizing the authority of the church, and by modeling that the mentor is still a disciple.

Intellectual Resource

Simplicianus, like Ambrose, appealed to Augustine as a thinking Christian who was trained in the liberal arts and understood the philosophers.[93] Though Augustine looked to Simplicianus as an intellectual resource, he first made note of Simplicianus's pious character, as he had done with Ambrose:

> I regarded him as your good servant, a man from whom your grace radiated. Moreover I had heard how from his youth he had lived for you in complete dedication and since he was an old man by now I

---

[90] *Sermon*, 216.1–2; Harmless, *Augustine and the Catechumenate*, 105.

[91] See Finbarr Clancy, *"Fide et Symbolo, De,"* ATTA, 360–61.

[92] The creed was also the subject of *Sermons*, 212–15; also Allan Fitzgerald, *"Symbolo ad Catechumenos, De,"* ATTA, 820.

[93] *Confessions*, 8.1.1–2; see Madec, "Christian Influences on Augustine," ATTA, 151; and Brown, *Augustine*, 95, 97.

assumed that after following your way of life for long years and with such noble zeal he must be rich in experience and deeply learned.[94]

As Augustine's faith concerns at this point were intellectual, Simplicianus was qualified and available to dialogue with him over some of the key issues.[95] Burns understands that Simplicianus was especially helpful in explaining the "union of the divine and human in Christ."[96]

Simplicianus also encouraged Augustine by recounting the story of Marius Victorinus, a Platonist who had become a Christian in large part through dialogue with Simplicianus.[97] While Ponticianus's account of the holy man Antony had profoundly touched Augustine's heart on his journey to conversion, Simplicianus's account of a Platonist coming to Christ equally moved him to have the courage to confess Christ. Augustine recounted, "On hearing the story I was fired to imitate Victorinus; indeed it was to this end that your servant Simplicianus had related it."[98] If Ambrose, Simplicianus, and Marius Victorinus were educated and thinking Christians, then Augustine could also be a Christian.

Though Augustine's faith would become less speculative after his ordination as presbyter and bishop, the example of Simplicianus appeared later to impact the manner in which Augustine prepared for baptism those from an intellectual background. In *On the Instruction of Beginners*, Augustine instructed Deogratias to take into account the superior knowledge of the Scriptures that someone trained in the liberal arts would have compared to someone less educated and to orient the training program to the level of understanding of the educated catechumen.[99]

---

[94] *Confessions*, 8.1.1; also *Letter* 37.1.
[95] *Confessions*, 8.1.1; 2.3.
[96] See Burns, "Ambrose Preaching to Augustine," 377.
[97] *Confessions*, 8.2.4.
[98] Ibid., 8.5.10.
[99] *On the Instruction of Beginners*, 8.12.

Authority of the Church

Through his account of Marius Victorinus, Simplicianus also emphasized to Augustine the spiritual authority of the church. Although Victorinus initially did not see the relationship between the four walls of the church and his faith, he did not want to cause problems for himself socially and professionally. So Simplicianus insisted that he needed to experience salvation and declare his faith within the church.[100] This message was intended for Augustine, and he ultimately responded by being baptized in the church and remaining in it for the rest of his life. As Augustine's ecclesiology developed, Simplicianus's impact was surely felt, for Augustine would later affirm in his preaching and writing that salvation needed to be experienced within the spiritual authority of the church and that being a Christian required fellowship with other believers.[101]

Mentor as Disciple

Simplicianus demonstrated that a mentor should still be a learner by writing to Augustine, as well as Ambrose, posing theological questions.[102] The teacher was asking a former student for help! As we will see, Augustine also demonstrated the posture of a learner, progressing in his understanding and practice of the Christian life as he served as a bishop and mentor to spiritual leaders.

Valerius

Each of Augustine's mentors mentioned to this point were those who either influenced him prior to his conversion or in his first years as a Christian. Yet, when considering Augustine's preparation for pastoral ministry, the activity that filled most of his days for the final 40 years of his life, there is another mentor who is largely overlooked in the study of Augustine—his predecessor, bishop Valerius

---

[100] *Confession*, 5.8; 6.4; 8.2.4; Rousseau, "Augustine and Ambrose," 153.

[101] *Exposition on the Psalms*, 132.2; Possidius, *Life of Augustine*, 3; *On Baptism*, 3.13.18; 4.1.1; 4.2.2; also Jourjon, "Le Saint Évêque d'Hippone," 130.

[102] *Letter* 37.

of Hippo (d. 397).[103] In fact, in a perusal of key encyclopedias and dictionaries of early Christianity, one is hard pressed to find a single entry dedicated to Valerius.[104] Even the excellent volume *Augustine Through the Ages*, which hardly leaves a stone unturned regarding Augustine's life and work, contains no article on Valerius. Although what is known about Augustine's predecessor is scant, being limited to a few letters and sermons of Augustine and to Possidius's biography, this evidence is sufficient for a profitable study.[105]

The greater issue is whether Valerius is important to the study of Augustine. My argument is that upon Augustine's ordination and preparation for a lifetime of pastoral ministry, Valerius was his most significant mentor—particularly from Augustine's ordination as presbyter in 391 until Valerius's death in 396 or 397. Valerius mentored Augustine in four distinct ways: by selecting him for ministry, by maintaining a personal mentor-disciple relationship, by involving him increasingly in ministry, and by releasing him to ministry.

Selection

Possidius wrote that, for some time before Augustine's visit to Hippo in 391, the aging, native-Greek-speaking bishop had been in search of a presbyter: one "capable of building the Lord's church by preaching the word of God and salutary doctrine."[106] While Valerius was concerned about the future leadership for the church of Hippo,

---

[103] A form of this section first appeared in my article "An Unrecognized and Unlikely Influence? The Impact of Valerius of Hippo on Augustine," *Irish Theological Quarterly* 72:3 (2007): 251–64. I am especially thankful to Thomas O'Loughlin, Alan Fitzgerald, and Michael Conway for their feedback on the article and this section.

[104] See *The Catholic Encyclopedia*, Charles G. Herberman, ed. (New York: Appleton, 1912). *Enciclopedia Cattolica* (Roma: Città del Vaticano, 1953); *The Harper Collins Encyclopedia of Catholicism*, Richard McBrien, ed. (San Francisco: Harper Collins, 1995); *The Oxford Dictionary of the Christian Church*, F. L. Cross, ed. (Oxford: Oxford University Press, 1997); *Encyclopedia of Early Christianity*, 2nd ed., Everett Ferguson, ed. (New York; London: Garland, 1997); *Encyclopedia of the Early Church*, Angelo DiBerardino, ed. (Cambridge: James Clarke & Co., 1992); and *ATTA*.

[105] See Mandouze, *Prosopograhie*, 1139–41. Valerius had also been treated in Brown, *Augustine*; Bardy, *Saint Augustin*; van der Meer, *Augustine the Bishop*; Michelle Pellegrino, *True Priest*; Bacchi, *Ordained Ministry*; and Gerald Bonner, *St. Augustine: His Life and Controversies* (Norwich: Canterbury, 1986).

[106] Possidius, *Life of Augustine*, 5.2.

it seems that he was also looking for someone to serve in areas where he was weak. Though some have suggested that Valerius was not a strong theologian or that he was incapable of mounting an effective apologetic against the growing Donatist movement in Hippo, it is safest to conclude that Valerius's main weakness was language. Having immigrated or perhaps come as a missionary to Africa, he was searching for someone who could effectively communicate and preach in Latin.[107]

Valerius began to pray and let the need be known for a qualified presbyter in Hippo. Then, with Augustine present in the church assembly on that momentous Sunday in 391, Valerius repeated to the congregation their great need for another minister, which forced something of a selection by stealth.[108] Though Augustine was clearly not comfortable with the events, this manner of setting apart leaders was nevertheless common in his day and served as Valerius's official means of selecting Augustine to an office of spiritual leadership.[109]

Though Valerius had orchestrated the ordination by force because of the great needs of the Hippo church, his decision was still risky. Would he let a former Manichean serve and teach in the church? It was precisely for this reason that Megalius of Calama, the senior ranking bishop in Numidia, initially opposed Augustine's ordination. Yet Valerius stood firm and succeeded in having Augustine ordained as presbyter for the church of Hippo.[110]

How could Valerius take such a chance on Augustine and not give in to the pressure of those who opposed his choice of presbyter? It seems that Valerius knew something of Augustine's reputation as a "servant of God" in Tagaste. Augustine admitted in a sermon many years later that at the time of his ordination he had "already

---

[107] See Andre Hamman, *Etudes Pabristiques: Methodogie, Liturgie, Histoire* (Paris: Beachesne), 273; Brown, *Augustine*, 132; and Mandouze, *Prosopographie*, 1139.

[108] Possidius, *Life of Augustine*, 4.1; Bardy, *Saint Augustin*, 157; and van der Meer, *Augustine the Bishop*, 4.

[109] *On Adulterous Marriages*, 2.20.22; also Pellegrino, *True Priest*, 18; and Possidius, *Life of Augustine*, 4.2. This manner of ordination had also been the experience of Ambrose, Gregory of Nyssa, and Gregory of Nazianzus.

[110] *Against Two Letters of the Pelagians*, 3.16.19; also Brown, *Augustine*, 198; Bonner, *St. Augustine*, 120; and Possidius, *Life of Augustine*, 5.4.

begun to acquire a reputation of some weight among the servants of God."[111] Similarly, Possidius affirmed, "The catholics already knew of Augustine's way of life and teaching."[112] Despite Augustine's Manichean background, Valerius was able to mitigate the risk in his selection because Augustine had spent the previous three years in Tagaste living according to the moral principles taught in the Scriptures, teaching sound doctrine, and exercising spiritual gifts and natural talents that could help the church.

Second, Valerius was willing to take a risk with Augustine because he recognized his potential for church ministry. Pellegrino explains, "Valerius judged the new priest to be fully fit for the exercise of the priestly ministry, whereas Augustine himself, with his better and deeper knowledge of himself, was convinced he could not face it without a more searching preparation."[113] Pellegrino is referring to Augustine's request of Valerius to take a period of concentrated study in the Scriptures before assuming his duties as presbyter.[114] While Augustine was aware of his own shortcomings, there is no indication that Valerius ever wavered on his choice of Augustine.

Valerius's selection of Augustine in 391 charted a new and perhaps unforeseen life direction for Augustine. While one cannot pretend to know what Augustine was thinking about a future in ministry in late 390, he was nevertheless not on any observable course for the ministry. Rather, since his conversion four years earlier and following his contact with monasteries in Milan and Rome, he had returned to Africa and fulfilled his plan of establishing a community of "servants of God" in Tagaste.[115] His experience there was something of a "holy leisure" (*otium sanctum*) characterized by prayer, reading, dialogue, and writing—a world away from the burden (*sarcina*) of the ministry in Hippo.[116] So when Valerius ordained Augustine in

---

[111] *Sermon*, 355.2; also Bardy, *Saint Augustin*, 158.

[112] Possidius, *Life of Augustine*, 4.1.

[113] Pellegrino, *True Priest*, 33.

[114] *Letter* 21.

[115] *Confessions*, 8.6.15; *On the Catholic and Manichean Ways of Life*, 1.33.70; and *Sermon*, 355.2.

[116] "Burden" (*sarcina*) was Augustine's preferred term to describe the ministry. See *Letters* 31.4; 69.1; 71.2; 85.2; 86; 101.3; 149.34; 242.1; 20*.4; Maurice Jourjon, "L'évêque et le People de Dieu Selon Saint Augustin," Maurice Jourjon et al, eds., *Saint Augustin Parmi*

The baptistry attached to the basilica of peace in Hippo.

391, he had a vision for Augustine's potential that Augustine did not seem to have for himself. Yet Augustine did not reject this vision, nor did he depart from it in the next five years with Valerius, or in the nearly 40 years that he spent in church ministry in Hippo.[117] Augustine needed a catalyst like Valerius in his life, not only to see his potential but also to "push him in the water" by actively calling him to the ministry.

During his 34 years as bishop of Hippo, Augustine also valued the recruitment of qualified men for the needs of the ministry, and he saw a steady flow of men join him in the monastery in Hippo and serve the church of that city.[118] While Augustine would ordain

---

Nous (Paris: Éditions Xavier Mappus, 1954), 155–57; George Lawless, "Augustine's Burden of Ministry," *Angelicum* 61 (1984): 295–315; Thomas F. Martin, "*Clericatus Sarcina (ep. 126.3)*: Augustine and the Care of the Clergy," *The Practice of Christianity in Roman Africa*, http://ccat.sas.upenn.edu/jod/augustine.html, accessed May 28, 2004; Lienhard, "Ministry," *ATTA*, 568; and Bacchi, *Ordained Ministry*, 79.

[117] See Mandouze, *L'aventure*, 218.
[118] Possidius, *Life of Augustine*, 5.1; *Sermons*, 355–56.

many men in Hippo and elsewhere, he broke with Valerius on the practice of ordination by force. This is most evident in his refusal to allow Pinian to be ordained by force in Hippo in 411.[119]

Mentor-Disciple Relationship

In his only letter to Valerius, Augustine addressed him as "sincerely beloved father" and "father."[120] In letters to others, Augustine referred to him as "most blessed and venerable father" or "most blessed father."[121] Augustine's esteem for Valerius seemed to be strengthened by the aging bishop's holy character. In a letter to the Donatist bishop of Hippo, Augustine described Valerius as a man who "desires peace, . . . not tossed about by the inanity of vain pride."[122] In a letter to Aurelius of Carthage, Augustine called Valerius "a man of such modesty and gentleness and also of such prudence and solicitude in the Lord."[123] Possidius joined in the chorus by calling him "a devout and God-fearing man."[124]

Augustine also respected Valerius's authority as the bishop of Hippo. Again, in *Letter* 21, Augustine addressed him as "most blessed and venerable lord" and "your holiness" and repeatedly referred to him as old (*senex*).[125] This last title, though perhaps strange or even disrespectful to the modern reader, was Augustine's sign of respect for his bishop. Augustine's respect for the authority of his bishop seems significant in that just a few years prior he had been critical of clergy in general.[126]

Though Valerius was in a position of authority over Augustine, the old bishop regarded his young presbyter with respect. As noted,

---

[119] *Letter* 126.

[120] *Letters* 21.1; 21.3; unless otherwise noted, English translations of *Letters* 1–149 are from WSA pt. 2, vol. 3, ed. John E. Rotelle (Hyde Park, NY: New City Press, 2001); *Letters* 150–269 are from http://www.newadvent.org/fathers/1102.htm; *Letters* 1*–29* are from *Saint Augustine: Letters Vol. VI (1*29*)*, trans. Robert B. Eno, in FC vol. 81, ed. Thomas P. Halton et al. (Washington, D.C.: Catholic University of America Press, 1989)

[121] *Letters* 33.4; 31.4.

[122] *Letter* 31.4.

[123] *Letter* 22.4.

[124] Possidius, *Life of Augustine*, 5.2.

[125] *Letters* 21.1; 21.4; 21.5, 6; 29.7, 11; Possidius, *Life of Augustine*, 8.1.

[126] Possidius, *Life of Augustine*, 4.3.

Augustine petitioned Valerius for a period of study before reporting to Hippo, to which Valerius apparently consented.[127] While Hamman suggests that Augustine was granted one year for study, in which he succeeded in memorizing the Scriptures, neither assertion can be supported from Augustine's writings.[128] Nevertheless, Valerius's agreement to a preassignment study sabbatical, a rarity in most any profession, revealed respect for the new presbyter; Valerius was allowing Augustine to have a say in what he needed to be successful in the ministry.

Yet Valerius did not restrict Augustine from continuing in the monastic lifestyle that had been his practice in Tagaste. Rather, Valerius gave him the freedom to pursue his convictions and desires and effectively become his own kind of presbyter. Valerius went a step further and gave him some land on which to build a house in the garden by the Hippo church, where he could establish a community of clergy and "servants of God."[129] Thus, instead of imposing controls on his new presbyter, Valerius empowered and resourced Augustine to live out his own vision of the ministry.

While Valerius demonstrated respect for his young and talented presbyter, it is also apparent that he was not threatened by Augustine.[130] We recall that Valerius had deliberately recruited someone better than himself for preaching. How many bishops in Valerius's day, or at any point in the history of the church, would have demonstrated such humility? When Augustine's reputation as a teacher and apologist increased, Valerius did not try to suppress his presbyter; rather, he sought to create even more opportunities for him to shine. Paulinus of Nola appropriately referred to Valerius as "that blessed old man, whose most pure mind has never been touched by any stain of jealous envy."[131] Clearly, Valerius was thinking more about the present and future needs of the Hippo church

---

[127] *Letter* 21; *Sermon*, 355.2.

[128] In *Letter* 21.4, Augustine asked for "a short time for myself, say, up to Easter." See Hamman, *Etudes*, 273–74.

[129] *Sermon*, 355.2; see Bacchi, *Ordained Ministry*, 4; Bardy, *Saint Augustin*, 160; and Brown, *Augustine*, 133.

[130] Bonner, *St. Augustine*, 114.

[131] *Letter* 32.2.

than his own career ambitions, modeling what Augustine would later articulate as the "burden" of the ministry.

While loving Augustine as a son and giving him the freedom to become his own type of minister, Valerius was also courageous to give his protégé significant tasks for which Augustine did not feel prepared—beginning with his ordination. Valerius asked him to preach on the morning of the feast of St. Leontius to give what would surely be an unpopular message against the drunken excesses that typically accompanied the festival. Augustine later confessed that Valerius "did not hesitate to lay upon my shoulders the very dangerous burden of commenting on the words of the truth on their account."[132] After getting through that challenging message, Valerius made Augustine preach yet a second time to those who came to the church in the afternoon. Augustine added, "Though I was reluctant, since I now wanted so perilous a day to be over with, old Valerius forced me under an order to say something to them."[133] This account shows that Valerius did not mind forcing Augustine into some awkward and uncomfortable situations because he believed in his presbyter and continued to see his potential even when Augustine did not. Though Augustine would have much rather been somewhere else on that day, the experience would prepare him for many other confrontational sermons that he would give in his career.

During Augustine's time as bishop, his relationship with his clergy was also characterized by a clear sense of authority. By his nature he had been the driving force and natural leader of the pre-monastery in Tagaste as well as the monastery in Hippo before his consecration as bishop.[134] Yet the authority (*auctoritas*) he possessed as bishop of the church in Hippo also extended to its clergy and at times was expressed in disciplining wayward clergy.[135] Augustine's belief in the authority of a spiritual mentor can be further traced

---

[132] *Letter* 29.7.

[133] *Letter* 29.11.

[134] Possidius, *Life of Augustine*, 5.1.

[135] *Letters* 65.2; 78; 82; 85; 96; 186; 209; 219; *City of God*, 20.9.2; *Sermons*, 46–47; 355–56; *Expositions in Psalms*, 126; 132; *On the Sack of the City of Rome*, 15; see Jan M. Joncas, "Clergy, North African," *ATTA*, 215; and Bardy, *Saint Augustin*, 163.

through the authority that was assigned to the monastic superior in his *Rule*.[136]

Though Augustine had authority through his spiritual stature and his position as bishop, the clergy in the monastery seemed more motivated to follow him because of his holy life.[137] Possidius wrote, "I believe, however, that they profited even more who were able to hear him speaking in church and see him there present, especially if they were familiar with his manner of life among his fellow human beings."[138] The clergy in the Hippo monastery were the ones most intimately aware of who he really was. Possidius's intended response was to "emulate and imitate him in the present world."[139] Hence, it seems that Augustine also experienced an intimate mentoring relationship with his fellow clergy in the monastery at Hippo—which was by nature a community of friends.

Finally, in the same way that Valerius allowed Augustine the freedom for some initial time of study and to start a monastery in Hippo, Augustine demonstrated to his clergy a level of respect in developing their own convictions about ministry. Possidius recorded that though Augustine did not allow property willed to the church to be held in a trust, he let other clergy make this decision for themselves. Although he was not interested in building buildings, he did not forbid other clergy from doing so given that they were reasonably modest.[140]

Involving in Ministry

Valerius was looking for a man superior to himself in communication, and he found that man in Augustine. Early in Augustine's ministry as presbyter, Valerius began to give the former teacher of rhetoric teaching assignments of increasing responsibility. As Cyprian had done with his presbyters and probably deacons as well, Valerius entrusted Augustine with teaching catechumens as they

---

[136] *Rule*, 6.3; 7.1.
[137] Luc Verheijen, "Saint Augustin: Un Moine Devenu Prêtre et Evêque," *Estudios Agostinos* 12 (1977): 315; *Confessions*, 10.36.58–59; *Letter* 22.9.31; *Expositions in Psalms*, 116.3.
[138] Possidius, *Life of Augustine*, 31.9.
[139] Ibid., 31.11.
[140] Ibid., 24.9, 11.

prepared for baptism.[141] In this role Augustine had the opportunity to "hand over" the Creed that he had received from Ambrose and Simplicianus just a few years before.

Valerius probably invited opposition from the North African bishops by setting Augustine apart to preach in the Hippo church while he was still a presbyter.[142] Having come from the Eastern church, where this was not an uncommon practice, Valerius apparently did not mind going against the tradition of the North African churches because Augustine's teaching ability, which was superior to his own, was benefiting the church.[143] According to Pellegrino, the North African bishops were justified in their concern about allowing a presbyter to preach because of the legacy of the presbyter Arius, who had spread his heresy from the pulpit in Alexandria.[144] In light of the bishops' concern, Valerius's resolve to have Augustine preach was significant.

Before Valerius is unduly cast as a rebel or someone starstruck by newfound talent, involving Augustine in preaching seems consistent with Valerius's overall mentoring program. Possidius sheds some light: "[Valerius] gave his priest permission to preach the gospel in church even when he himself was present."[145] Hence, instead of merely setting Augustine free to preach where and when he liked, Valerius supervised Augustine in this greater task.

Possidius also recorded that, in addition to having him preach in the church, Valerius encouraged Augustine to use his gifts by "holding frequent public discussions."[146] This was surely a reference to Augustine's debate in Hippo with Fortunatus the Manichean as well as Augustine's teaching of an apologetic nature "against all the African heretics, especially the Donatists, the Manicheans, and the pagans."[147]

---

[141] *Sermons*, 214–216; also Brown, *Augustine*, 134.

[142] Possidius, *Life of Augustine*, 5.3; also Bacchi, *Ordained Ministry*, 4; Bardy, *Saint Augustin*, 164; and Brown, *Augustine*, 133.

[143] Ibid., 5.4.

[144] See Pellegrino's commentary on Possidius, 5.3, in John E. Rotelle, ed., *Life of Saint Augustine* (Villanova: Augustinian Press, 1988), 48.

[145] Possidius, *Life of Augustine*, 5.3.

[146] Ibid.

[147] Ibid., 6; 7.1.

If Augustine's preaching in Hippo had not already raised concerns among the North African bishops, there was probably some resistance to the presbyter of only two years and a former Manichee addressing the council of bishops in Hippo in 393. According to Bonner, Augustine's purpose for speaking was to resource the large number of uneducated bishops with teaching on the Creed.[148] While it cannot be proven that Valerius orchestrated Augustine's prominent role in this council, he must have at least allowed Augustine this influential opportunity through his authority as Augustine's bishop.[149] Hence, by not standing in his way, Valerius seems to allow Augustine another ministry opportunity of increasing responsibility.

As Valerius involved his presbyter in ministry, Valerius gave him assignments in ministries that corresponded with Augustine's strengths and talents. Augustine was a gifted communicator, teacher, writer, and orator in debate. Valerius put him to work where those skills were needed in the church and where Valerius himself was unable to meet the need. Though later as a bishop Augustine performed duties that he did not care for or that left him drained, Valerius's wisdom to involve Augustine in ministries that corresponded with his strengths seems to be an important quality of a mentor.[150]

While serving as bishop, Augustine also involved clergy in ministries where he was weak or limited and where they were gifted. For example, in the final years of his ministry, he set apart Eraclius, his eventual successor, to relieve him of the load of rendering civil judgments as well as administering church property so that he could concentrate on studying and writing.[151] Augustine was also happy to entrust to Alypius and Evodius the task of traveling to Italy on church-related business; Augustine despised travel, and Alypius's background in law made him more qualified to appeal to the secular authorities about issues facing the church.[152] Finally, though his appointment of Antoninus as bishop of Fussala was a colossal fail-

---

[148] Bonner, *St. Augustine,* 115.

[149] It seems evident that Bishop Aurelius of Carthage used his influence to put Augustine's gifts to use at the African church councils from 393 to 427.

[150] This principle can also be found in Ambrose, *On the Duties of Ministers,* 1.215.

[151] *Letter* 213.5; also Bacchi, *Ordained Ministry,* 32, 39.

[152] *Confessions,* 6.9.15; *Letters* 44; 10*; 15*; 16*; 22*; 23A*; also Bacchi, *Ordained Ministry,* 28; Brown, *Augustine,* 156; O'Donnell, "Evodius of Uzalis," *ATTA,* 344.

ure, Augustine did at least one thing right: he attempted to ordain a Punic-speaking bishop.[153] As Fussala was located some 40 miles from Hippo, Augustine or one of his presbyters could have made the journey at least on occasion to preach and minister there except for the fact that they could not speak Punic. Like Valerius years before, Augustine was humbly seeking to recruit a man who could most effectively communicate the Scriptures in the language of the people.[154]

With regard to his decision to have Augustine preach while still a presbyter, Valerius seems to have brought some innovation to the North African church in this area. In *Sermon* 20, Augustine also encouraged the practice of presbyters preaching and modeled this by having his own presbyter Eraclius preach under his supervision.[155] Augustine's *Letter* 41 indicates that Aurelius had also adopted the practice with his Carthaginian presbyters.[156] Finally, Possidius recorded that presbyters throughout North Africa began to be involved in preaching, a development that certainly came through the influence of Aurelius and Augustine—both of whom were probably influenced by Valerius.[157]

Releasing to Ministry

In the initial four years of his ministry, through faithfulness and success in assignments of increasing levels of responsibility, Augustine was realizing the potential Valerius saw in him. According to Possidius, Valerius began to fear that Augustine would be "selected" for another place of ministry in much the same manner Valerius had conscripted him in 391. Thus, after consorting

---

[153] *Letters* 209; 20*; also Bacchi, *Ordained Ministry*, 19–22; and Brown, *Augustine*, 468. Though we do not know anything about Augustine's initial choice for bishop for Fussala, the fact that his second choice was a Punic speaker and that Fussala was a Punic-speaking area makes probable that his first choice would have been a Punic speaker as well.

[154] Similarly, in *Letter* 84 to bishop Novatus of Sitifis, Augustine requests the services of the deacon Lucillus for the ministry in the region of Hippo as Lucillus was a Punic speaker and able to minister to the needs of the non-Latin speakers in the diocese. Verheijen, *Saint Augustin*, 332–33.

[155] *Sermon*, 20.5; see Pellegrino in Rotelle, *Life of Saint Augustine*, 48; and van der Meer, *Augustine the Bishop*, 413.

[156] *Letter* 41; also Bardy, *Saint Augustin*, 165.

[157] Possidius, *Life of Augustine*, 5.5.

with the bishops of Carthage and Calama, as well as presenting the idea to the congregation at Hippo, Valerius made Augustine his cobishop in 395.[158] Despite Augustine's resistance to the idea and Valerius's apparent oversight of the canons of Nicea, which forbid two bishops serving in the same church, Valerius succeeded in having Augustine ordained bishop.[159]

Indeed, demonstrating his burden for the ministry, Valerius wanted to see the church of Hippo in the capable hands of Augustine for many years to come;[160] but Possidius added that what Valerius really wanted "was not so much a successor as a fellow bishop here and now."[161] Paulinus of Nola, in a letter to Augustine about Valerius's decision, wrote, "That blessed old man . . . now gathers from the Most High fruits worthy of the peace of his heart, for he has now merited to have as a colleague the man whom he simply desired to have as his successor in the priestly office."[162] At this stage of the ministry, Valerius was recruiting Augustine to be his equal, which testifies once again to Valerius's humility and to the fact that he was not threatened by Augustine. Rather, for the sake of the church, he was happy to share the work of ministry and to release a young leader to service and responsibility.

Augustine was well aware of his strengths and weaknesses in his ministry as bishop.[163] He humbly entrusted tasks of administration, civil judgments, lobbying, traveling, and preaching in another language to those who were better qualified than he. He released men with the authority and responsibility to minister. Possidius recorded that the Hippo monastery became an important training center for

---

[158] Ibid., 8.1–3.

[159] *Letter* 213.4. Pellegrino cites canon 8 of the council of Nicea in his commentary of Possidius, 8.5 in Rotelle, *Life of Saint Augustine*, 54. Although we cannot know for sure whether Valerius, along with Aurelius and Megalius, was ignorant of the canons of Nicea or simply ignoring them to help his cause in getting Augustine ordained bishop, we must note that he would not be the first spiritual leader to ignore church canons when setting apart a key leader. This was also the case of Basil's ordination of Poemenius of Satala. Basil, *Letters* 102–103; also Andrea Sterk, *Renouncing the World yet Leading the Church* (Cambridge, MA: Harvard University Press, 2004), 87.

[160] *Letter* 31.4; also Mandouze, *L'aventure*, 141, 143.

[161] Possidius, *Life of Augustine*, 8.2.

[162] *Letter* 32.2.

[163] Possidius, *Life of Augustine*, 19.6.

church leaders and that at least 10 North African bishops were sent out from there.[164]

Yet unlike Valerius Augustine did not attempt in any observable way to hold back a minister from another church that was in need. Instead, Possidius indicated that Augustine freely "gave [clergy] upon request to the various churches."[165] Valerius had a vision for resourcing the local church at Hippo, but Augustine was committed to resourcing the universal church in North Africa. In addition, having clearly apprehended the canons of Nicea, which forbade ordaining two bishops in the same church, Augustine (unlike Valerius) was careful to honor this church legislation; and, as a result, Eraclius was not consecrated as bishop of Hippo until Augustine's death.

Summary

When we look more closely at Augustine's mosaic, especially those who shaped him into what he would become, the influences were diverse. A simple and uneducated mother modeled prayer and piety, emphasized practical faith, remained sound in doctrine, and raised him as a Christian. Friends were simply there with him on the delicate journey to faith; one rebuked him for strange ideas while another brought out his greatness in dialogue. A distinguished and eloquent bishop showed him the kindness of a father, opened the Scriptures to him for the first time, communicated in a medium he understood, and probably personally oversaw his initiation into the church. Another educated man, available to him for intellectual dialogue, impressed upon Augustine the necessity of the church while demonstrating the posture of a lifelong disciple. Finally, a humble, fatherly figure with an accent ordained him to the ministry, gave him the freedom to become his own type of minister, involved him increasingly in the work of ministry, and then released him to his own work. With this mosaic in mind, we may now begin to consider how Augustine served to shape and color the mosaics of the spiritual leaders of his day.

---

[164] Ibid., 11.1–3.
[165] Ibid., 11.3.

Chapter Four

AUGUSTINE'S APPROACH TO MENTORING

rom the time of his ordination as presbyter in 391 until his death in 430, Augustine had relationships with hundreds of clergy in Hippo, in the provinces of North Africa, and beyond. This chapter will treat in detail the most significant, repeated approaches to mentoring observed in Augustine's relationship to the clergy.

Augustine and the Offices of Spiritual Leadership

During Augustine's tenure as bishop, the number of clergy in North Africa was large, and the clerical offices were well developed.[1] At the council of Carthage in 411, catholic bishops alone numbered 268. Most towns had their own bishop, and some, like Hippo, even had presbyters and deacons serving in the church. According to Victor de Vita, Carthage had around 500 clergy at the time of the Vandal conquest in 439.[2]

---

[1] *Letter* 43, written to some Donatist leaders, gives us some indication of the structure of the bishop and clerical offices going back to the time of the schism's beginning; see Daniel E. Doyle, *The Bishop as Disciplinarian in the Letters of St. Augustine* (New York: P. Lang, 2002), 178.

[2] See Joncas, "Clergy, North African," *ATTA*, 216.

Though many in Augustine's day aspired to the office of bishop for honor or even wealth, Augustine's ordinations as presbyter in 391 and cobishop to Valerius in 395 were preceded by great reluctance on his part. Mandouze correctly refers to Augustine as a "bishop despite himself."[3] As shown, his intention since the time of his conversion was to begin a community of "servants of God" (*serui Dei*) pursuing a monastic lifestyle in a type of "holy leisure" (*otium sanctum*).[4] He was often critical of the clergy and purposefully avoided churches for fear of being ordained by force—the very thing that happened to him. Thus, Augustine arrived at his ordination not by ambitious motives but more out of surrender to what he believed was a divine call, one that he would not abandon in nearly 40 years of ministry.[5]

As mentioned in the previous chapter, Augustine most often referred to ministry, particularly his work as a bishop, as a "burden" (*sarcina*), which Bacchi defines as "responsibility for the spiritual health and well-being of the flock."[6] Augustine most often used *sarcina* in his correspondence with other spiritual leaders to imply that he regarded himself as a servant of the church.[7] Though he would have preferred a quiet life of contemplation with like-minded friends, the needs of the church beckoned him from his leisure in Tagaste to use his gifts to serve the church.[8] Lienhard

---

[3] *Letters* 21.1; 125.2; Possidius, *Life of Augustine*, 4.1–2; 8.3; *Sermon*, 355.2; see Michelle Pellegrino, *The True Priest: The Priesthood as Preached and Practiced by Saint Augustine*, trans. Arthur Gibson (Langley, UK: St. Paul, 1998), 22; and Mandouze, "L'évêque et le Corps Presbytéral au Service du Peuple Fidèle Selon Saint Augustin," in H. Bouësse, ed., *L'évêque dans L'Eglise du Christ* (Paris: Desclée, 1963), 142.

[4] Possidius, *Life of Augustine*, 2.2; 3.1; also George Lawless, *Augustine of Hippo and His Monastic Rule* (Oxford: Clarendon, 1987), 41.

[5] Possidius, *Life of Augustine*, 4.1, 3; *Letter* 124.2; see Pellegrino, *True Priest*, 23–26; Bardy, *Saint Augustin: L'homme et l'oeuvre*, 7th ed. (Paris: Bibliothèque Augustenenne, 1948), 158–60; and van der Meer, *Augustine the Bishop*, 14–15.

[6] See Lee Bacchi, *The Theology of the Ordained Ministry in the Letters of Augustine of Hippo* (San Francisco: International Scholars, 1998),79.

[7] *Letters* 31.4; 69.1; 71.2; 85.2; 86; 101.3; 149.34; 242.1; 20*.4; also Bacchi, *Ordained Ministry*, 75–80.

[8] In this sense his ordination to ministry is comparable to that of Basil of Caesarea and Gregory of Nazianzus, who left their own ascetic retreat in Pontus to join the battle against unsound doctrine. Their "retreat" (*aprogmon* in Greek) is rendered *otium* in Latin; see Gregory of Nazianzus, *Orations*, 43.30–31; Basil, *Letter* 8; also Phillip Rousseau, *Pachomius: The Making of a Community in Fourth-Century Egypt* (Berkley: University of California Press, 1985), 88.

writes that the word *ministerium*, which could refer to many contexts of service, meant "church ministry" for Augustine.[9] He adds that ministers are "defined by the one whom they serve," meaning that they are "ministers of God," "ministers of Christ," and "ministers of the church."[10] He expressed this conviction of service over personal rights in a letter to the presbyter Eudoxius and his monks at Capraria, a group resisting ordination: "Do not prefer your leisure to the needs of the church. If no good men were willing to minister to her as she brings to birth new children, you would not have found a way to be born in Christ."[11] Hence, the ordained ministry was a calling to service that required great sacrifice because of the needs of the church.

Finally, Augustine valued carrying the burden of the ministry in humility. Bacchi asserts that Augustine's letters presented "the ordained ministry as one characterized by and exercised in humility," and Pellegrino suggests that Augustine considered humility "the virtue he considers to be the foundation of the Christian life."[12] Having been mentored by humble men like Ambrose, Simplicianus, and Valerius, Augustine's greatest statement of humility for a spiritual leader was his *Confessions*—a work penned from 397 to 401 while he was preaching from the *cathedra* in Hippo and influencing important church councils.

Augustine as Bishop

Augustine shared some details of his daily routine in a sermon preached on the anniversary of his ordination. He asked his people not only to obey him but also to pray for him as he confronted his daily challenges:

[9] See Joseph T. Lienhard, "Ministry," *ATTA*, 568; also *Expositions in Psalms*, 118.32.8; *Tractates on the Gospel of John*, 34.1; *Letter* 34.1.

[10] See Lienhard, "Ministry," *ATTA*, 568; Pellegrino, *True Priest*, 24–25; 59–88; and *Expositions in Psalms*, 102.13; *Tractates on the Gospel of John*, 51.12; *Letters* 134.14; 228.10,12; *Sermon*, 46.2; 340.1; *On the Work of Monks*, 29.37.

[11] *Letter* 48.2. Unless otherwise noted, English translations of *Letters* 1–149 are from WSA; also *City of God*, 19.19; *Expositions in Psalms*, 103.9; *Sermon*, 355.2; *Letters* 101.3; 128; *Tractates on the Gospel of John*, 57.4.

[12] See Bacchi, *Ordained Ministry*, xiii; and Pellegrino, *True Priest*, 156.

The turbulent have to be corrected, the faint-hearted cheered up, the weary supported; the gospel's opponents need to be refuted, its insidious enemies guarded against; the unlearned need to be taught, the indolent stirred up, the argumentative checked; the proud must be put in their place, the desperate set on their feet, those engaged in quarrels reconciled; the needy have to be helped, the oppressed to be liberated, the good to be given your backing, the bad to be tolerated; all must be loved.[13]

On another occasion he added that his duties required him "to preach, to refute, to rebuke, to build up, to manage for everybody."[14] From these general descriptions, let us summarize his main roles as the bishop of Hippo.

Preaching. Like Ambrose, Augustine regarded his primary responsibility to be preaching and expositing the Scriptures.[15] He wrote in *Confessions*, "My pen serves me as a tongue, but when will it find eloquence enough to recount all those exhortations and threats, all that encouragement and guidance, by which you led me to this position where I must preach the word and administer the sacrament to your people?"[16] Augustine often described this responsibility to preach through various word pictures. In *Sermon* 95, he described the task of interpreting the Scriptures as breaking bread for the church while in *On Teaching Christianity* he likened it to Jesus taking the fish and loaves of bread and distributing them to the crowds.[17] He believed that as soon as he learned something in the Scriptures, he should quickly pass it on for the edification of the church. He confessed, "I feed you on what I am fed on myself. . . . I set food before you from the pantry which I too live on."[18] He wrote to Jerome, "If I have some ability in this area, I use it completely

---

[13] *Sermon*, 340.1.

[14] *Sermon*, 339.4.

[15] See Mandouze, *L'aventure*, 145.

[16] *Confessions*, 11.2.2; also *Letters* 21.3; 261.

[17] For a thorough survey, see George Lawless, "Preaching," *ATTA*, 675–77; and Pellegrino, *True Priest*, 90–104; also *On Teaching Christianity*, 1.1.1; and Peter Brown, *Augustine of Hippo: A Biography*, rev. ed. (Berkley: University of California Press, 2000), 155.

[18] *Sermon*, 339.3.3.

for the people of God. But on account of my work for the church I cannot at all have the leisure of training scholars in more details than the people will listen to."[19]

During his career Augustine preached more than 500 sermons, 124 on John's Gospel, another 10 on John's first epistle, as well as an undetermined number of homilies on the Psalms.[20] Like Ambrose, Augustine was known for unraveling difficult texts with the aid of allegory. *On Teaching Christianity* revealed his thoughts on how to interpret Scripture, and the fourth book was essentially an early manual for delivering sermons.[21] In addition to his preaching in Hippo, he also delivered sermons while traveling in Carthage and other North African cities. His sermons were routinely transcribed by a stenographer and circulated to other churches and sent to resource preachers of lesser ability.[22]

A North African worship assembly in Augustine's day was often a rowdy affair with the audience shouting and expressing emotion throughout the sermon. Augustine, seated on his chair (*cathedra*), spoke rather extemporaneously, though his preparation was indeed thorough. Although he followed the rules of rhetoric in speaking, he was more concerned with the substance of a message than its form of delivery.[23] Like Ambrose he communicated eloquently but not at the expense of nourishing content.

Overseeing with authority. A second role for Augustine was overseeing the church. Joncas asserts that Augustine believed in a bishop's firm authority (*episcopalis auctoritas*) to direct the people

---

[19] *Letter* 73.2.5.

[20] The number of homilies on Psalms has not been determined because some of them were only dictated. For a helpful summary of Augustine's sermons see Daniel Doyle, "The Bishop as Teacher," in Kim Paffenroth and Kevin Hughes, *Augustine and Liberal Education* (Aldershot, UK: Ashgate, 2000), 85; and Bacchi, *Ordained Ministry*, 10–12.

[21] Book 4 was penned in 426 and 427, at the time of his *Reconsiderations* after a lengthy preaching career. Books 1–3.25, 37 were written in 396. See "Augustine's Works (Dates and Explanations)," *ATTA*, xliv.

[22] See Othmar Perler, "Les Voyages de Saint Augustin," *Recherches Augustiniennes* 1 (1958): 10–20; *On Teaching Christianity*, 4.29.63; *Letter* 16*.1; Gerald Bonner, *St. Augustine: His Life and Controversies* (Norwich: Canterbury, 1986), 145; and Bardy, *Saint Augustin*, 209.

[23] See Frederick van der Meer, *Augustine the Bishop*, trans. B. Battershaw and G. R. Lamb (London: Sheed & Ward, 1961), 169–70, 394; Bacchi, *Ordained Ministry*, 9; *On Teaching Christianity*, 4.2.3; 12.28.

and affairs of the church.[24] Bacchi argues that the bishop's burdens required such authority and that bishops will give an even greater account of their ministries on the Day of Judgment than other spiritual leaders.[25] Their burdens included dealing with troublemakers in the church, seeking to reform unholy practices such as the *laetitia* festival that led many astray, and dealing with heresy.[26] Bishops were also charged with the spiritual oversight of other clergy associated with his church and parish.

Presiding over the sacraments. Augustine wrote to his colleague Honoratus describing his ongoing ministry around the altar even in the midst of the Vandal siege: "Do we not consider how many people of both sexes and of every age usually rush to the church, some demanding baptism, others reconciliation, still others acts of penance, and all of them the administration and conferral of the sacraments?"[27] Hence, a third significant responsibility for Augustine was presiding over the sacraments.[28] Though van der Meer correctly asserts that Augustine used the term *sacrament* (*sacramentum*) in a general sense, Augustine seemed to make a special distinction in his use of sacrament or mystery (*mysterium*) when he referred to baptism and the Eucharist.[29] In his reply to Januarius's general questions about the sacraments, Augustine wrote about "sacraments, which are in number very few, in observance most easy, and in significance most excellent, as baptism solemnized in the name of the Trinity, the communion of His body and blood, and such other things as are prescribed in the canonical Scriptures."[30] Like Ambrose, Augustine was personally involved in initiating new believers—both adults and children—into the church

---

[24] See Joncas, "Clergy, North African," *ATTA*, 215; also *City of God*, 20.9.2; *Sermon*, 46–47; *Expositions in Psalms*, 126; 132; *Letter* 186.

[25] *Letter* 31.4; *Sermon*, 339.1; also Bacchi, *Ordained Ministry*, 80.

[26] *On the Catholic and Manichean Ways of Life*, 1.32.69; see Brown, *Augustine*, 200–2. Some of the "troublemakers" included members of the clergy themselves (*Letters* 78; 85; 209; *Sermon*, 355–56). Also *Letters* 22; 105.13; *Sermon*, 129; and Bacchi, *Ordained Ministry*, 80–81.

[27] *Letter* 228.8; see Pellegrino, *True Priest*, 41.

[28] See Pellegrino, *True Priest*, 38; Bacchi, *Ordained Ministry*, 73; and *Letters* 69.1; 261.2; 259.2.

[29] See van der Meer, *Augustine the Bishop*, 280. Joncas ("Clergy, North African," *ATTA*, 215) includes penance and ordaining clergy as other sacramental roles.

[30] *Letter* 54.1.

through baptism.[31] The period preceding Lent was a key evangelistic period for Augustine as he pleaded with the unbaptized who frequented the church at Hippo to submit their names for baptism. During Lent, Augustine instructed these catechumens in the Scriptures, taught them the Lord's Prayer, and handed over the Creed—a preparation which culminated in their baptism at Easter.[32] Once baptized, these believers were allowed to join the faithful in celebrating the Eucharist. While Augustine presided over the Eucharist for the congregation on Sunday, there was also a daily celebration primarily for clergy, monks, and servants of God, which was also open to the laity.[33]

Serving as a judge. The *Theodosian Code* gave power to bishops to render judgments in Roman civil courts, and the *Justinian Code* allowed them to serve as mediators in other cases.[34] Like Ambrose, Augustine functioned in this role, though not without complaint as he could spend an entire morning waiting to speak to an official about a given case.[35] Indeed, serving in this capacity took him away from other ministries like studying and writing until he was able to delegate this responsibility to his successor Eraclius in the final years of his ministry.[36] Though Augustine did not prefer this aspect of the ministry, he still did it and allowed other bishops to serve in this way in hopes that they might influence the civil court with principles from the Scriptures.[37]

---

[31] See Bacchi, *Ordained Ministry*, 16; Joncas, "Clergy, North African," *ATTA*, 215; *Sermon*, 227–29; 272; and *Letter* 98.5.10.

[32] For a thorough treatment of the stages in preparation for baptism in Ambrose and Augustine's day, see Edward Yarnold, *The Awe Inspiring Rites of Initiation: The Origins of the R.C.I.A.* (Edinburgh: T&T Clark, 1994), 1–33; also Odo Casel, *The Mystery of Christian Worship* (New York: Herder & Herder, 1962), 9–49; and van der Meer, *Augustine the Bishop*, 347–87.

[33] See Yarnold, *Rites of Initiation*, 40–54; *Letter* 54.3.4; also Joncas, "Clergy, North African," *ATTA*, 215; and van der Meer, *Augustine the Bishop*, 294.

[34] See Bacchi, *Ordained Ministry*, 32.

[35] *Letters* 33.5; 24*.1; Possidius, *Life of Augustine*, 19.2–4; also Bacchi, *Ordained Ministry*, 32; van der Meer, *Augustine the Bishop*, 260; Henry Chadwick, "The Role of the Christian Bishop in Ancient Society," in Edward C. Hobbs and William Wuellner, eds., *The Role of the Christian Bishop in Ancient Society*, Protocol to the Thirty-Fifth Colloquy (Berkley: Center for Hermeneutical Studies in Hellenistic and Modern Culture), 6; and Pellegrino, *True Priest*, 52.

[36] *Letter* 213.5; see Bacchi, *Ordained Ministry*, 32.

[37] Possidius, *Life of Augustine*, 19; *Letter* 133; see Bacchi, *Ordained Ministry*, 32.

Administering church property. It was common in Augustine's day for the wealthy to donate or will property to the church, and the responsibility for administering the newly acquired funds or property fell on the bishop. This was another task that Augustine particularly loathed and also delegated to Eraclius.[38] This required assimilating a gift into the church's treasury and distributing resources where there was need. During his ministry the needy included the poor as well as the kidnapped that were in need of being ransomed. Hence, like Cyprian, Basil, and Ambrose, Augustine played an active role in meeting the material needs of the church and community.[39]

Participation in church councils. Augustine also continued in the tradition of Cyprian, Ambrose, Basil, and other bishops through his participation in church councils. Beginning around the time of Augustine's ordination as presbyter in 391, Aurelius, the metropolitan bishop of Carthage, sought to convene the bishops annually "where doctrinal, liturgical, and disciplinary questions could be resolved and a renewed sense of purpose instilled in the episcopate."[40] After 407, however, the African bishops, concluding that meeting once a year was too difficult, decided to meet only when there were issues that affected the entire African church. Like Cyprian, Augustine considered the church councils an important means of maintaining the unity of the church. Bishops assembled to agree on points of doctrine and practice that they would then uphold throughout the region. The most common reason for convening a council was to deal with heresy. As we will explore further in this chapter, the main heretical groups addressed by the church councils of Augustine's day were the Donatists and Pelagians.

Augustine's Clergy

Augustine's clerical staff resembled that of Cyprian, Basil, and Ambrose. The higher orders included presbyters and deacons, while the lower orders were made up of subdeacons, acolytes, and readers.

---

[38] *Letters* 125–26; 213.5; see Bardy, *Saint Augustin*, 208–9; and Bacchi, *Ordained Ministry*, 39.
[39] Possidius, *Life of Augustine*, 24; *Sermon*, 339.4; see Bacchi, *Ordained Ministry*, 39; Bardy, *Saint Augustin*, 208–9; and Mandouze, "L'évêque," 136.
[40] See Merdinger, "Councils of North African Bishops," *ATTA*, 249.

Because presbyters were assistants to the bishops, their duties varied according to the needs of their bishops,[41] and they ended up fulfilling many of the same roles as the bishop. Lienhard asserts that because of the growth and increasing needs of the North African church in Augustine's day, presbyters were often sent to minister in churches where there was no bishop. In these cases especially the presbyter essentially functioned as a bishop. Presbyters counseled, preached, and presided over the sacraments.[42] Presbyters in North Africa rarely preached until Valerius involved Augustine in preaching at Hippo. Soon others such as Aurelius followed suit and released their presbyters to preach, which helped to meet the needs of the growing church.[43]

Deacons also served under a particular bishop and were "attached" (*adiunctus*) to the bishop's ministry.[44] They were responsible for leading congregational prayer, reading the Scripture during the liturgy, serving the wine during the Eucharist, and instructing catechumens before baptism.[45] This last responsibility was the subject of Augustine's book *On the Instruction of Beginners*.

According to his sermons and letters, some subdeacons lived with him in the Hippo clerical monastery, and their main responsibility was carrying letters.[46] Though little is known about the acolytes, their primary role was delivering letters.[47]

Readers led the singing of psalms and read the Scriptures during the worship assembly. Augustine probably incorporated the

---

[41] *Letter* 22.1; see Bacchi, *Ordained Ministry*, 72; Lienhard, "Ministry," *ATTA*, 569; and Pellegrino, *True Priest*, 72.

[42] *Letter* 21.3; see Bacchi, *Ordained Ministry*, 72; and Lienhard, "Ministry," 569.

[43] *Sermon*, 196.4.4; 20.5; 137.11.13; *Letters* 41.1; 105.4; and Lienhard, "Ministry," 569.

[44] See Joncas, "Clergy, North African," *ATTA*, 215. *Adiunctus* was used to describe the deacon Deogratias of Carthage in *On the Instruction of Beginners*, 1.1. Also Charles J. Hefele, *A History of the Councils of the Church: From the Original Documents, Vol. II* (Edinburgh: T & T Clark, 1896), 413.

[45] *Letter* 55.31; *Sermon*, 356.1; 304; also Hefele, *History of the Councils*, 2:414; Bacchi, *Ordained Ministry*, 71; Joncas, "Clergy, North African," *ATTA*, 215; and Lienhard, "Ministry," 569.

[46] *Sermon*, 256; *Letters* 39.1; 222.3; see Lienhard, "Ministry," 569; Joncas, "Clergy, North African," *ATTA*, 216; and Bacchi, *Ordained Ministry*, 66–67.

[47] *Letters* 191.1; 192.1; 193.1; 194.1; see Lienhard, "Ministry," *ATTA*, 568.

Psalms into the liturgy, following Ambrose's practice in Milan.[48] As was the case under Cyprian, Ambrose, and Basil, the readers who served with Augustine were youth whose voices were clear for reading and singing.[49] As noted at the end of chapter 2, the clergy needed a certain level of education in order to read the Scriptures for themselves and to make them accessible for others.[50] Thus, the reader was not merely selected for his clear voice or spiritual qualifications; he was also required to have a good level of reading to perform his ministry. Finally, like Cyprian, Augustine placed great value on Scripture reading in the church. This is apparent in *Sermon* 356 when Augustine took the Scriptures, which had already been read by a deacon, and said: "I too want to read. It gives me more pleasure, you see, to be reading these words than to be arguing my case with my own words."[51]

How Did Augustine Mentor?

The most instructive primary sources on Augustine's mentoring are his *Confessions*, sermons, letters, and the *Rule*, as well as Possidius's *Life of Augustine*. These reveal that Augustine's most significant mentoring forms included the monastery, letters, books, church councils, and personal visits.

The Monastery

Since his youth Augustine had demonstrated a strong need for others. As a professor of rhetoric in Milan, he formed a community of philosophically minded friends in pursuit of the "happy life." It is no surprise that once Augustine became a Christian he would also want to pursue his faith in the context of friends. Ladner writes:

---

[48] *Sermon*, 17.1.1; *Expositions in Psalms*, 32.2.1.5; 138.1; *Letter* 64.3; see Lienhard, "Ministry," 568; and van der Meer, *Augustine the Bishop*, 326.

[49] See Joncas, "Clergy, North African," *ATTA*, 216.

[50] See Gamble, *Books and Readers*, 9–10; and Paul Achtemeier, "*Omne Verbum Sonat*: The New Testament and the Oral Environment of Late Western Antiquity," *JBL* 109 (1990): 15–16.

[51] *Sermon*, 356.1.

Augustine's whole life since his conversion was in one
sense a "monastic itinerary" and the monastic impulse
of his nature must have been a very personal one. A
good deal of it was due to Augustine's strong need for
friendship, for the sharing of the deepest interests of
his soul with like-minded friends.[52]

Besides his personal bent toward friendship and community,
Augustine was further influenced toward a monastic way of life
while in Italy. As noted in *Confessions*, one aspect that appealed
to Augustine as he approached conversion was the lifestyle of
Antony. He was also exposed to a community of monks living
under Ambrose's supervision on the outskirts of Milan and to
another community in Rome that he visited in 388 while in transit
to Africa.[53] His *On the Catholic and Manichean Ways of Life* reveals
that Augustine was drawn to Christian monasticism because of his
repulsion at the false asceticism of the Manicheans that he observed
firsthand during his nine-year involvement with the sect.[54] In addition to Augustine's exposure to monks in Milan, Ambrose probably
told Augustine about Eusebius of Vercelli (d. 371), the first Italian
bishop to unite clergy with monastic community.[55]

We will now explore the stages in Augustine's monastic itinerary: first, Cassiciacum (386–387) as he prepared for baptism in the
company of friends; second, the community of servant of God at
Tagaste (388–391); third, the garden monastery in Hippo (391–
395); and finally the clerical monastery in Hippo (395–430).

Cassiciacum. Following his conversion in 386 and just before
the period of vacation, Augustine retired to the country estate of his

---

[52] See G. B. Ladner, *The Idea of Reform: Its Impact on Christian Thought and Action in the Age of the Fathers* (New York: Harper & Row, 1967), 353.

[53] *Confessions*, 8.6.15; *On the Catholic and Manichean Ways of Life*, 1.33.70; also Brown, *Augustine*, 119.

[54] *On the Catholic and Manichean Ways of Life*, 1.18.34; 2.19.68; see Elizabeth Clark, "Asceticism," *ATTA*, 68; and J. Kevin Coyle, "*Moribus Ecclesiae Catholicae et de Mori-bus Manicheorum, De*," *ATTA*, 571.

[55] Ambrose, *Letters* 63.66; 66; 71; see Ladner, *Idea of Reform*, 352–53; Adolar Zumkeller, *Augustine's Ideal of the Religious Life*, trans. Edmund Colledge (New York: Fordham University Press, 1986), 45; and van der Meer, *Augustine the Bishop*, 199.

friend Verecundus at Cassiciacum.[56] He wrote that there he "found rest . . . from the hurly-burly of the world" and sought to attain "knowledge of God and soul."[57] He was joined at Cassiciacum by Monica, his son Adeodatus, his brother Navigius, his cousins Lastidianus and Rusticus, his students Licentius and Trygetius, as well as Alypius. This group of family and friends spent seven months together in the fall and winter of 386 and 387 before returning to Milan at Easter, where Augustine was baptized along with Adeodatus and Alypius.[58]

What was the purpose of Cassiciacum? Was it simply a philosophical school, or should it be regarded as Augustine's first monastery? To answer these questions we should consider the daily routine and activities of the group. Overall the schedule was rather flexible. The group rose for corporate prayer each day at daybreak and also ended the day in prayer. Augustine wrote that he personally spent time each day reading the psalms and seeking God.[59] Since Cassiciacum was a country estate on a farm, the group also worked in the fields during harvest time and performed other duties on the farm.[60] Living together as a family, they took meals together served by Monica, who functioned as a mother to the entire group.[61]

Augustine had decided to retire from teaching, but he did accept the job of tutoring the two boys—Licentius and Trygetius—in Vergil's *Aeneid*.[62] Though it is unlikely that the other members of the group joined the two boys in their course of study, as Kevane has suggested, Augustine did take on the role of teacher for the group in that he encouraged them in the disciplines of reading and

---

[56] The location of Cassiciacum is probably modern-day Cassiago di Brianza located 21 miles (34 km) northeast of Milan. See Di Berardino, "Cassiciacum," *ATTA*, 135.

[57] *Confessions*, 9.3.5; *Soliloquies*, 1.2.7 (translation from Zumkeller, *Augustine's Ideal*, 8).

[58] *Confessions*, 9.6.14; see Zumkeller, *Augustine's Ideal*, 9.

[59] See *On Order*, 1.8.25; *Letter* 3.4; Lawless, *Monastic Rule*, 30; Zumkeller, *Augustine's Ideal*, 9; *Confessions*, 9.4.8; and Bonner, *St. Augustine*, 94.

[60] *Against the Skeptics*, 1.5.15; 2.4.10; see Lawless, *Monastic Rule*, 30; Zumkeller, *Augustine's Ideal*, 9; and Bonner, *St. Augustine*, 93.

[61] *Against the Skeptics*, 1.9.25; 2.5.13; see Joan McWilliam, "*Academicos, Contra*," *ATTA*, 2–3; and Bonner, *St. Augustine*, 93.

[62] *On Order*, 1.8.26; 2.4.10; see Sabine MacCormack, "Vergil," *ATTA*, 865; and Lawless, *Monastic Rule*, 29.

studying.[63] The most significant form of learning at Cassiciacium was dialogue. During their leisure time in the midmorning or late afternoon, the group met for dialogues that have been preserved under the titles *Against the Skeptics, On the Happy Life*, and *On Order*.[64] Lawless summarizes the daily schedule at Cassiciacum as "work (both physical and intellectual), contemplation (both philosophical and Christian), prayer and serious dialogue on a variety of themes."[65]

Though Augustine's time at Cassiciacum and the recorded dialogues are most often studied by scholars through philosophical lenses, it would be shortsighted to regard Cassiciacum as a mere philosophical retreat in the classical Roman sense.[66] While the dialogues were certainly characterized by the pursuit of truth via philosophy and regular reference is made to the likes of Vergil and Cicero, the dialogues also reveal a group of friends who believed that answers were found in Christ, the church, and the Scriptures.[67] Because the day included prayer, Scripture reading, and work, the experience was more than a philosophical retreat. The fact that the attempt at a philosophical community in search of the "happy life" had failed only a few months prior to the gathering at Cassiciacum showed that the latter had greater purposes than just philosophical speculation.[68]

Although Cassiciacum was not simply about philosophy, it should not be regarded as Augustine's first monastery.[69] Communal living, prayer, Scripture reading, and manual labor were present, but the

---

[63] See Eugene Kevane, *Augustine the Educator* (Westminster, MD: Newman, 1954), 60–61; *Against the Skeptics*, 1.1.4; 1.3.6; 3.1.1; and Lawless, *Monastic Rule*, 31.

[64] See Zumkeller, *Augustine's Ideal*, 10. Augustine's *Soliloquies* was also recorded at Cassiciacum, but I have not grouped it with the others since it is a monologue.

[65] See Lawless, *Monastic Rule*, 36–37.

[66] See Bonner, *St. Augustine*, 93.

[67] *Against the Skeptics*, 3.20.43; *On the Happy Life*, 4.34–5; *Soliloquies*, 1.2.7; see McWilliam, "*Academicos, Contra*," *ATTA*, 4; McWilliam, "*Beata Vita, De*," *ATTA*, 94–95; McWilliam, "*Ordine, De*," *ATTA*, 602–3; and McWilliam, "*Soliloquia*," *ATTA*, 806–7.

[68] See Mandouze, *L'aventure*, 195–96.

[69] See Bardy "Les Origines des Écoles Monastiques en Occident," *Sacris Eruditi* 5 (1953), 94; R. J. Halliburton, "The Inclination to Retirement: The Retreat of Cassiciacum and the 'Monastery' of Tagaste," *Studia Patristica* 5 (TU 80) (1962): 329–40; and Mandouze, *L'aventure*, 201.

group still lacked the theological foundations and long-term commitment of Augustine's future community. Reflecting on the experience in *Confessions* some 10 years later, Augustine admitted that his work and writing at Cassiciacum had a "whiff of scholastic pride about it."[70] Toward the end of his life in his *Reconsiderations*, he utterly recanted some of his philosophical thought expressed in the Cassiciacum dialogues.[71] Zumkeller considers the Cassiciacum experience as a "time of transition" for Augustine, and Bonner regards it as a time of reflection and preparation for baptism.[72] Zumkeller adds, "Certainly, the circle of friends at Cassiciacum was not yet a monastic community, but the groundwork had been laid for the new way of life which was to be established at Tagaste and Hippo."[73]

In the context of this premonastic gathering at Cassiciacum, how did Augustine function as a mentor? First, he was the natural leader of the group. His vision, charisma, initiative, and natural disposition to friendship made him the catalyst that initially brought the group together and kept it going for seven months. Second, he mentored the group by serving as its primary teacher. At times his teaching methods included basic lecture in which the content was taken from a philosophical text or from the Scriptures. Yet Augustine's key method of teaching was initiating and facilitating group dialogue. His teaching philosophy was student centered, and discussion topics were driven by participants' interests because he believed that the external dialogue served to encourage the internal dialogue in each person.[74] Noting that dialogue had fallen out of vogue in the Roman world, Howie argues that Augustine still valued the form and that the dialogues have a distinct Ciceronian flavor to them.[75] In his *Soliloquies*, Augustine affirmed that "there is no better way of

---

[70] *Confessions*, 9.4.7.
[71] *Reconsiderations*, 1.1–3; see Zumkeller, *Augustine's Ideal*, 10.
[72] See Zumkeller, *Augustine's Ideal*, 10; and Bonner, *St. Augustine*, 94.
[73] See Zumkeller, *Augustine's Ideal*, 13; and Mandouze, *L'aventure*, 193.
[74] See *Against the Skeptics*, 2.10.28; see Kevane, *Augustine the Educator*, 63, 93, 98; Lucien Jerphagnon, *Saint Augustin, le Pédogogue de Dieu* (Paris: Découvertes Gallimard, 2002), 66; and Bardy, *Saint Augustin*, 121.
[75] See George Howie, *Educational Theory and Practice in St. Augustine* (New York: Teachers College Press, 1969), 164.

seeking truth than by the method of question and answer."[76] While
Augustine's key role was to inspire thought and facilitate discussion, he would at times exercise some authority by bringing closure
to a discussion while offering a conclusion.[77] Augustine probably
preferred the mode of dialogue partly as a reaction to his own experience as a student, when the emphasis was on rote learning and
eloquent communication.[78]

Tagaste. As Augustine and company traveled to Rome in 387 to
set sail for Carthage, they were unexpectedly held up by Maximus's
invasion of Italy and the subsequent closure of the Roman ports. The
group decided to wait out the events in neighboring Ostia, the little
port town where Augustine and Monica experienced their famous
vision together and where Monica was laid to rest.[79]

The delay in Rome allowed Augustine to visit and observe the
inner workings of several monasteries. He related in *On the Catholic
and Manichean Ways of Life*, written in 388 or 389 upon his return
to Africa, that he encountered groups of holy men living together
in houses, in a structured way of life, and focused on God. They
shared their possessions in common; adhered to discipline in their
diet; and followed a daily plan of prayer, Scripture reading, and dialogue.[80] Augustine's interaction with the monasteries in Rome not
only solidified his conviction that monasticism was an acceptable
way of life, but it also gave him some clear ideas and principles to
apply in Tagaste.[81]

Upon their arrival in Tagaste in 388, Augustine, Adeodatus,
Alypius, and Evodius were joined at Augustine's family estate
by Severus. This would become the second phase of Augustine's

---

[76] *Soliloquies*, 2.7.14; English translation from Howie, *Educational Theory and Practice*, 170.
[77] *Against the Skeptics*, 1.3.7; see Kevane, *Augustine the Educator*, and Bardy, *St. Augustin*, 119.
[78] *Confessions*, 1.18; 3.4; see Kevane, *Augustine the Educator*, 38, 41, 46.
[79] See Brown, Augustine, 121; and *Confessions*, 10.23–11.28.
[80] *On the Catholic and Manichean Ways of Life*, 1.33.70; 1.31.67–68; 71–3; see Lawless, *Monastic Rule*, 40.
[81] See Mary T. Clark, *Augustine* (Washington, DC: Georgetown University Press, 1994), 85.

monastic itinerary.[82] To better understand this community, let us again consider their daily activities and values.

Possidius recorded that the three years they spent in Tagaste were "lived for God in fasting, prayer, and good works and in meditating day and night on the law of the Lord."[83] As at Cassiciacum there was no fixed daily schedule although Bardy has argued that they followed a certain monastic rule that spelled out monastic values such as poverty and obedience and provided a daily schedule for reading and working.[84] Although Bardy's claim lacks support in Augustine's works, it is true that a day in the Tagaste community was characterized by prayer, fasting, good works, and reading Scripture as well as psalm singing and reading other spiritually oriented books.[85]

As at Cassiciacum the group valued learning together through discussion. *On the Teacher*, Augustine's dialogue with Adeodatus, portrays the group learning that went on at Tagaste, while *On Eighty-three Varied Questions*, a resource written for other spiritual leaders, was initially inspired by Augustine's conversations with the group.[86] As Possidius noted, the group also spent part of their day working. Unlike the manual labor performed at Cassiciacum or by Pachomius's monks, the servants of God at Tagaste carried out intellectual labor, including reading, study, and teaching.[87]

The Tagaste community was united around the common goal of progressing toward spiritual perfection, as evidenced by a daily regimen of spiritual disciplines. Because of their conviction that the community itself brought about spiritual growth, they were constantly together. Each member renounced private property, and all shared their possessions in common.[88] While Bardy notes the Egyptian monastic influence here, we should also note the more immediate influence

---

[82] Possidius, *Life of Augustine*, 3.1; see Bardy, *Saint Augustin*, 142.
[83] Possidius, *Life of Augustine*, 3.2; also Ps 1:2; Luke 2:37.
[84] See Bardy, *Saint Augustin*, 145, 161.
[85] See Lawless, *Monastic Rule*, 48.
[86] *Confessions*, 9.6.14; see Zumkeller, *Augustine's Ideal*, 25.
[87] See Lawless, *Monastic Rule*, 50.
[88] See Bardy, *Saint Augustin*, 145; *Letters* 5; 83.2; see Zumkeller, *Augustine's Ideal*, 29–30; and Mandouze, *L'aventure*, 209.

of Augustine's experience in Rome.[89] Finally, the community valued having a spiritual superior—a role fulfilled by Augustine.

Brown, commenting on Augustine's return to Tagaste, writes, "The center of gravity of Augustine's thought had begun to shift. He had returned to Africa without his textbooks, and his schemes for an intellectual program based on the liberal arts now seems distant."[90] The Tagaste group became much more concerned with spiritual growth.[91]

Though Augustine never referred to the experiment at Tagaste as a monastery (*monasterium*),[92] the daily activities and values do very much resemble the cenobitic monastic activity demonstrated by Pachomius and Basil.[93] Lawless, arguing that Tagaste was a legitimate monastery, writes, "Experience comes first, its articulation afterwards. Conceptualizations ordinarily represent an attempt to encapsulate an experience after it has crystallized."[94] Though this argument is appealing, I am still hesitant to assert that Tagaste was a monastery because the group seemed to lack an exclusively Christian monastic focus but continued philosophical speculation. This is most apparent in Augustine's "good works" or writings that were often inspired by group dialogue. His *On Music*, begun after his baptism in 387 and completed at Tagaste, is similar to the Cassiciacum dialogues and focuses on the philosophical themes of "particularity, connection, motion, and time."[95] *On the Teacher*, completed at Tagaste by 389, deals with the philosophical issues of signs, the meaning of signs, and signs representing

---

[89] See Bardy, "Les Origines des Écoles Monastiques en Occident," *Sacris Erudiri* 5 (1953): 95.

[90] See Brown, *Augustine*, 127; also *Letter* 15.1.

[91] See Zumkeller, *Augustine's Ideal*, 29.

[92] For more on this question see Lawless, "Augustine's First Monastery: Thagaste or Hippo," *Augustinianum* 25 (1985): 65–78; L. Johan van der Lof, "The Threefold Meaning of *Servi Dei* in the Writings of Saint Augustine," *Augustinian Studies* 12 (1981): 43–59; Halliburton, "Inclination to Retirement," *Studia Patristica* 5 (TU 80) (1962): 329–40; Zumkeller, *Augustine's Ideal*, 24–32; Mandouze, *L'aventure*, 201–9; and M. Mellet, *L'Itineraire et L'Ideale Monastique de Saint Augustin* (Paris: Desclée De Brouwer, 1934), 19.

[93] See van der Lof, "Threefold Meaning," 54.

[94] See Lawless, *Monastic Rule*, 58.

[95] See Nancy Van Deusen, "*Musica, De*," *ATTA*, 574.

This post-fourth century baptistery in Sufetula (modern Sbeitla, Tunisia) is one of the most well preserved in the Roman world (photo: Marcus Brooks).

reality.[96] Augustine's *On Eighty-three Varied Questions*, a work of replies on philosophy, theology, and Scriptural exegesis, was initiated in Tagaste in 388 and completed in Hippo in 396. The questions Augustine answered during the Tagaste period were almost exclusively philosophical.[97] His last work from Tagaste, *On True Religion*, was written to Romanianus with the goal of helping his friend depart completely from Manichean thinking and accept the Christian faith. Though the work is an apologetic, bridging from what Romanianus knew to Christianity, it still maintains a high regard for Plato.[98]

On the other hand, two of Augustine's six works completed at Tagaste are more concerned with purely Christian teaching. Both are also apologies against the Manicheans. In *On Genesis, Against*

---

[96] See Douglas Kries, "*Magistro, De,*" ATTA, 520.
[97] See Eric Plumer, "*Diversus Quaestionibus Octoginta Tribus, De,*" ATTA, 276–77.
[98] *Letter* 15; see Frederick Van Fleteren, "*Vera Religione, De,*" ATTA, 864.

the Manichees, he offered an exegesis of the Genesis account of creation to counter what Augustine regarded as a false teaching of the Manicheans.[99] In *On the Catholic and Manichean Ways of Life*, he defended the Hebrew Scriptures against Manichean attacks, showed the superiority of Christian asceticism, and presented the cardinal virtues of Christianity.[100]

Augustine's correspondence from Tagaste also gives insight into his focus. In his correspondence with Nebridius, which speaks of "Christ, of Plato, of Plotinus," four letters clearly dealt with philosophical questions, while two were theological.[101] His final letters from Tagaste were more spiritually oriented: to the pagan Maximus of Madaura, an apologetic for Christianity; to Caelestinus, a resource with theological understanding on the nature of God and Christ; to Gaius, an invitation to the truth that accords with the church; and to Antoninus, congratulations on his new Christian faith and encouragement to read the Scripture.[102]

The divided interests that kept the Tagaste group from being a full-orbed Christian monastery also became clear when Augustine was ordained by Valerius in 391. If the Tagaste group had been a functioning monastery where the reading and study of Scripture were a primary focus, why did Augustine ask Valerius for a period of study before assuming his duties as presbyter? Though Augustine had left his philosophy books behind in Italy, he continued to be occupied with philosophical speculation that characterized most of his writings at Tagaste. He still felt ill prepared in his knowledge of the Scriptures when called upon by Valerius to be ordained. Yet his later writings and letters from Tagaste do show an increased emphasis on theology and scriptural exegesis. His reputation as an

---

[99] See Coyle, "*Genesi Adversus Manicheos, De*," *ATTA*, 378–79.

[100] See Coyle, "*Moribus Ecclesiae Catholicae et de Moribus Manicheorum, De*," *ATTA*, 571.

[101] *Letter* 6.1. In *Letter* 7, he wrote on the relationship of images and memory; in *Letter* 9, he gave his thoughts on the cause of dreams; in *Letter* 13, he discussed the body and soul; and in *Letter* 14, he replied to questions on the relationship of bodies, the sun, planets, Christ, and God in the universe. See *Letters* 5–6, 8 for Nebridius's questions and responses. In *Letter* 11, he wrote on how the Son only had a body and his relationship to the Godhead; while in *Letter* 12, he followed up to the previous letter with more thoughts on the incarnation.

[102] *Letters* 17–20.

emerging apologist and teacher in his final year in Tagaste probably caught Valerius's attention.

A final reason I have difficulty considering Tagaste a monastery is that it lacked the focus of a community existing to serve the church and function under its authority. The monasteries of Pachomius, Basil, Ambrose, and those that Augustine observed in Rome consistently submitted to church authority and were normally supervised by a bishop or presbyter.[103] There is no evidence that Augustine and friends had aligned themselves in any way to the church when they set up the Tagaste community. Rather, Augustine at this time did not hold the African clergy in high regard.[104] Further, while most of the intellectual activity of Tagaste benefitted members of the group, it did little to resource the members of the local church in Tagaste.

Hence, Tagaste, though more spiritually inclined than Cassiciacum, still resembled a place of leisure more than a Christian monastery for much of its existence. Yet Augustine's later writings and letters from Tagaste do become increasingly concerned with scriptural exegesis and Christian apologetics. In the final year at Tagaste, Augustine, through his writings and teaching, seems to have become a resource for the wider Christian community, which kept him busy.[105] Thus, Tagaste was also a period of transition between the more contemplative gathering at Cassiciacum and the full-fledged, church-focused monastery at Hippo. Therefore, I tend to agree with those who regard Tagaste as proto-monastic or a "premonastery."[106]

How, then, did Augustine function as a mentor? First, as at Cassiciacum, he continued to act as a mentor by being the catalyst for the group in both its inception and continuation. Second, Augustine emerged more at Tagaste as the superior for the group,

---

[103] *On the Catholic and Manichean Ways of Life*, 1.33.70. Though the Pachomian koinonia was not directly supervised by a clergy, Pachomius nevertheless maintained a submissive posture toward the church and Athanaisus. See William Harmless, *Desert Christians: An Introduction to the Literature of Early Monotheism* (Oxford: Oxford University Press, 2004), 119.

[104] Possidius, *Life of Augustine*, 4.3.

[105] *Letters* 13–14.

[106] See Charles Brockwell, "Augustine's Ideal of Monastic Community: A Paradigm for His Doctrine of the Church," *Augustinian Studies* 8 (1977): 95; Christine Mohrman, *Etudes sur le Latin des Chrétiens, Vol. IV* (Roma: Edizioni di storia e letteratura, 1977), 300; and Lawless, "Augustine's First Monastery," 66–67.

meaning that he not only gave direction to the daily spiritual activities, but he also exercised a certain authority over the group. Third, he continued his practice from Cassiciacum of teaching through dialogue. Fourth, by writing books and letters, he began to resource Christians and spiritual leaders outside the Tagaste community, particularly in the last year. Finally, through apologetic material written and perhaps delivered orally against the Manicheans and pagans, Augustine began to develop a conviction for orthodox doctrine and the primacy of Scripture.

The garden monastery at Hippo. In early 391, Augustine traveled the 60 miles to Hippo to see about setting up a community of servants of God there and to visit a man who might join them.[107] Because Hippo had a bishop, Augustine felt safe enough to attend the church. Yet, when Valerius selected him for ministry that day, he set a new course for Augustine's monastic itinerary. The bishop was happy that his new presbyter would continue to practice a monastic lifestyle and resourced him to that end by giving him a plot of land in the church garden to build a house for his community. The newly ordained monk-presbyter's community would break with Tagaste and become a veritable monastery under the authority of the church and functioning for its benefit.[108]

The Tagaste community continued, but Alypius, Severus, and Evodius moved to Hippo with Augustine.[109] Kevane writes that the new Hippo monastery attracted "members in considerable numbers" of "various ages and levels of education" including youth, former slaves, peasants, common laborers, as well as the wealthy and distinguished.[110] Some were natives of Hippo; others came from other parts of Africa. The new monks included clergy, laymen, even catechumens.[111]

Unlike Cassiciacum and Tagaste, the Hippo community followed a strict schedule. As the daily routine included personal and

---

[107] *Sermon*, 355.2; Possidius, *Life of Augustine*, 3.1; see Zumkeller, *Augustine's Ideal*, 33.
[108] See Mandouze, "L'évêque," 145.
[109] *Letters* 31; 33.2; see Bardy, *Saint Augustin*, 160.
[110] See Kevane, *Augustine the Educator*, 119; *Letter* 209.3; *On the Work of Monks*, 22.25; 25.33; and Zumkeller, *Augustine's Ideal*, 37.
[111] *Letter* 64.3; *Sermon*, 356.4; see Zumkeller, *Augustine's Ideal*, 37.

corporate prayer, the garden monastery probably contained a cell for each monk to facilitate personal prayer but also an oratory for group prayer. The day consisted of Scripture reading as well as reading from other spiritually nourishing books facilitated by a library in the house.[112] Everyone in the monastery had work to do each day. The clergy were occupied with church work, and the laymen were involved in physical labor that may have included working as copyists. The entire monastery took each meal together.[113]

What values characterized the Hippo monastery? First, it was focused on the church. Like Ambrose in Milan and the unnamed presbyter in Rome, Augustine presided over the community through his authority as presbyter of the church of Hippo. The labor performed by the monks, whether large or small, was focused on the needs of the church. Augustine sought to impress this on the monks of Capraria in his letter to them in 398.[114] Zumkeller summarizes, "More and more he recognized that service to the church was a task pleasing to the will of God, to which the comfortable tranquility of monastic communities must always give place."[115]

A second and related value was training clergy. When Augustine returned to Africa, he found the church besieged by the Manicheans, Donatists, Arians, and pagans. Even worse, he discovered that most of the African clergy were ill prepared to teach the Scriptures or mount an apologetic against the church's rivals. One reason he taught on the creed at the council of Hippo in 393 was to educate bishops and clergy who were weak in their theological understanding.[116] Trapé observes, "He saw this form of life not only as a significant way to live out the gospel . . . but equally an efficient means for giving renewed vigor to the church in Africa."[117] The daily

---

[112] *On the Work of Monks*, 18.21; *Rule*, 2.2; 5.10; see Zumkeller, *Augustine's Ideal*, 36–38.

[113] *Rule*, 5.8–9; 3.2; *On the Work of Monks*, 29.37; *Exposition in Psalms*, 99.12; see Zumkeller, *Augustine's Ideal*, 38.

[114] *Letter* 48; also *Letters* 130; 147; 217; 231; *On the Work of Monks*, 29.37; Brockwell, "Augustine's Ideal of Monastic Community: A Paradigm for His Doctrine of the Church," 105; and Lawless, *Monastic Rule*, 62.

[115] See Zumkeller, *Augustine's Ideal*, 35.

[116] See Agostino Trapé, *Saint Augustine: l'homme, le Pasteur, le Mystique* (Paris: Fayard, 1988), 119; Hamman, *Etudes Palristiques*, 276; and Bonner, *St. Augustine and His Controversies*, 115.

[117] See Trapé, *Saint Augustine*, 119 (trans. my own).

disciplines of prayer, scriptural study, and reading, as well as regular interaction with Augustine's teaching, prepared many monks for a possible future in church ministry. As a result some members of the Hippo monastery began to be ordained as clergy. Alypius was ordained a bishop before Augustine, set apart to serve the church of his native Tagaste in 394.[118]

Finally, Augustine brought with him from Tagaste the conviction that all personal property should be renounced and everything shared in common. Possidius described the Hippo monastery as "following the way of life and rule that had been established under the holy apostles. The most important provision was that no one in that community was to have any property of his own, but rather they were to have all things in common."[119] As Augustine invited men to join him in the monastery, they were not admitted until they had renounced their property, taken a vow of poverty, and committed themselves to simplicity.[120] Therefore, prior to any articulation of a monastic rule, Augustine and his community followed the basic principles of the Jerusalem church articulated in Acts 4:31–35.

In the four years that he spent as a monk-presbyter overseeing the monastery in Hippo, how did Augustine mentor? First, as at Cassiciacum and Tagaste, his initiative and leadership drew men to himself and to his vision. In *Sermon* 355, he recalled the beginning of the monastery: "I began to gather together brothers of good will, my companions in poverty, having nothing just like me and imitating me."[121] Second, he began to select men to join him. Instead of accepting just anyone who was drawn to the idea of monastic living, he received only those who agreed to follow the rule of the apostles and who were committed to living a holy life.[122] Third, as a presbyter, he mentored from a position of clear spiritual authority

---

[118] Augustine was not opposed to qualified monks being ordained to the ministry as he indicated in *Letters* 48; 60.1; Possidius, *Life of Augustine*, 11; *City of God*, 10.19. Also Mandouze, *L'aventure*, 219; Trapé, *Saint Augustine*, 117; *Letter* 24; and Bardy, "Les Origines," 209.

[119] Possidius, *Life of Augustine*, 5.1.

[120] *Sermon*, 355.2; *Expositions in Psalms*, 75.16; *Letter* 243; see Zumkeller, *Augustine's Ideal*, 37–39.

[121] *Sermon*, 355.2.

[122] *Letters* 243; 78.9.

over the men. Fourth, he mentored the monks through his teaching from the Scriptures. Possidius wrote, "At home and in the church Augustine was preaching and teaching the word of salvation."[123] For Augustine, to be preaching "at home" (*in domo*) meant teaching the brothers in the monastery. It also seems plausible that he continued to employ dialogue as a teaching tool as he had done at Cassiciacum and Tagaste and probably included discussion during meals. Fifth, through apologetic discourses delivered against the Donatists, Manicheans, and pagans, as well as books and sermons "based on the authority of the sacred Scriptures," Augustine modeled for his monks the importance of sound teaching and the primacy of Scripture.[124] Indeed, the "outstanding doctrine and the sweet fragrance of Christ" that "were diffused and made known throughout Africa" certainly had a primary impact on the men who shared his house.[125] Finally, as Hippo gained the reputation as a training center for North African clergy, Augustine began to set apart some monks to serve in the ordained ministry.

The clerical monastery (*monasterium clericorum*). When Valerius succeeded in ordaining Augustine as his cobishop in 395, he also directed Augustine to the next stage of his monastic itinerary. Mandouze suggests that Augustine had been a "monk-presbyter" following his ordination in 391, a "monk-bishop" in 395, and finally a "bishop-monk" upon Valerius's death in 396 or 397.[126] That is, Augustine's monastic and ecclesiastical roles became intertwined to the point that his burden for the ministry and "active life" (*uita actiua*) took precedent over the "contemplative life" (*uita comtemplatiua*) of the monastery.[127] He would wrestle with this tension for the duration of his ministry as a bishop-monk. Like Athanasius and Basil before him, he was a monk living in the city and occupied with the work of the church. This transition is illustrated by his establishment of a clerical monastery (*monasterium clericorum*) in

---

[123] Possidius, *Life of Augustine*, 7.1.
[124] Ibid., 7.1, 3.
[125] Ibid., 7.4.
[126] See Mandouze, *L'aventure*, 219.
[127] *City of God*, 19.19; see Verheijen, "Saint Augustin," 285; van der Lof, "Threefold Meaning," 50; and Ladner, *Idea of Reform*, 334, 398.

the bishop's house when Valerius passed away.[128] The door of this new monastery was open to visitors and those in need. Augustine described this in *Sermon* 355:

> I arrived at the episcopate. I saw that the bishop is under the necessity of showing hospitable kindness to all visitors and travelers; indeed, if a bishop didn't do that he would be said to be lacking in humanity. But if this custom were transferred to the monastery it would not be fitting. And that's why I wanted to have a monastery of clergy in the bishop's residence.[129]

Thus, Augustine invited clergy and probably some of his closest companions from the garden monastery to accept ordination and join him in the clerical monastery. Though Alypius had already departed for Tagaste when the new monastery began, Augustine was joined by Severus, Evodius, and Possidius as well as ordained ministers from every rank of clerical office.[130]

The daily schedule of the clerical monastery resembled that of the garden monastery. They rose early for morning vigils and observed set hours throughout the day for personal and corporate prayer.[131] While the garden monastery monks prayed in the oratory in their house, the clergy probably met for prayer and singing the psalms in the Basilica of Peace (*Basilica Pacis*), a church beside the bishop's house.[132] In addition to the corporate prayer service, they celebrated the Eucharist each day, often joined by laity in Hippo.[133] The clergy also spent time each day reading the Scriptures and other spiritually

---

[128] For a physical description of the church grounds and bishop's house in Hippo, see van der Meer, *Augustine the Bishop*, 20.

[129] *Sermon*, 355.2.

[130] *Letter* 60.1; see Zumkeller, *Augustine's Ideal*, 40; and Bardy, *Saint Augustin*, 209. A complete list of those who were living with Augustine in 425–426 at the outbreak of the clerical scandal is given in *Sermon*, 356.

[131] *Expositions in Psalms*, 118.29.4; *Rule*, 2.1; see Zumkeller, *Augustine's Ideal*, 46, 182.

[132] *Letter* 55.18.34; *Expositions in Psalms*, 46.1; *Confessions*, 9.7.15; see Zumkeller, *Augustine's Ideal*, 47–49.

[133] *Letter* 54; *Against Faustus, a Manichean*, 19.11; see Zumkeller, *Augustine's Ideal*, 50–51.

oriented books from their library.[134] They worked each day serving the needs of the church according to their clerical roles. They took two meals together each day except fast days.[135]

Within the clerical monastery, quite a few of the values that characterized the previous stages of the monastic itinerary continued to be present. First, they continued to believe that the group itself was the key to intellectual and spiritual growth. Second, the rule of the apostles—the renunciation of private property, commitment to sharing everything in common, and commitment to poverty and simplicity—continued to be upheld as it had been in the garden monastery and to some degree in Tagaste.[136] Lawless maintains, "Lack of evidence for a monastic code to guide the bishop's clerical community from the date of his episcopal ordination in 395–396 suggests that Acts 4:32–35 is, in effect, its basic rule of life."[137] Third, like the garden monastery, the clerical monastery demonstrated the value of training clergy for ministry both in Hippo and in the African church.

Two final monastic values seemed unique to this stage of Augustine's monastic journey. First, Augustine required that each of his men practice celibacy, a rule that applied to those who were married as well as those who had previously been married.[138] Following in the cenobitic tradition, celibacy was thought to be among the best means of making progress toward the perfect life.[139] A second related value was personal holiness and integrity. Crespin asserts, "Holiness was, in [Augustine's] eyes, inseparable from the clerical state."[140] One simple way that he required holi-

---

[134] *Letters* 55.21, 39; 132; *Sermon*, 219; *On the Work of Monks*, 17.20; 29.37; Possidius, *Life of Augustine*, 31; see Brown, *Augustine*, 195; and Zumkeller, *Augustine's Ideal*, 46, 187–88.

[135] *On the Work of Monks*, 27.35; 29.37; *City of God*, 19.19; *Sermon*, 356.13; see Zumkeller, *Augustine's Ideal*, 42, 195.

[136] *Letter* 243; *Sermon*, 355–56; Possidius, *Life of Augustine*, 5.1; 22; see Bardy, *Saint Augustin*, 163; and Zumkeller, *Augustine's Ideal*, 38, 43.

[137] Augustine did not publish his *Rule* until 399; see Lawless, *Monastic Rule*, 160.

[138] See Brockwell, "Augustine's Ideal," 102.

[139] *Letters* 210–11; *On Adulterous Marriages*, 2.20.22; see Mandouze, *L'aventure*, 176; and Zumkeller, *Augustine's Ideal*, 41.

[140] Remi Crespin, *Ministère et Sainteté* (Paris: Études Augustiniennes, 1965), 183 (translation my own); also *Expositions in Psalms*, 126.3; 132.4; and *Sermons*, 46.2; 49.2; 179.7;

ness was through his absolute intolerance of gossip during meal times. Possidius wrote that to remind the men of this conviction "he had these words inscribed on the table: 'Let those who like to slander the lives of the absent know that their own are not worthy of this table.'"[141] Augustine also forbid women from entering or coming near the monastery. When a woman needed to see Augustine, he would arrange the meeting in the presence of other clergy.[142] Like Ambrose he exhorted his men to avoid entanglements with the world by refusing all invitations to dinner in the city.[143] Perhaps the greatest example of Augustine's commitment to holiness was his transparency in handling the scandal in the clerical monastery in 425–426.[144] Not only did he expose the sin of his clergy before the congregation; he also reaffirmed the standards of the apostolic rule, called upon the unholy clergy to repent, and promised expulsion to those who refused.[145]

The clerical monastery provides us with the clearest form of Augustine interacting in community with the clergy. How did he go about mentoring spiritual leaders in this final stage of his monastic itinerary? First, in light of the daily Scripture reading program as well as the opportunities the men had to hear him preach and teach, Augustine trained them in how to interpret the Scriptures and teach them to others. Possidius's reference to Augustine's "divine teachings" being heard by "men who were serving God in the monastery with and under the direction of holy Augustine" gives evidence for Augustine's regular teaching program.[146] Possidius described

---

270.1; 340.1.

[141] Possidius, *Life of Augustine*, 22.6.

[142] Ibid., 26.1–3; see Zumkeller, *Augustine's Ideal*, 43.

[143] See Possidius, *Life of Augustine*, 27.4–5 and Ambrose, *On the Duties of Ministers*, 1.86. Augustine also forbade them to arrange marriages and to recommend men for military service.

[144] According to *Sermon*, 355.3, the scandal began when it was discovered that the presbyter Januarius had violated the rule of the apostles by concealing property and then trying to will it to the church while disinheriting his children in the process. Augustine then investigated the affairs of every member of the monastery and gave a full report to the congregation in *Sermon*, 356.2–11, 15.

[145] *Sermon*, 355.3; 356.2, 6; 355.6; 356.1; 356.14; see van der Meer, *Augustine the Bishop*, 203–6.

[146] Possidius, *Life of Augustine*, 11.1.

Augustine's disciples who left Hippo for other places of service as "venerable men of continence and learning" who went to serve in various places as "zeal for the spread of God's word increased."[147] These descriptions not only give us an idea of their level of training in the Scriptures, but also their convictions for teaching them. As Augustine's first request of Valerius had been a period of concentrated study in the Scriptures, Augustine would also impress upon his men this value and make the study of Scripture the primary focus of their monastic training program.[148]

Second, Augustine mentored the clergy by providing intellectual training. African church leaders in his day were poorly prepared to teach the Scriptures and inept at defending Christianity against heretics and pagans. As Ambrose and Simplicianus convinced Augustine he could be a thinking Christian, Augustine also imparted to his men their need to develop intellectually in light of the hostile and difficult situations in which they would serve.[149] Through a program of reading facilitated by a private library, as well as through observing Augustine engaging regularly the enemies of the church, his men progressed toward becoming defenders of the faith.[150] Possidius reported that Augustine's ministry of apologetics and debate led to renewal in the African church: "The result was that by the grace of God the catholic church of Africa began to lift its head after having long been prostrated, led astray, weighed down and oppressed."[151] Yet we can also infer from Possidius that the church was strengthened by Augustine's disciples—a corps of men thoroughly trained in apologetics, theology, and even aspects of the liberal arts.[152]

Third, Augustine mentored his men by continuing the practice of dialogue. Dialogue had characterized Augustine's relationships

---

[147] Ibid., 11.3–4.
[148] See Martin, "*Clericatus Sarcina (Letter 126.3)*: Augustine and the Care of the Clergy," 2, http://ccat.sas.upenn.edu/jod/augustine.html.
[149] *Letter* 60.1; see Jerphagnon, *Saint Augustine*, 68; van der Meer, *Augustine the Bishop*, 200; and Brown, *Augustine*, 137.
[150] *On the Work of Monks*, 29.37; Possidius, *Life of Augustine*, 31; see Zumkeller, *Augustine's Ideal*, 187; Brown, *Augustine*, 195; and Harry Gamble, *Books and Readers*, 165–67; also Possidius, *Life of Augustine*, 6; 7; 9; 11; 13; 14; 16–18.
[151] Possidius, *Life of Augustine*, 7.2.
[152] Ibid., 11.4–5; 13.

with Alypius in the villa near Milan leading up to his conversion, with Simplicianus in Milan, at Cassiciacum, with Evodius in Rome, at Tagaste, and initially at Hippo. Possidius described his dialogue with the clergy in the monastery: "His real delight was to speak of the things of God . . . at home in familiar converse with his brothers."[153] Augustine also used the two common meals that the clergy took together to institute a form of "table talk." Possidius wrote, "Even at table he found more delight in reading and conversation than in eating and drinking."[154] The mealtime discussions included at least these aspects. First, following in the tradition of Basil, the clergy read spiritually nourishing books.[155] This meant, of course, that one person read aloud followed by a discussion about the book. Brown suggests that the reading list included books devoted to the lives of figures such as Perpetua, Felicitas, and Cyprian, and that the ensuing discussion dealt with imitating their examples.[156] Second, in their discussions they would at times address a philosophical, theological, or exegetical question. Bardy argues that such discussions helped to clarify Augustine's thought on some issues and that the table talk served as the inspiration for several of his books.[157] Finally, at table Augustine and his clergy discussed what they had experienced during the day in their ministries in the church. Possidius recorded that the group once discussed Augustine's sermon that day and specifically why he had digressed from his topic.[158] Hence, this third aspect of table talk allowed the group to reflect on the day by sharing victories and failures while finding renewed courage and vision to carry on in the work of ministry. We could consider this a "help session," for they wrestled with church-related issues, engaged in problem solving, and shared wisdom. Ironically, some of the clergy who had left Hippo to serve the church in North Africa returned as refugees during the Vandal

---

[153] Ibid., 19.6.

[154] Ibid., 22.6.

[155] Ibid., 22.6; *Rule*, 3.2; see Zumkeller, *Augustine's Ideal*, 42. Basil's practice of reading at table is recorded in John Cassian, *Institutes*, 4.17. Also Pellegrino's commentary on Possidius, 22.6 in Rotelle, *Life of Saint Augustine*, 93.

[156] See Brown, *Augustine*, 151–52.

[157] See Bardy, "Les Origines," 196; and Zumkeller, *Augustine's Ideal*, 42.

[158] Possidius, *Life of Augustine*, 15.

siege and once again benefited from discussion around Augustine's table.[159]

Fourth, Augustine also mentored by opening his door and demonstrating hospitality to visitors as Basil had done in the hospice in Caesarea.[160] One of Augustine's guests was the Spanish presbyter Paul Orosius, who had come to study under him in 414 while fleeing the Vandal conquest in Spain. Others included the Bishops Paul and Eutropius, who came to learn more about the heresies that challenged the church.[161] Augustine's hospitality ran the risk of welcoming an unworthy or disruptive visitor into the monastery, but he maintained the conviction of showing hospitality. He wrote to Profuturus, "In receiving unknown guests, after all, we usually say that it is much better to put up with an evil man than perhaps to turn away a good man through ignorance."[162] Augustine not only ministered to travelers who visited the monastery but also modeled the importance of hospitality to his disciples.

A fifth way Augustine mentored the clergy in the monastery was through correction and discipline. If the men did something as seemingly insignificant as swear an oath while at table, they were penalized one of their allotted glasses of wine. As already noted, once Januarius's dishonest activity came to his attention, he thoroughly investigated the matter and exposed the sin of his clergy to the congregation.[163] Further, he maintained the apostolic standard of the monastery and threatened expulsion to those who would not repent.

Sixth, Augustine mentored through the clerical monastery by involving his clergy in the monastery's work. Each year Augustine assigned a different clergy to serve as "provost of the bishop's house" (*praepositus domus ecclesiae*), giving the clergy responsibility over the administration and finances of the monastery. Possidius wrote,

---

[159] Ibid., 28.13; also 29.1–2; and Brown, *Augustine*, 409.

[160] *Sermon*, 356.10; see Brown, *Augustine*, 195; John Cassian, *Conferences*, 14.4.2; and Ladner, *Idea of Reform*, 332.

[161] *Letters* 166.1; 169.13; See William Frend, "Orosius, Paulus," *ATTA*, 615–17; and Bardy, 295.

[162] *Letter* 38.2; see Zumkeller, *Augustine's Ideal*, 43.

[163] Possidius, *Life of Augustine*, 25.1; *Sermon*, 180.10; 307.5; 355–56.

The administration of the house attached to the church and of all its possessions he used to delegate to the more capable among the clergy, letting each of them have the task in turn. He never kept the key or wore the ring. Instead, those in charge of the house kept a record of all income and expenditures and gave an account to him at the end of the year.[164]

Augustine not only entrusted the provost with the task but also empowered him for it by giving him the necessary tools of administrative authority—the signet ring and key to the house. Indeed, he demonstrated great trust in the provost by reviewing the financial records only once a year. Finally, Augustine involved many different clergy in this ministry as a new provost was appointed each year. We know from Augustine's correspondence that he did not enjoy administrative aspects of ministry and considered them his areas of weakness. Like his mentor Valerius, he was happy to entrust such tasks to other more qualified clergy.[165]

Finally, Augustine mentored by releasing many of his men to serve the church throughout North Africa. Possidius said that these were men "Augustine gave upon request to the various churches."[166] In this respect Augustine broke with Valerius in that he did not try to detain any of his clergy in Hippo from serving elsewhere. While Valerius was committed to resourcing the Hippo church by setting apart Augustine as his cobishop in 395, Augustine had more of a vision to resource the universal church in Africa.

Though Eusebius of Vercelli and Basil of Caesarea had certainly embraced the lifestyle of a monk-bishop and invited other clergy to form some sort of a community, Augustine's clerical monastery had no precedent in the history of the Christian movement. Lawless asserts that Augustine culminated his monastic itinerary by effectively clericalizing the monk and monasticizing the cleric.[167]

---

[164] Possidius, *Life of Augustine*, 24.1; see Zumkeller, *Augustine's Ideal*, 43.
[165] *Letter* 213.5.
[166] Possidius, *Life of Augustine*, 11.3.
[167] See Lawless, *Monastic Rule*, 62; and Mandouze, *L'aventure*, 168–69.

Outcomes of Augustine's monastic mentoring. Augustine's monastic itinerary began at Cassiciacum as a sort of Christian retreat characterized by philosophical and spiritual pursuits. Though philosophical speculation continued at Tagaste, the Hippo community was much more focused on the Scriptures and spiritual growth. Once he was ordained, he established the garden monastery at Hippo, which existed for the church and under church authority. Finally, Augustine's monastic itinerary found its fulfillment in the clerical monastery, a community of clergy dedicated to serving the church.

What were the specific outcomes of Augustine's work of mentoring leaders through the clerical monastery? As alluded to already, his most significant legacy was "numerous clergy," the men he sent out as leaders for the North African church.[168] Possidius wrote:

> Other churches therefore began eagerly to ask and obtain bishops and clerics from the monastery that owed its origin and growth to this memorable man. . . . I myself know of about ten holy and venerable men of continence and learning, some of them quite outstanding, whom blessed Augustine gave upon request to the various churches.[169]

Aside from Possidius himself, who was ordained bishop of Calama in 400, the group included Alypius, who left the garden monastery in 394 to become bishop of Tagaste.[170] The other nine included Profuturus, who was ordained bishop of Cirta in 395; Severus, who became bishop of Milevus in 397; Evodius, who was ordained bishop of Uzalis before 401; Peregrinus, who was set apart as a deacon in Thenae; Urbanus, who was ordained bishop of Sicca; Paul, who was consecrated bishop of Cataqua; Servilius and Privatus; and Antoninus, who became bishop of Fussala.[171]

---

[168] Possidius, *Life of Augustine*, 31.8.

[169] Ibid., 11.2–3.

[170] *Letter* 101; see Pellegrino in Rotelle, *Life of Saint Augustine*, 60.

[171] See *Letters* 32.1; 158.9, 11; 31.9; 149.34; 85.1; 209.3; Pellegrino in Rotelle, *Life of Saint Augustine*, 60; Mandouze, *Prosopographie*, 928–30, 1070–75, 367, 852–53, 1232–33, 842, 920, 1063, 73–75; Othmar Perler, *Les Voyages de Saint Augustin* (Paris: Etudes Augustiniennes, 1969), 156; Bardy, "Les Origines," 209; and O'Donnell, "Evodius of Uzalis," *ATTA*, 344.

In reality, only half of the men continued in ministry in a long-term capacity; for Profuturus, Servilius, and Privatus died prematurely and Paul and Antoninus were removed from their places of ministry because of immoral behavior. So how could Possidius, writing years after Augustine's death, mention "numerous clergy" as part of Augustine's legacy? The answer seems to be that those who remained faithful in ministry also invested time mentoring other potential leaders. Possidius added that Augustine's men "founded monasteries in their turn."[172] We know of two monasteries, one for women and one for lay monks, that grew out of the garden monastery in Hippo. Sometime after 410, two more monasteries were founded at Tagaste under Alypius's direction. Before becoming bishop of Uzalius, Evodius was involved in setting up a monastery in Carthage.[173] Another monastery was apparently initiated at Carthage though it is unclear whether it was founded by Augustine or Aurelius. This may have been the community of monks who refused to work, which prompted Aurelius to ask for Augustine's intervention through his work *On the Work of Monks*. Zumkeller claims that by the end of the fifth century there were 38 monasteries in North Africa.[174] Some of these were certainly founded by Augustine's clerical monks sent out from Carthage while the rest were surely influenced by Augustine's monastic contribution.

Letters

Augustine continued the practice of Cyprian, Basil, and Ambrose by equipping and edifying the clergy by writing letters. Hamman writes that Augustine, "on account of his letters and writings, became a mentor of the clergy and the bishops through correspondence. He is the most consulted man in the western church."[175] Augustine's surviving letters total 252, which includes the general collection of 224 as well as a group of 28 letters discovered by Johannes Divjak

---

[172] Possidius, *Life of Augustine*, 11.3; also *Letter* 157.4.39; and Mandouze, *L'aventure*, 238.

[173] *Sermon*, 356.10; see Lawless, *Monastic Rule*, 62; Trapé, *Saint Augustine*, 25; *Letter* 24.3; and commentary in WSA, 2.1.71.

[174] See Zumkeller, *Augustine's Ideal*, 58, 84–5.

[175] See Hamman, *Etudes Patristiques*, 277 (translation my own).

and published in 1981.[176] Most were written after his ordination as presbyter in 391, yet up to 16 letters survive from the five years prior to his move to Hippo.

Augustine's letters provide a good picture of church life in the fourth and fifth centuries and the challenges that he faced as a bishop. The Pelagian controversy, the Donatist schism, church councils, and the problems of unworthy clergy come to life in this correspondence. A deeply warm and personal individual, Augustine regarded letters as a conversation between friends separated by distance.[177] He met some of these friends, particularly Paulinus of Nola and Jerome, only through correspondence. In Augustine's letters we meet someone committed to resourcing his correspondents according to their needs. Though he wrote fewer letters than Basil, his letters are generally much longer, some being short books or treatises.[178]

Of the 236 letters written during his ministry as presbyter and bishop of Hippo, 105 were addressed to ordained clergy.[179] One hundred contain a definite quality of mentoring about them.[180] Twenty-one were written to spiritual leaders who were serving in Hippo or who had left the clerical monastery to serve elsewhere in Africa.[181] The clergy who received the most correspondence from Augustine were Jerome, who received nine letters, and Paulinus of

---

[176] Augustine's letters also include an additional 50 letters written to him and seven others that are neither from him nor to him though most refer to Augustine. I am following the argument of Robert Eno and others (Eno in *FC*, 81.3) that the Divjak letters include 28 letters from Augustine since *Letters* 23* and 23*A seem to be addressed to two different people. Henry Chadwick ("New Letters of St. Augustine," *JTS* 34 [1983], 425), on the other hand, only counts 27.

[177] See for example: *Letters* 29.1; 40.1.1; 48.4; 138.1; 166.1; 194.2; See Eno, "*Epistulae*," *ATTA*, 298.

[178] See for example: *Letters* 54–55; 128; 140; 146–47; 166–67; 174–76; 185; 187; 211.

[179] Augustine probably only wrote five letters while serving as presbyter (*Letters* 21–23; 26; 28). Though it is unclear whether the abbot Valentinus of Hadrumetum was ordained, I have included Augustine's letters to him (*Letters* 214–15; 215A) in this study because: (1) As an abbot, he was also likely ordained (*Letter* 48), (2) Augustine's role as a mentor to Valentinus and his monks is significant in the context of the Pelagian controversy.

[180] Aside from *Letter* 21 written to his mentor Valerius, *Letters* 212; 227; 269; and 25* are not included in our study as they are basically short notes of information.

[181] *Letters* 29; 38; 62–63; 83; 85; 110; 122; 125; 159; 162; 164; 169; 213; 245; 7*; 9*; 10*; 15*; 22*; 23A*.

Nola, who received seven.[182] While Augustine primarily wrote to clergy serving in the Western, Latin-speaking church, he also wrote to a few leaders of the eastern church.[183]

How did Augustine mentor spiritual leaders through his letters? Like Basil, Augustine demonstrated a clear sense of peer mentoring in a large number of his letters. Some letters served as a theological and exegetical resource; other letters were written to influence spiritual leaders toward maintaining sound teaching. In still other letters he gave direction in practical ministry by addressing various church issues. He also wrote a smaller number of letters offering his perspective on ministry, exhorting some leaders to spiritual growth, encouraging others, and initiating reconciliation. In many cases Augustine used the same letter to fulfill multiple mentoring purposes.

Peer mentoring. Augustine wrote 23 letters to five different leaders in which we observe him mentoring and being mentored by those we would regard as his peers. In *Letter* 37, he responded to a set of theological questions posed by his former mentor Simplicianus in 396 around the time that he succeeded Ambrose as bishop of Milan. Though he served Simplicianus as an exegetical resource through his responses, Augustine continued to regard Simplicianus as a mentor, inviting his feedback on his responses by asking him to "assume the role of censor to correct them."[184] This relationship had shifted from mentor-disciple to peer.

Augustine's four letters to Aurelius of Carthage also reflected peer mentoring. In *Letter* 22, written while still a presbyter, Augustine discussed with Aurelius a strategy for reforming the drunken excesses related to the *laetitia* festival. In *Letter* 41, penned around 396, Augustine affirmed Aurelius for his decision to allow the presbyters of Carthage to preach in the church under his supervision. Augustine, who had personally been involved in Valerius's

---

[182] *Letters* 28; 40; 67; 71; 73; 82; 166–67; 19* were to Jerome. *Letters* 27; 31; 42; 45; 80; 95; 186 were to Paulinus, while all but *Letters* 27 and 186 were addressed to Paulinus and his wife Theresia.

[183] *Letters* 179; 4*; 6*.

[184] *Letter* 37.3; the letter was probably accompanied by the work *To Simplicianus*, which addressed several passages in Kings and Romans; see James Wetzel, "*Simplicianum, Ad*," *ATTA*, 798–99.

innovation in this area, did not conceal his enthusiasm or influence on the subject:

> Let those go first, and let these follow, having become imitators of them as they are in Christ. May the route of the holy ants be fervent; may the activity of the holy bees spread its perfume; may their fruit be borne in patience with salutary perseverance up to the end.[185]

While providing Aurelius with input in this letter, Augustine asked for prayer as well as feedback on the initial drafts of *On Teaching Christianity*.[186] In *Letter* 60, written in 401, Augustine rather persuasively advised Aurelius on the issue of ordaining monks who had quit the monastery before seeking ordination.[187] Though he did not withhold his thoughts on the matter, Augustine clearly communicated a humble posture toward the bishop of Carthage: "I do not dare speak in opposition to your Wisdom, your Honor, and your Charity, and I, of course, hope that you will do what you see will be salutary for the members of the church."[188] Finally, in *Letter* 16*, written around 419, Augustine asked Aurelius for news regarding Alypius's trip to Rome, inquired of Aurelius's encyclical letter to the Numidian bishops following the 419 council of Carthage, and indicated that he had sent a copy of two sermons to resource Aurelius.[189]

Augustine's seven letters to Paulinus of Nola reveal a growing, intimate friendship between two spiritual leaders desperate to learn from each other. In *Letter* 27, written in 396, Augustine responded to Paulinus's initial letter, expressing how he had been encouraged by it and that he desired to get to know this new friend in Christ.[190] In *Letter* 31, written the following year, Augustine wrote that he was so

---

[185] *Letter* 41.1.
[186] *Letter* 41.2.
[187] *Letter* 60.1.
[188] *Letter* 60.2.
[189] *Letter* 16*.1, 3.
[190] *Letter* 27.1–3. In *Letter* 25.1, Paulinus acknowledged receipt of Augustine's "Pentateuch Against the Manichees" that he had sent via Alypius. According to Paulinus's *Letter* 6.2, Aurelius originally told Paulinus about Augustine's works. See Mandouze, *Prosopographie*, 107.

excited to get to know Paulinus that he questioned the letter carriers at length about his new friend. Augustine was also so encouraged by Paulinus's previous letter that he had shared it with the men in the Hippo monastery.[191] Finally, Augustine communicated that he had sent the three books *On Free Will* to resource Paulinus while request-ing Paulinus's book *Against the Pagans*.[192] In *Letters* 42 and 45, written in 398, Augustine lamented that he had heard nothing from Paulinus and reiterated his request for Paulinus's book.[193] Around 404, he wrote *Letter* 80 inquiring from Paulinus about how to discern God's will.[194] In *Letter* 95, penned around 408, Augustine dialogued with Paulinus over the notion of eternal life while also responding to Paulinus's questions about the nature of the resurrection body.[195] Also, Augustine posed once again a question about Christian lei-sure that Paulinus had apparently failed to address.[196] Finally, *Letter* 149, written in 415, was purely an exegetical resource in response to Paulinus's questions on passages in the Psalms, in Paul, and in the Gospels. Augustine concluded the letter by conceding his own need to learn as well as affirming Paulinus for his desire to grow.[197]

Although much attention has been given to Augustine's relation-ship with Jerome because of their famous feuds, Augustine's nine letters to the monk-presbyter of Bethlehem also provide evidence for a peer mentoring relationship.[198] Augustine sent *Letter* 28 to Jerome via his disciple Profuturus in 394 or 395, though Profuturus was unable to fulfill the mission because he was ordained bishop of Cirta in 395.[199] Meanwhile, the letter took nine years to get to Bethlehem, having taken a detour in Rome, which led Jerome to believe that Augustine was waging a public campaign against

---

[191] *Letter* 31.2–3.
[192] *Letter* 31.7–8.
[193] *Letter* 45 was coauthored by Alypius.
[194] *Letter* 80.2.
[195] *Letter* 95.2, 5, 7–8.
[196] *Letter* 95.9.
[197] *Letter* 149. 1.3–10; 149.2.11–30; 149.3.31–34.
[198] One of the key reasons for the misunderstandings between Augustine and Jerome was that the delivery of letters between Hippo and Bethlehem was often unreliable, as Augustine pointed out in *Letter* 73.2.5. See Robert J. O'Connell, "When Saintly Fathers Feuded: The Correspondence Between Augustine and Jerome," *Thought* 54 (1979): 344–64.
[199] *Letter* 71.1.2.

him.[200] Augustine's main issue in *Letter* 28 was his contention with Jerome's exegesis of Gal 2:11–14, in which he taught that Paul had lied about Peter's failure to live correctly according to the gospel.[201] Though Augustine was rather severe in his reproof of Jerome, he also invited the same scrutiny from Jerome toward his own writings.[202] Hence, through this letter and others, Augustine valued doctrinal purity over personal feelings.

Letter 40 also encountered difficulty making it to Bethlehem; because it was discovered on an island in the Adriatic Sea in 398, a year after it had been written, before it was redirected to Jerome. Again, Augustine took up the issue of Jerome's exegesis of Galatians and, this time, called on Jerome to recant his views.[203] Despite this serious concern Augustine wrote that he and his men had benefited from Jerome's book *On Illustrious Men*, a catalogue of Christian writers that also functioned as an apologetic against pagan opponents to Christianity.[204] Augustine went on to ask Jerome if he could resource them further with a book summarizing the heresies that existed.[205] In addition to the exegetical tangling in the letter, we should also note Augustine's warmth in communicating with Jerome: "Hence, enter into this conversation by letter with us so that we do not allow bodily absence to do much to keep us apart, though we are united in the Lord by oneness of the Spirit."[206]

In 403, Augustine wrote *Letter* 67, even though he still had not received a reply from Jerome to his two previous letters. He wrote to defend himself against a rumor that he had written a book against Jerome and sent it to Rome. In the spirit of his mentor Simplicianus, Augustine communicated his desire to learn from Jerome, even if the two disagreed. He wrote, "I am not only fully prepared to hear as a brother what you hold to the contrary, if something disturbs you

---

[200] See commentary on *Letter* 28 in WSA, 2.1.90–91.

[201] *Letter* 28.3.3–5.

[202] *Letter* 28.4.6.

[203] *Letter* 40.3.3–4.7.

[204] *Letter* 40.2.2; see Stefan Rebenich, *Jerome* (London and New York: Routledge, 2002), 97.

[205] *Letter* 40.6.9.

[206] *Letter* 40.1.1.

in my writings, but I also beg and demand this of you. For I will rejoice either over my correction or over your good will."[207]

Though Jerome finally replied in 402 to Augustine's initial letters, Augustine sent *Letter* 71 in 403. He raised the issue of Jerome's translation of Job from Hebrew into Latin and asked for a guide to determine the variant readings from Jerome's previous translation of the same book from Greek into Latin. Augustine further shared his apprehensions about a direct Hebrew-to-Latin translation because he highly regarded the Septuagint. Nevertheless, he asked Jerome to help him understand the variant passages that came as a result of a Hebrew-Latin translation. Finally, Augustine praised Jerome for his new translation of the Gospel from Greek into Latin.[208]

Following two rather strong letters from Jerome in 402 and 403, Augustine responded with *Letter* 73.[209] At the outset of the letter, he complained about Jerome's harsh communication in the two previous letters. He asked, "When you reply so that you give offense, what room is left for us to enter upon the discussion of the Scriptures without rancor?"[210] Yet he continued to pursue the relationship by calling Jerome to engage him in decent and respectful dialogue: "I ask you, if it is possible, that we investigate and discuss something between us in order that our hearts may be nourished without the bitterness of discord."[211] Augustine went on humbly to ask Jerome's forgiveness for any offense he may have caused while communicating a renewed desire to learn from him. He emphasized this commitment by expressing his intent to send one of his disciples to study under Jerome and then return to Hippo to enlighten Augustine and his clergy.[212]

In 404 or 405, Augustine responded in *Letter* 82 to three significant letters from Jerome.[213] Augustine began the letter with a strong reproof to Jerome's concluding words in *Letter* 81: "Let us playfully

---

[207] *Letter* 67.2.2.

[208] *Letter* 71.2.3–4; 71.4.6.

[209] *Letters* 68 and 71 in Augustine's letters.

[210] *Letter* 73.1.1.

[211] *Letter* 73.3.9.

[212] *Letter* 73.1.1, 2.3–5.

[213] *Letters* 72; 75; 81 in Augustine's letters.

exercise on the field of the Scriptures without causing injury to each other."[214] Augustine replied:

> You ask or rather you command with the confidence of love that we playfully exercise on the field of the Scriptures without causing injury to one another. As far as I am concerned, I prefer to do this seriously rather than playfully . . . not like someone playing on the field of the Scriptures, but like someone gasping for air in the mountains.[215]

Augustine's quote not only reveals the seriousness with which he regarded the Scriptures but also his task to interpret and apply them in the context of his ministry in Hippo, far from the leisurely and contemplative situation Jerome enjoyed in Bethlehem. In the same letter, he expressed his conviction that the writings of the philosophers were worthless compared to the revelation of Scripture, which certainly testified to Augustine's intellectual and spiritual development from his days in Cassiciacum and Tagaste.[216] Also, he passionately continued his conversation with Jerome over his interpretation of Paul's actions in Galatians—a dialogue that was 10 years old by this point![217] Despite the intensity of this letter, Augustine began by asking whether Jerome had forgiven him for his offenses.[218] He renewed his appeal for loving dialogue and respectful disagreement, especially as others were observing their behavior:

> Hence, let us rather teach, with as much insistence as we can, our dearest friends who most sincerely foster our labors that they may know that it is possible that among friends one contradicts the words of another, though love is, nonetheless, not diminished and though

---

[214] *Letter* 81.
[215] *Letter* 82.1.2.
[216] *Letter* 82.2.13.
[217] *Letter* 82.2.4–3.29.
[218] *Letter* 82.1.1.

the truth, which is owed to friendship, does not give
birth to hatred.[219]

He added that if it were not possible to dialogue in a righteous
manner, then perhaps they ought to cease their interaction: "That is,
may we do this in fraternal love with a spirit that is not displeasing in
the eyes of God. But if you do not think that this is possible between
us without a harmful offense to love itself, let us not do this."[220] He
thanked Jerome for warning him about the errors of the Ebionite
and Nazarean heresies and conceded that Jerome had convinced
him of the importance of translating the Hebrew Scriptures directly
into Latin as opposed to relying solely on the Septuagint.[221]

Augustine's final three letters to Jerome, written at the height of
the Pelagian controversy in 415 and 416, indicate that the two men
had made peace with each other and were strong allies in the fight
against heresy. In *Letter* 166, Augustine responded to Jerome's recommendation that he write something on the origin of the soul.[222]
Though he acknowledged his limitations on addressing this question
and invited Jerome's input, Augustine nevertheless made a significant effort to treat the subject.[223] Similarly, in *Letter* 167, Augustine
wrote to Jerome inviting his insights on James 2:10 and provided
his own thoughts. Augustine argued that any violation of the law
is a violation of love and challenged the two common beliefs that
all sins are equal and that one possesses all virtue if he has one virtue. Augustine concluded the letter by asking Jerome to reply and
correct any erroneous thinking he may have.[224] Jerome did reply
briefly yet did not take issue with any points in order to maintain
solidarity against the Pelagian opposition.[225] In his final letter to
Jerome, *Letter* 19*, Augustine shared some news about the ongoing Pelagian controversy and requested that Jerome confirm that he

---

[219] *Letter* 82.4.32.
[220] *Letter* 82.5.36.
[221] *Letter* 82.2.15 (refers to Jerome's assertions in *Letter* 75.4.13); and *Letter* 82.5.34; also
City of God, 18.43.
[222] In *Letter* 165, Jerome had referred Marcellinus to Augustine on this question.
[223] *Letter* 166.1.1; 2.3; 9.28.
[224] *Letter* 167.1.1; 167.16–20; 167.4.14–15; 167.2.4–3.12; 167.5.21.
[225] *Letter* 172.

received his letter. Augustine also made a point to sign them in his own hand in order to avoid the previous problems of letters getting lost or being difficult to verify.[226]

Related to his correspondence with Jerome, Augustine sent *Letter* 74 to Praesidius, a fellow Numidian bishop, asking him to forward *Letter* 73 to Jerome.[227] More than merely asking him to have the letter delivered, Augustine asked Praesidius to read the two previous letters exchanged between the feuding leaders and invited him to point out where Augustine may have been wrong. He wrote, "If I wrote something that I ought not to have or in a way in which I ought not to have, do not write to him about me, but rather write to me myself out of fraternal love in order that, having been corrected, I may ask his forgiveness if I myself recognize my fault."[228] Hence, instead of looking for an ally in his conflict with Jerome, Augustine humbly invited another spiritual leader to provide him with objective feedback.

Augustine's final peer mentoring letters were *Letters* 190 and 202A, written to Bishop Optatus in 417 and 418. In the first letter Augustine resourced Optatus with his thoughts on the origin of the soul, as he had Jerome in *Letter* 166, yet admitted his limited understanding on the subject and expressed his desire to read what Optatus had written on it.[229] Augustine followed up in *Letter* 202A with a long treatment of the question and complained that he had still not heard anything from Jerome on the matter since he had written *Letter* 167 some years prior.

Theological and exegetical resource. Augustine wrote another 31 letters in which he resourced spiritual leaders by responding to their theological and exegetical questions.[230] In 408, he wrote *Letter* 92A to Cyprian, a presbyter serving with him in Hippo who had apparently delivered letters for Augustine in the past.[231] His main purpose

---

[226] *Letter* 19*.4.

[227] *Letter* 74.1.1.

[228] *Letter* 74.1.

[229] *Letter* 190.1–2, 20–21, 26.

[230] Though I count *Letters* 37; 149; 166–67; 190; and 202A among Augustine's theological and exegetical letters, I will not treat them in this section as they were adequately discussed in the previous section.

[231] *Letters* 71.1.1; 73.1.1.

was to give instructions to Cyprian on delivering *Letter* 92 to a certain Italica—a letter addressing the issue of whether God could be perceived in bodily form. Though the issue was raised by Italica, Augustine took the time in *Letter* 92A to educate his presbyter more on the issue, which effectively equipped Cyprian in how to deal with the heresy himself. Finally, Augustine wanted Cyprian to let him know if others were holding this view. Augustine addressed the same issue in 410 in *Letter* 148 to an unnamed bishop.[232] In *Letter* 98, written between 408 and 414, Augustine responded to queries on infant baptism received from Boniface of Cataqua. Augustine wrote that the faith of a baptized child may not be negatively affected by his parents' faith, and he also argued for the saving necessity of baptism.[233]

Around 409, Augustine resourced the presbyter Deogratias of Carthage in *Letter* 102 with answers to several exegetical questions that someone else had posed to Deogratias. Though writing a thorough response to each question, Augustine made a point to affirm Deogratias's own ability to handle these questions himself.[234] Augustine treated questions pertaining to the resurrection of both Christ and Lazarus, the time of Christ's appearing in history, the differences in the sacrifices found in the Scriptures, the interpretation of Matt 7:2, the assertion that according to Solomon God did not have a son, and Jonah's experience in the belly of a whale.[235] In 416, Augustine penned *Letter* 173A to the Carthaginian presbyters Deogratias and Theodorus. The letter served as a brief explanation of the Trinity, especially in light of 1 Cor 6:19–20 and Deut 6:13. For more in-depth reading, Augustine referred them to his *On the Trinity*.

Between 414 and 415, Augustine wrote four letters to his longtime friend Evodius, who had left the Hippo monastery to serve as the bishop of Uzalis. Evodius's theological questions were speculative, reminiscent of his dialogues with Augustine in Rome in 388. Though Augustine had moved on to carry greater burdens and was not terribly excited about Evodius's questions, he did take time to

---

[232] *Letter* 148.1.1.
[233] *Letter* 98.2, 10.
[234] *Letter* 102.1.
[235] *Letter* 102.2–37.

respond to them.[236] In *Letter* 159, Augustine replied to Evodius's question about the soul taking on another bodily form after death, a notion he rejected. In *Letter* 162, he reluctantly responded to Evodius's queries on the nature of reason and God, the incarnation of Christ, and the possibility of seeing God in bodily form. Though Augustine answered these questions on reason to some extent, he referred him to his books *On the Trinity, On True Religion*, his works on Genesis, and reminded him of their dialogues recorded in *On the Greatness of the Soul* and *On Free Will*. He concluded that God was spirit and could not be seen in bodily form.[237] In *Letter* 164, Augustine thoroughly responded to Evodius's request for an explanation of 1 Pet 3:18–20 and particularly the meaning of Christ's descending.[238] In *Letter* 169, he again reluctantly replied to Evodius's questions on the Trinity, the relationship of the dove at Christ's baptism to the Trinity, as well as Paul's writings to the Corinthians and to Timothy. He followed up on Evodius's previous question about seeing God in bodily form by asserting that God is best perceived in a spiritual sense. He declined Evodius's request to revise *On the Trinity*, citing the priority of other pressing ministry concerns. Nevertheless, he did agree to resource Evodius with copies of portions of *City of God* and *Expositions in Psalms*, given that Evodius could send someone to Hippo to copy them.[239]

Augustine's *Letter* 174, written in 416, was a theological resource to Aurelius and his clergy at Carthage that was accompanied by at least portions of *On the Trinity* that he had been working on since 399.[240] In 418, Augustine responded with *Letter* 196 to Donatius's request that Augustine write to a certain clergy named Asellicus who had an unhealthy fascination with Judaism. Augustine showed Asellicus from the Scriptures that dietary and ceremonial laws from the Hebrew Scriptures were irrelevant for Christians. In 419,

---

[236] *Letters* 162.1; 169.1.1.
[237] *Letter* 162.2, 8.
[238] *Letter* 164.1.2.
[239] *Letters* 169.1.1–4.
[240] Apparently Evodius's prodding in the previous year or two proved effective in convincing Augustine to continue working on *On the Trinity*. See Perler, *Les Voyages*, 328–29.

Augustine sent *Letter* 23* along with his book *On the Soul and Its Origin* to Renatus of Caesarea.[241]

Augustine wrote two exegetical letters to Bishop Hesychius of Salome in 419. *Letter* 197 responded briefly to Hesychius's questions about the prophets and the end of the world. Augustine sent this letter with some books that Jerome had already written on the subject instead of addressing the matter entirely on his own.[242] Apparently dissatisfied with Jerome's answers, Hesychius responded with another letter asking for clarification.[243] Augustine replied with *Letter* 199, addressing some of the theories found in the Scriptures related to the time of Christ's return, and also commented on the signs related to the end of the age. Yet Augustine encouraged Hesychius to focus less on knowing the precise time of Christ's return, something not even the apostles knew, and urged him to prepare himself for Christ's return by living well in the present world.[244]

Around 420, Augustine wrote *Letter* 207 to Bishop Claudius in Italy. His letter was accompanied by books written to refute the heresy of Julian of Eclanum, who essentially propagated Pelagius's teaching. Later around 428, while still in the midst of the battle with Julian, Augustine wrote two letters to Quodvultdeus, a deacon of Carthage who had asked Augustine for a book summarizing the heresies facing the church together with a response for each one.[245] In *Letter* 222, Augustine responded that such a task would be difficult in light of his present responsibilities; instead, he suggested a similar work written in Greek by a certain Philastrus. He invited Quodvultdeus to take the book and have it translated into Latin for his colleagues in Carthage. Yet, in response to the deacon's repeated request, Augustine wrote *Letter* 224, agreeing to write the book once he had finished with his latest books against Julian. But Augustine

---

[241] Although Renatus was probably a nonordained monk, he had inquired of Augustine about the nature of the soul on behalf of Bishop Optatus and other clergy in Mauretania Caesarea. See *Letter* 190.1; and Mandouze, *Prosopographie*, 959–60.

[242] *Letter* 197.5.

[243] *Letter* 198.7.

[244] *Letter* 199.17–33; 199.4–6, 12; 199.1–4, 9, 52–54.

[245] *Letter* 221.2–3.

was only able to produce the incomplete *On Heresies* before his death in 430.[246]

Augustine penned a number of letters to clergy and spiritual leaders affected by Pelagius's teaching. In 418, Augustine sent *Letter* 194 to Sixtus, a presbyter in Rome. In a significant portion of the letter, he resourced Sixtus with teaching on the errors of the Pelagians by providing a thorough treatise on the nature of man, original sin, and the gift of faith.[247] Around 420, he wrote *Letter* 6* to Atticus of Constantinople, refuting the Pelagian teaching on sex and marriage that was spreading in his area. Around 426, Augustine wrote *Letters* 214, 215, and 215A to the abbot Valentinus and his monks at Hadrumetum. Each letter contained teaching on the nature of the will in an effort to steer the monks away from the Pelagian heresy. More than simply mentoring by letter, Augustine received two of Valentinus's monks, Cresconius and Felix, at Hippo where they spent time with Augustine and his men and received teaching as well as some books to take back to their community at Hadrumetum. The result was that Valentinus responded to Augustine with a humble declaration of his orthodoxy as well as reverence for Augustine's position as bishop of Hippo.[248] Augustine sent three final exegetical or theological letters to resource clergy. In the undated *Letter* 249, Augustine wrote to a certain Restitutus, referring him to the writings of Tyconius, the Donatist bishop who had developed a set of hermeneutical rules. Augustine was influenced by Tyconius in developing his rules for interpretation in *On Teaching Christianity*. In *Letter* 5*, written around 416, Augustine responded to two exegetical questions from a certain Bishop Valentianus. To Valentianus's question on why a newly baptized believer should recite the Lord's Prayer, which included confession, Augustine responded that ongoing confession was required because of man's continual struggle with sin, even after baptism. In response to his query on the meaning of Gen 6:3, Augustine first provided a better translation of the verse compared to the bishop's poor Latin translation and then

---

[246] *Letter* 224.1–2; see Roland Teske, "*Haeresibus, De*," *ATTA*, 412–13.

[247] *Letter* 194.3–46.

[248] *Letters* 214.1; 215.1; the books were *On Grace and Free Will* and *On Admonition and Grace*; also *Letter* 216; 215A had been written uniquely to Valentinus.

gave some further commentary on the verse.[249] Finally, in *Letter* 29*, Augustine politely refused Paulinus of Milan's request that he write an account of the lives of the saints. Augustine's refusal was a bit ironic since it was Augustine who had asked Paulinus to write the *Life of Ambrose*. Nevertheless, Augustine referred Paulinus to the work he had already done in commemorating the saints' lives through his sermons.

Toward maintaining sound teaching. In another 18 letters, Augustine wrote influencing and urging his fellow clergy to maintain sound doctrine. Most of these letters addressed battles with the Priscillianists, Donatists, Julian, and the Pelagians; but two do not seem to be related to any heresy or church controversy. In 401, Augustine wrote *Letter* 64 to admonish the presbyter Quintianus of Carthage to read only the canonical Scriptures in the church, reminding him of the canons of the councils of 393 and 397, which affirmed the canonical books.[250] In *Letter* 148, cited in the last section, Augustine wrote to an unnamed bishop via Fortunatianus of Sicca, challenging his belief that God may be perceived in bodily form. Augustine made his appeal based on the teachings of the church fathers as well as what was taught in the Scriptures.[251]

In *Letter* 237, an undated letter to Ceretius of Gaul, Augustine denounced a certain Argirius, who was caught up in the Priscillianist heresy. While condemning their claim that a certain hymn belonged in the Scriptures, Augustine himself appealed to the authority of the canonical Scriptures and chastised Argirius and his group for misusing them.[252]

Around 412, Augustine wrote *Letter* 28* to support Novatus of Sitifis whose church was experiencing a reunion of catholics and Donatists in the aftermath of the council of Carthage in 411, which condemned the Donatists and ordered them to unite with the catholic church. Augustine encouraged Novatus to use this opportunity

---

[249] *Letter* 5*.2–3.

[250] In *Letter* 64.3, Augustine cited canon 38 of the council of Hippo of 393 and canon 47 of the council of Carthage of 397.

[251] *Letter* 148.2.10–4.15.

[252] *Letter* 237.1–3, 7, 9; For a concise explanation of the Priscillianist heresy, see Roland Teske, "*Priscillianists, Contra*," *ATTA*, 684–85.

to teach his congregation about the nature of the church by reading the proceedings of the council of Carthage in church during Lent, which had also been the practice in Hippo, Carthage, Tagaste, Cirta, and probably Mauretania Caesarea.[253]

Also noted in the previous section, Augustine's *Letter* 207 to Bishop Claudius was accompanied by books intended to refute Julian's heresy, which was spreading in Italy. The letter and books were theological resources that served to encourage Claudius and the clergy toward maintaining sound doctrine.

Augustine's final 13 letters related to maintaining sound doctrine were addressed to clergy affected by the Pelagian controversy.[254] In 416, Augustine penned *Letter* 178 to a certain Bishop Hilary, warning him about Pelagian thinking and explaining some of its errors. In 417, Augustine wrote Paulinus in *Letter* 186, also recounting Pelagius's teaching. As this was probably difficult news for Paulinus, who apparently had a relationship with Pelagius, Augustine showed sensitivity by coauthoring the letter with Alypius, who had personally visited Paulinus in Italy. In 418, Augustine encouraged Sixtus of Rome with *Letters* 191 and 194 by affirming him as an apologist against the Pelagians.[255] Sixtus appears to have been led astray by Pelagian thinking at some point but then renounced it and actively joined Augustine and others in the fight against it. Finally, in *Letter* 190, one already considered, Augustine warned Optatus about the dangers of falling into the Pelagian heresy.[256]

In two letters Augustine communicated with bishops in the East, investigating how Pelagius was acquitted by a church council in Palestine and endeavoring to influence them in their thinking about the heresy. In *Letter* 179, written in 416, Augustine appealed to Bishop John of Jerusalem, raising the issue of the teaching that Pelagius's disciples had been spreading. He also requested a copy

---

[253] *Letter* 28*.1–2. See Robert Eno's comments in *FC*, 6.187.

[254] In the previous sections we treated *Letters* 190; 194; 6*; 214–15; 215A, which were written to resource the clergy with theological instruction and also to steer them away from the errors of the Pelagians. To avoid being redundant, we will not consider *Letters* 6*; 214–15; 215A in this section.

[255] *Letter* 194 served the purpose of being a theological resource as well as an encouragement to fight heresy.

[256] *Letter* 190.22.

of the acts from the 415 council of Diospolis that had acquitted Pelagius. This situation required Augustine to gather all the facts in order to pin down Pelagius in his heresy. Augustine took the opportunity to relate what he knew about Pelagius and essentially make an argument against Pelagius to John.[257] In *Letter* 4*, written the following year to Cyril of Alexandria, Augustine acknowledged that he had received from Cyril a copy of the acts, which John had failed to send.[258] Augustine took them and produced his *On the Deeds of Pelagius*, an apologetic against Pelagius that he sent as a resource to Aurelius of Carthage. He also sent a certified copy to Cyril via his courier Justus. Finally, Augustine urged Cyril to beware of Latin speakers in Alexandria propagating Pelagius's teaching and generally encouraged him to fight against heresy.[259]

Finally, in 416, Augustine wrote two letters in collaboration with other African bishops to influence Pope Innocent I on the matter of Pelagius. In *Letter* 176, Augustine communicated the decision of the 416 council of Milevus in which Pelagius was condemned. While giving their theological position on man's sinful nature supported by numerous passages from the Scriptures, Augustine and the bishops of Numidia wrote to inform their chief shepherd of what was happening in the African church and to persuade him to their position.[260] In *Letter* 177, written the same year, Augustine wrote on behalf of bishops Aurelius, Evodius, Possidius, and Alypius. Again, by using arguments from the Scriptures and sending Pelagius's own book to Innocent, Augustine laid out the heart of the Pelagian issue—man's nature.[261] While it may seem odd to assert that Augustine, along with his fellow bishops, was mentoring the pope through his letters, he was nevertheless attempting to influence Innocent toward sound doctrine as he had done in letters to John and Cyril. Augustine's correspondence seemed effective, for Innocent responded to each

---

[257] *Letter* 179.2–7, 9, 10.
[258] Apparently John had disregarded Augustine and his request in light of Augustine's association with his enemy Jerome.
[259] *Letter* 4*.2, 5.
[260] *Letter* 176.1–3.
[261] *Letter* 177.1, 7–8.

letter affirming the bishops for their commitment to sound teaching and condemning the errors of Pelagius.[262]

Practical church matters. In 35 letters, Augustine mentored his fellow clergy by giving direction and insight into practical matters related to leading the church.[263] Ten of these letters were written to resource disciples who had left Hippo to serve the African church as bishops. Alypius was Augustine's key correspondent, receiving six letters. In *Letter* 29, written in 395 while Augustine was still a presbyter, he recounted to Alypius the ordeal of preaching to the crowds in the midst of his battle to reform the *laetitia* festival. Though the letter was very much one minister sharing an experience with another minister, Augustine indirectly impressed upon Alypius the necessity of dealing with such church problems by holding up the Scriptures as the final authority for church practice.[264]

In *Letter* 83, written around 404, Augustine wrote to Alypius regarding a certain Honoratus of Thiava, one of Augustine's monks at Hippo who had died. The church at Thiava, a congregation under Alypius's supervision, was demanding that Honoratus's possessions be returned to the church. While responding to Alypius's request for help in the matter, Augustine certainly honored his friend's jurisdiction over the Thiava church by dealing with the problem in cooperation with Alypius. As the matter was apparently pressing, Augustine asked Alypius to sign a letter that he had already written to the church, given that Alypius agreed with its contents. Augustine also took the opportunity to discuss some principles related to the issue—that a monk should settle his estate before entering a monastery and that clergy should avoid the appearance of evil with regard to money matters.[265]

Between 419 and 423, Augustine wrote *Letters* 15* and 9* to resource Alypius in his role as a judge and leader of the clergy.[266]

---

[262] *Letters* 182–83.

[263] Augustine's *Letters* 41 and 60 to Aurelius of Carthage deal with practical church matters. Since they were adequately treated in the section on peer mentoring, they will not be discussed here.

[264] *Letter* 29.2–11. Augustine's repetition of "taking up the book" (*codicem etiam accepi statimque . . . accepto codice recitaui*) in *Letter* 29.4, 10 is significant.

[265] *Letter* 83.1–4.

[266] *Letter* 15* was also written to the clergy serving with Alypius in Tagaste.

A man in Tagaste had raped a nun from the convent, and Alypius's clergy responded by beating the man. The man appealed to Pope Caelestinus, who demanded that the clergy be judged and punished for their actions. As Alypius was preparing to deal with this awkward situation, his longtime friend wrote to support and encourage him as well as to give him some direction. Though Augustine did not seem too concerned about the actions of the clergy except for the possibility that they used excessive force, he urged Alypius to investigate the facts before rendering a judgment, a principle that can be observed repeatedly throughout his own ministry.[267]

In *Letter* 22*, written around 420, Augustine mentored Alypius by involving him in a specific ministry related to his previous training as a lawyer—sending him to Rome to intercede before the pope on church matters.[268] On this journey Augustine asked him to speak with the pope about the problem of recruiting clergy from certain classes, the possible need for a secular defender for the church, and the appointment of the unworthy Honorius as bishop of Mauretania Caesarea.[269] While Alypius was still in Rome, Augustine wrote *Letter* 10* asking him also to appeal to secular leaders over the crisis of abduction and slavery that was happening in Africa. In maintaining his practice of thoroughly investigating a matter, Augustine supplied Alypius with a statute to help him in his efforts.[270]

In *Letters* 62 and 63, written in 402, Augustine wrote to Severus of Milevus about a deacon named Timothy who had been dishonest with Augustine, Alypius, and Samsucius of Turris.[271] Timothy had begun as a reader in the church at Subsanna near Hippo, left to go to Milevus to serve with Severus, and then wanted to return to Subsanna.[272] In *Letter* 63, Augustine endeavored to work through the awkward situation involving his close friend by sharing that he had corrected Timothy through "reprimands, by admonitions and by prayers."[273] Though he left the decision to Severus, he asked him

---

[267] *Letter* 9*.1–3.
[268] The letter was also addressed to Bishop Peregrinus of Thenae.
[269] *Letter* 22*.1–2, 4, 6–7.
[270] *Letter* 10*.2–4, 6.
[271] The three bishops coauthored *Letter* 62.
[272] *Letters* 62.2; 63.1.
[273] *Letter* 63.2.

to free Timothy from his commitment to the Milevus church and allow him to return to Subsanna.[274]

Around 401, Augustine wrote *Letter* 245 to his friend and eventual biographer Possidius. He responded to Possidius's request about how to deal with church members wearing gold, expensive dress, using skin pigments, and wearing amulet earrings. Augustine encouraged Possidius not to prohibit people from presenting themselves in a certain way but to have them consider what the Scriptures taught about true beauty and what was honorable between husbands and wives. Regarding amulets, however, he reminded Possidius that he had a strong warrant from Scripture to denounce such superstitions. Finally, Augustine advised Possidius against ordaining a man who had been baptized as a Donatist.[275] In *Letter* 23A*, probably written to Possidius around 419, Augustine inquired about Alypius's travels to Italy on behalf of the African church.[276] In other church business, Augustine affirmed a certain Bishop Donatianus and sent a copy of the acts that acquitted the Bishop Maurentius. Finally, Augustine shared with his friend about his recent writing projects.[277]

Augustine wrote 11 letters to clergy specifically dealing with issues of church leadership. Around 402, he penned *Letter* 59 to Bishop Victorinus, who had waged something of a campaign against Xantippus for the position of primate of Numidia. While encouraging Victorinus to resolve the issue directly with Xantippus, he also rebuked him for the inappropriate manner in which he had pursued the office.[278] Augustine wrote *Letter* 65 to the same Xantippus, who ended up becoming primate in 402. In his letter Augustine was actually making Xantippus aware of what had transpired with a clergy named Abundantianus, who had been found guilty of embezzlement and sexual immorality. While informing him about the matter, Augustine was indirectly modeling how to deal with immoral clergy by taking his time to investigate the matter thoroughly, removing

---

[274] *Letter* 63.4.
[275] *Letter* 245.1–2.
[276] For arguments on authorship of this letter see Chadwick, "New Letters of St. Augustine," 448–49.
[277] *Letter* 23A*.1, 3–4.
[278] *Letter* 59.1.

him from his place of ministry, and dealing with him in a compassionate manner.[279]

In 422, Augustine wrote *Letter* 209 to Pope Caelestinus regarding the fallen Bishop Antoninus of Fussala, who had been removed from his position by Augustine and then appealed to Pope Boniface.[280] In the letter Augustine recounted the affair by first relating the great burden he had had for the region of Fussala, an area strongly influenced by the Donatists.[281] As Fussala was primarily composed of Punic speakers, Augustine, surely influenced by Valerius, was convinced of the need to set apart a Punic-speaking bishop.[282] When his first choice of bishop refused to be ordained, Augustine made a hasty decision in ordaining Antoninus, a reader who had grown up in the Hippo monastery. Though the purpose of this letter was to inform Caelestinus of what had gone on, Augustine did indirectly influence the pope in how he handled the affair. First, Augustine responded to Antoninus with both discipline and grace. He wrote:

> We so mixed clemency with severity in our sentence, that while reserving to him his office of bishop, we did not leave altogether unpunished offenses which behoved neither to be repeated again by himself, nor held forth to the imitation of others. We therefore, in correcting him, reserved to the young man the rank of his office unimpaired, but at the same time, as a punishment, we took away his power, appointing that he should not any longer rule over those with whom he had dealt in such a manner that with just resentment they could not submit to his authority.[283]

Although Antoninus's authority as bishop was taken away, he was not actually stripped of his title. In fact, Augustine wondered if he himself and the other Numidian bishops had been too lenient.[284]

---

[279] *Letter* 65.1.
[280] *Letter* 209.6–9.
[281] *Letter* 209.2.
[282] *Letter* 209.3.
[283] *Letter* 209.5.
[284] *Letter* 209.7.

Second, despite Antoninus's behavior Augustine still loved him as a son and longed to treat him with compassion. In the letter Augustine was actually appealing to Caelestinus for compassionate treatment for both Antoninus and the people of Fussala.[285] Finally, Augustine took responsibility for his poor choice in Antoninus. He admitted that he hastily selected Antoninus under the pressure of inconveniencing the aging primate of Numidia, who was already en route to Fussala.[286] Perhaps he also feared embarrassment from the rival Donatist party that was active in Fussala. Augustine was willing to take responsibility to the point of resigning from his own office over his mistake.[287]

In *Letter* 78, written prior to 408 to the people and clergy of Hippo, Augustine openly related the case of a priest named Boniface who had accused a monk of immorality and then was accused by the same monk in return. Augustine again modeled to the clergy how to deal with potential immorality by being completely transparent about the issue and by considering the accused innocent until proven guilty.[288] Similarly, in the undated *Letter* 13* to the presbyter Restitutus, Augustine gave advice on dealing with a particular deacon who had shared his bed with a nun. Again, as Augustine was investigating the matter, he encouraged Restitutus to consider the deacon innocent until proven guilty. Yet, if the congregation became agitated, Augustine urged Restitutus to read *Letter* 13* to the church.[289]

In *Letter* 85, written before 408, Augustine wrote to Paul of Cataqua confronting him about worldliness, which had injured the church. This letter must have been difficult for Augustine, who regarded Paul, an alumnus of the clerical monastery, as "not only my brother, but my colleague." Though Paul's offense was not explicitly mentioned in the letter, Augustine hinted failure to repent would result in his removal as bishop: "Unless the Lord delivers you from

---

[285] *Letter* 209.9.
[286] *Letter* 209.3.
[287] *Letter* 209.10.
[288] *Letter* 78.2, 8.
[289] *Letter* 13*.2–3. In *Letter* 18*.1–2 we learn that the deacon was found guilty.

all your worldly concerns and burdens and calls you back to a genu-
ine episcopal manner of life, such a wound cannot be healed."[290]

In *Letter* 236, written to Deuterius of Caesarea, Augustine indicated that he was sending back to Caesarea a subdeacon who had
been serving in the region of Hippo yet who had become involved
in the Manichean sect. Augustine, acting on his convictions for
sound doctrine, demonstrated absolutely no tolerance for heresy. In
Letter 219, however, written to Bishops Proculus of Marseille and
Cillenius of Gaul in 426, Augustine commended a monk named
Leporius to them. Leporius appears to have fled Gaul because of his
heretical views on the incarnation. Augustine received him in Hippo
and spent time mentoring him toward an orthodox understanding of
the incarnation before sending him back to Gaul with a statement
recanting his heresy and embracing orthodoxy.[291] Through this letter Augustine modeled restorative grace to the two Gallic clergy.
Finally, in the undated *Letter* 26* to Honoratus, Augustine refused
to recommend the unworthy and unreliable Donantius to be named
deacon in Suppa.[292]

In *Letter* 84, written before 411 to Novatus of Sitifis, Augustine
denied Novatus's request for his brother Lucillus, a deacon serving
in Hippo, to be transferred back to Sitifis. Augustine first appealed to
his burden for the ministry and the needs of the church over any personal desires. He wrote, "For the sake of the world to come . . . we
set the needs of our mother, the church, before the needs of our own
time."[293] Second, Lucillus was a Punic speaker, and his language
ability was greatly needed in the region of Hippo. Again, following
the influence of Valerius, Augustine valued overcoming language
barriers in ministry by finding capable communicators. In *Letter*
28*, a letter treated in the previous section, Augustine resourced the
same Novatus in his role as a judge in an upcoming case.[294]

---

[290] *Letter* 85.1.
[291] His declaration of orthodoxy happened in the context of the council of Carthage in 418. See Hefele, *Histoire des Conciles d'apres les Documents Originaux, Vol. II* (Paris: Letouzey et Ané, 1908), 2.1.215–16; and Mandouze, *Prosopographie*, 123.
[292] *Letter* 26*.1–2.
[293] *Letter* 84.1.
[294] *Letter* 28*.7.

Letter 213, written on September 9, 426, contains the proceedings of Augustine's nomination of the presbyter Eraclius to succeed him as bishop. Augustine purposefully employed notaries to record the event so as to avoid the confusion and disputes that had occurred in other churches during a change of leadership. Augustine clearly wanted to leave the Hippo church in good hands after he passed away. He wrote, "I know that churches are wont to be disturbed after the decease of their bishops by ambitious or contentious parties, and I feel it to be my duty to take measures to prevent this community from suffering."[295] Hence, the record of the transfer of leadership in Hippo served as a good model for other churches to follow. Two aspects of Augustine's ordination of Eraclius are noteworthy. First, Augustine made sure that the clergy and congregation of Hippo were behind the decision to have Eraclius as their new bishop. Second, he broke with Valerius and upheld the canons of Nicea by not ordaining Eraclius as his cobishop. Instead, Eraclius continued serving as a presbyter until Augustine's death, focusing on administrative tasks and serving as a judge, which allowed Augustine the freedom to study and write more.[296]

In other practical church matters, Augustine wrote *Letter* 36 in 397 to the African presbyter Casulanus, responding to his question of whether believers should fast on the Sabbath. Though providing an answer, Augustine encouraged Casulanus to use his own "fine mind" (*ingenio*) to find solutions to such matters.[297] Following the teaching of Ambrose, Augustine advised Casulanus that in situations where there was no direct command from Scripture, it was acceptable to follow the traditions of one's church.[298] In *Letter* 61, written in 401, Augustine gave advice to the deacon Theodorus of Carthage on receiving former Donatist clergy into communion.[299] Before 423, Augustine wrote *Letter* 115 to Fortunatus of Cirta, asking him to deliver a letter on his behalf to the governor regarding a certain Faventius who had sought refuge in the church of Hippo and

---

[295] *Letter* 213.1.
[296] *Letter* 213.1–6.
[297] *Letter* 36.2.3.
[298] *Letter* 36.1.2; 36.14.32.
[299] *Letter* 61.1.

was then arrested. Through his letter Augustine essentially involved Fortunatus in this ministry of interceding for a refugee and appealing to the secular authorities. In *Letter* 191 to the presbyter Sixtus, a letter previously treated, Augustine gave some insights for dealing with heresy in the church. He urged a balance between being gentle with those needing to be taught while disciplining those who intentionally propagated false teaching.[300]

Augustine addressed one of his last letters, *Letter* 228, to Honoratus in 429. Honoratus, like Quodvultdeus, had written asking how the clergy should respond to the danger posed by the Vandal invasion and whether it was acceptable for them to flee if necessary.[301] Augustine responded decisively that, while personal safety was important, a shepherd should never abandon his flock. When church members were in need of ministry, especially during volatile times, a minister must be present. Augustine also encouraged Honoratus not to fear death, for he possessed eternal life.[302]

In *Letter* 250, written before 420, Augustine confronted the young Bishop Auxilius for excommunicating a man along with his entire family. While pressing the bishop for a Scriptural basis for his decision, he encouraged him to pardon the excommunicated man. Finally the aging Augustine related to Auxilius that bishops also made mistakes so they should admit them and move on.[303] In *Letters* 253 and 254, written sometime after 395, Augustine wrote to Benenatus, who had hastily arranged a marriage for a young girl who was a ward of the church. While discussing the issue in *Letter* 254, Augustine concluded that the girl was too young to be married. He sent the undated *Letter* 3* to the deacon Felix, counseling him over the issue of a woman who had committed her daughter to virginity during a time of illness and later wanted to have her released from the vow. Augustine advised Felix that the woman should keep the oath and that her daughter ought to become a nun.[304]

---

[300] *Letter* 191.2.
[301] *Letter* 228.1.
[302] *Letter* 228.8, 11.
[303] *Letter* 250.1, 3; also *Letter* 1*.
[304] *Letter* 3*.1, 3; see Chadwick, "New Letters of St. Augustine," 428.

In 426, Augustine wrote *Letter* 7* to Faustinus, a deacon serving with him in Hippo. Briefly, Augustine sent Faustinus to Novatus of Sitifis to make him aware of a financial gift previously pledged by Count Boniface that had been withdrawn by his widow. Augustine wanted Novatus to appeal directly to the higher secular authority, Count Sebastian. Though Faustinus was involved in this work of the church by communicating to Novatus on the matter, Augustine provided clear instructions in the letter for how to proceed. He entrusted Novatus with an assignment and then wrote providing support and direction.[305] Augustine also wrote the undated *Letter* 8* to Bishop Victor regarding a church financial matter. Apparently Victor had purchased land for the church from an elderly woman who did not legally own it, and her son responded by demanding back his property from the church.[306] Though Victor had initially refused the man's request, Augustine encouraged him to return the man's land and to be careful about entangling the church in any potential legal problems.

Perspective on ministry. Augustine wrote two letters that shared his perspective on ministry. As noted, Augustine's motivation for the ministry was encapsulated in the word *burden*. Hence, it should come as no surprise that the two letters in question also communicated this value. Earlier in this chapter we cited Augustine's *Letter* 48 to the presbyter and abbot Eudoxius and his monks of Capraria. Augustine exhorted the men toward serving the church and achieving a proper balance between the active and contemplative lives.[307] He indirectly communicated the same idea to Bishop Memorius of Apulia around 408 in *Letter* 101. Augustine was writing to apologize for being unable to send Memorius a corrected copy of *On Music*, a set of books that he had authored nearly 20 years before. He described the period of his life when he was writing this work as "the beginning of our leisure, when my mind was free from greater and more important cares." Yet after nearly two decades as a presbyter and bishop of Hippo, he admitted, "After the burden of the cares about the church was imposed on me, all

---

[305] *Letter* 7*.1–2.
[306] *Letter* 8*.1.
[307] *Letter* 48.3.

those trifles fled from my hands so that I can now scarcely find the manuscript."[308] While excusing himself for being unable to fulfill a request, Augustine actually communicated more of his ministry philosophy than anything else.

Toward spiritual growth. Three of Augustine's letters show him mentoring members of the clergy toward their own spiritual growth. In 397, Augustine wrote *Letter* 38 to Profuturus in which he followed up on a previous conversation and exhorted Profuturus to guard against being carried off by anger and hatred.[309] In *Letter* 64 to Quintianus, a letter that we have already treated in part, Augustine wrote to this Carthaginian presbyter following an apparent conflict with Bishop Aurelius. While not usurping the authority of his friend Aurelius, Augustine sought to encourage Quintianus—especially urging him toward patience.[310] Finally, Augustine wrote *Letter* 125 to Alypius in 411 in the aftermath of the Pinian controversy in Hippo. In response to the jeering and false accusations made by the faithful at Hippo, Augustine urged his friend to model a life of integrity before his accusers. He further encouraged Alypius through his good example to heal the suspicion of Albina, Pinian's mother, that the church was greedy and only interested in her son's money.[311]

Encouragement. Augustine sent another five letters to encourage various clergy in their faith and ministry. He addressed *Letter* 110 to Severus of Milevus, thanking his longtime friend for his letter of encouragement and affirming Severus in their continuing friendship.[312] Similarly, Augustine's purpose in *Letter* 192 to Caelestinus in 418 was to express warmth and friendship to his coworker in ministry.[313]

In 409, Augustine wrote *Letter* 111 to Victorianus in order to encourage this presbyter who was troubled by violence resulting

---

[308] *Letter* 101.1, 3.

[309] *Letter* 38.2.

[310] *Letter* 64.1.

[311] *Letter* 125.1–2. Pinian was a wealthy layman whom the faithful at Hippo unsuccessfully attempted to ordain by force. In the aftermath they accused Alypius of taking Pinian from them to Tagaste.

[312] *Letter* 110.1. The date of *Letter* 110 is not certain and has been dated between 401 and 426.

[313] *Letter* 192.

from the Vandal invasion. Augustine began the letter by empathizing with Victorianus in his grief while reminding him that the Scriptures taught that one should not be surprised by such events. He went on to encourage Victorianus with two holy models who stood strong during suffering—the prophet Daniel and the niece of Severus of Milevus. In light of the models from Scripture, Augustine exhorted Victorianus to believe the Scriptures, teach them, and resist murmuring while continuing steadfast in prayer and believing that God would deliver him from harm.[314]

In 410, Augustine sent *Letter* 122 to the faithful of Hippo, both laity and clergy. While apologizing for his absence from Hippo, he encouraged them to persevere through any temporal difficulty they might face in light of the eternal glory that awaited them. He concluded by exhorting them to continue in good works, especially in caring for the poor.[315] Finally, in 412, Augustine addressed *Letter* 142 to Saturninus, Eufrates, and a group of clergy who had returned to the catholic church from the Donatist party.[316] Augustine rejoiced with them in their good decision, exhorted them to carry out their ministries in the church, and encouraged them to pray for those still in Donatism.[317]

Reconciliation. In Augustine's final two mentoring letters to the clergy he modeled humility and Christian fellowship by initiating reconciliation with two individuals that he had apparently offended. In *Letter* 148, a letter we have previously considered for its theological value, Augustine wrote through the intermediary of Fortunatianus of Sicca to reach out to a bishop that he had offended. Though Augustine does not hedge from his theological position, he repeatedly asks the bishop's forgiveness for the manner in which he communicated and demonstrates a desire to learn from this man.[318] Similarly, sometime after 418, Augustine and Alypius wrote *Letter* 171 to their former colleague from Hippo, Peregrinus, asking him to send their apologies to a doctor named Maximus, whose

---

[314] *Letter* 111.1–4, 6–7, 9.
[315] *Letter* 122.1–2.
[316] The letter also addressed laymen associated with these clergy.
[317] *Letter* 142.1, 4.
[318] *Letter* 148.1.1, 4; 148.5.18.

letter they were unable to answer because of other commitments. While there is no indication that Maximus was offended, Augustine was sensitive enough to inquire via Peregrinus.

Books

Possidius affirmed that Augustine, through the aid of stenographers, resourced spiritual leaders in Africa and beyond through his books and treatises. His writings became known in his lifetime to the entire Latin-speaking church and were ultimately preserved in the library at Hippo.[319] Some were even translated in Greek. Many were inspired by theological and exegetical dialogue during mealtime discussions in the Hippo monastery; others, as Pellegrino notes, were "written at the request (often repeated and insistent) of persons who wished to be enlightened on various points of doctrine; or they arose out of the urgent demands of polemical controversy with heretics and pagans."[320]

Augustine clearly believed that books were an invaluable resource for mentoring the clergy as well as the laity. As noted in our survey of Augustine's letters, he sometimes responded to a question by sending a relevant book written by another author.[321] Yet, in light of the time he gave to writing and the amount of material he produced, even in the midst of a busy pastoral ministry, Augustine believed that his books could also have a mentoring impact. He summarized this conviction in *Letter* 151:

> In so far as leisure is granted me from the work imperatively demanded by the church, which my office specially binds me to serve, I have resolved to devote the time entirely, if the Lord will, to the labor of studies pertaining to ecclesiastical learning; in doing which I think that I may, if it please the mercy of God, be of some service even to future generations.[322]

---

[319] Possidius, *Life of Augustine,* 7.3–4; 11.4; 18.10; 31.6; see Bardy, "Les Origines," 212.

[320] Pellegrino, *True Priest,* 46; also Bardy, "Les Origines," 196; and Kevane, *Augustine the Educator,* 121.

[321] *Letters* 197; 222; 240.

[322] *Letter* 151.13.

Not including his sermons and letters, Augustine's surviving works are listed under 117 titles.[323] Our focus in this section will be to consider the books that were written expressly to spiritual leaders to resource them in their ministries although the argument could be made that all of Augustine's writings could have served to edify the clergy. In 19 books Augustine resourced clergy in areas of theology and exegesis, apologetics toward maintaining sound doctrine, practical church matters, and toward spiritual growth. In response to some of his correspondents' questions, he included another 10 books, not originally intended for the clergy, also to resource them regarding theological, exegetical, and doctrinal issues.

Theological and exegetical works. Augustine sent eight theological and exegetical works to clergy who had written him letters. In *Letter* 16*, we learn that he sent two sermons to Aurelius in what seemed to be a regular practice of aiding the bishop of Carthage in this manner.[324] As noted in the last section, in *Letter* 29*, he refused the request of Paulinus of Milan to write a *Life* commemorating some saints; yet Augustine referred him to the body of sermons that he had already preached on the martyrs. Augustine's *Letter* 162 to Evodius was accompanied by copies of *On True Religion*, his works on Genesis, as well as their Roman dialogues *On the Greatness of the Soul* and *On Free Will*.[325] In *Letter* 169, Augustine also offered Evodius a copy of a finished portion of the *City of God* and some of his *Expositions in Psalms*. And in *Letter* 23*, Augustine sent a letter to Renatus with his book *On the Soul and Its Origin* to resource him and other clergy in Mauretania Caesariensis on the nature of the soul.[326] Even though none of these works were originally intended to mentor the clergy, Augustine sent them in response to the needs of these leaders.

During his ministry in Hippo, Augustine wrote eight theological or exegetical works for the express purpose of resourcing members of the clergy. His first work, *On Faith and the Creed*, was a written revision of his address to the African bishops at the council of

---

[323] This number is taken from "Augustine's Works," *ATTA*, xxxv–il.
[324] *Letter* 16*.1.
[325] It was probably *On the Literal Interpretation of Genesis*; *Letter* 162.2.
[326] *Letter* 190; see Bonner, "*Anima et Eius Origine, De*," *ATTA*, 22.

Hippo in 393. Since one aim of this council was to adopt a Latin translation of the Nicene Creed, Augustine's work was essentially a commentary on the Creed.[327] While taking time to attack the thought of heretics, most likely the Manicheans, Augustine suggested that understanding the Creed was the initial step toward understanding the Scriptures.[328] He concluded by writing, "This is the faith which in few words is given in the Creed to Christian novices, to be held by them. And these few words are known to the faithful, to the end that in believing they may be made subject to God; that being made subject, they may rightly live; that in rightly living, they may make the heart pure; that with the heart made pure, they may understand that which they believe."[329] Because many of the North African bishops were uneducated and ill equipped to teach, it was important that they first be resourced with teaching on the Creed in order to properly teach their congregations.

A second work, the *Unfinished Commentary on the Letter to the Romans*, was basically the record of his question-and-answer session with some clergy in Carthage during a reading of Romans in 394 or 395.[330] While continuing to teach against the Manichees, Augustine put forth his initial thoughts on grace, faith, free will, and conversion, and also discussed the four stages of the history of redemption.

Less than two years later, in 396, Augustine wrote *To Simplicianus* replying to his former mentor's theological questions and specifically addressing passages from Romans and Kings. The most remarkable aspect of this book is that, from the first part of book 1 to the second part, Augustine completely shifted his view of grace from a high regard for human freedom to a stronger belief in God's sovereignty.[331] Augustine, commenting on this development in his

---

[327] As Clancy notes, Augustine's Creed was a mixture of the Nicene, Roman, and Milanese Creeds. For further works related to the Creed by Augustine, see *Sermon*, 212–15; also Finbarr Clancy, "*Fide et Symbolo, De*," *ATTA*, 360–61.

[328] *On Faith and the Creed*, 1.1; 2.2; 4.8, 9; 6.13; 9.17, 20; 10.22.

[329] *On Faith and the Creed*, 10.25, English translation from www.newadvent.org/fathers/1304.htm.

[330] *Reconsiderations*, 1.23.1; see Paula Fredriksen, "*Expositio Quarandum Propositionum ex Epistula Apostoli ad Romanos*," *ATTA*, 345–46.

[331] See Wetzel, "*Simplicanum, Ad*," *ATTA*, 798.

thinking in his *Reconsiderations*, wrote, "In resolving this question, I really worked for the free choice of human will, but the grace of God won out."[332]

Augustine began *On Eighty-Three Varied Questions* around 388 upon his return to Tagaste. As previously noted, during his preordination years, he largely dealt with anti-Manichean or philosophical themes.[333] Yet, from 391 to 396, he resourced spiritual leaders by treating exegetical questions related to Scripture, especially Paul's letters.[334]

In 422, Augustine wrote *On the Care of the Dead* in reply to Paulinus of Nola's question about the value of burying someone near the body of a saint. Though Augustine acknowledged the benefits of praying for the dead, he related that one's soul was ultimately in the hands of God and was not really affected by the place of burial.[335]

Around 428, Augustine addressed *On the Predestination of the Saints* to Prosper of Aquitaine and Hilary, two Gallic monks who were probably ordained clergy involved in the monastic movement in Gaul led by John Cassian and Vincent of Lérins.[336] Reflecting what has come to be known as a semi-Pelagian position, the men took issue with Augustine's teaching on sovereign grace in his book *On Admonition and Grace*, through appealing to his earlier works that gave more freedom to the human will.[337] Though Augustine did not hedge on his position of divine sovereignty, he explained that prior to writing *To Simplicianus* he simply did not understand the concept of election by grace, which allowed him to maintain his new position.[338]

Around 426, Augustine completed his 15 books *On the Trinity* that he dedicated to Aurelius of Carthage. Augustine began writing this work around 399 probably as the outcome of table talks in the

---

[332] *Reconsiderations*, 2.1; English translation from Wetzel, "*Simplicanum, Ad*," ATTA, 798.
[333] See Eric Plumer, "*Diversis Quaestionibus Octoginta Tribus, De*," ATTA, 276–77.
[334] *On Eighty-Three Varied Questions*, 51–75; 82; see Plumer, "*Diversis Quaestionibus Octoginta Tribus, De*," ATTA, 276–77.
[335] *On the Care of the Dead*, 1.3; 2.4; 18.22; see Plumer, "*Cura Mortuis Gerenda, De*," ATTA, 259.
[336] See Bonner, "*Praedestinatione Sanctorum, De*," ATTA, 669.
[337] *Letters* 225–26; they were referring to his works *Expositions on Six Questions: Raised by Pagans and Commentary on Statements in the Letter to the Romans*. See Bonner, "*Praedestinatione Sanctorum, De*," ATTA, 669.
[338] *On the Predestination of the Saints*, 3.7; 4.8.

Hippo monastery. While composed as a prayer and meditation, it also sounded the depths of the theology of the Godhead. Williams writes, "The genius of [*On the Trinity*] is its fusion of speculation and prayer, its presentation of trinitarian theology as, ultimately, nothing other than a teasing out of what it is to be converted and to come to live in Christ."[339] In the first four books, Augustine exegeted passages related to the incarnation while treating scriptural terms related to the Trinity. Books 5 to 7 were more apologetic in nature and addressed Arian claims.[340] In the final eight books, Augustine, admitting the inadequacy of language, considered the analogies relevant to the Trinity. He was also careful to assert the equality of the members of the Godhead.[341] In the concluding books of this work, he showed the relation of the Trinity to the process of sanctification in the believer. Williams adds, "We are not here thinking about an image that is simply an aid to more accurate conceptualizing: the realizing of the image is inseparable from the whole process of sanctification."[342] Through this work Augustine resourced Aurelius and the African clergy with a theological work that ministered to them intellectually and spiritually. He dedicated it to Aurelius but also referred it to Evodius, Deogratias, and Theodorus in reply to their questions.[343]

Augustine's final resource to the clergy was an exegetical work *On Teaching Christianity*. Begun in 396 shortly after his consecration as cobishop of Hippo, Augustine completed the final portion in 426 while writing *Reconsiderations*.[344] Kevane suggests that the work may have originated at the request of Aurelius and was designed to serve clergy, monks, and Christians.[345] Like *On Faith and the Creed*, it was especially needed because the North African church lacked clergy skilled in interpreting the Scriptures. Although van der Meer refers to *On Teaching Christianity* as a manual for

---

[339] See Rowan Williams, *"Trinitate, De,"* *ATTA*, 850.

[340] Ibid., 846.

[341] *On the Trinity*, 15.19.33; see Williams, *"Trinitate, De,"* *ATTA*, 847.

[342] See Williams, *"Trinitate, De,"* *ATTA*, 850.

[343] *Letters* 174; 162; 173A.

[344] *Reconsiderations*, 2.4; see O'Donnell, *"Doctrina Christiana, De,"* *ATTA*, 278.

[345] See Kevane, "Augustine's *De Doctrina Christiana*: A Treatise on Christian Education," *Recherches Augustiniennes* 4 (1966): 100–1, 128; and Ladner, *Ideal of Reform*, 373.

preachers, and Kevane argues that it was essentially a Christian approach to reforming classical education, I will consider this work as a mentoring resource to clergy charged with communicating the Christian faith.[346] Based on the presupposition that the Scriptures were authoritative and that the teacher must have a pious heart, the work was comprised of four books intended to teach hermeneutics to help benefit the church rather than satisfy the speculation of scholars.[347] Augustine expressly wrote that his intention was to serve this aim:

> So [that] the man who is in possession of the rules which I here attempt to lay down, if he meet with an obscure passage in the books which he reads, will not need an interpreter to lay open the secret to him, but, holding fast by certain rules, and following up certain indications, will arrive at the hidden sense without any error, or at least without falling into any gross absurdity. And so although it will sufficiently appear in the course of the work itself that no one can justly object to this undertaking of mine, which has no other object than to be of service.[348]

In book 1, Augustine treated Christian doctrine in a style similar to *On Faith and the Creed*. In book 2 he dealt with resolving the apparent ambiguities of Scripture by employing tools such as the original languages (Greek and Hebrew), science, and philosophy.[349] In book 3 he moved closer to the text of Scripture by giving some instruction on how to discern the literal or figurative meaning of a given passage. Also, working off of the rules of Tyconius the Donatist, Augustine articulated his own hermeneutical principles. In the final book he instructed spiritual leaders in actually delivering a message. Clearly influenced by Ambrose's example and instruction

---

[346] See Kevane, "Augustine's *De Doctrina Christiana*," 137.
[347] *On Teaching Christianity*, 2.8.31; 2.37.41; 2.7.9–11; 2.41.62; 3.1.1; 4.15.32; 4.30.63; "Preface" 1, 9; 1.35.39; 4.31.64.
[348] *On Teaching Christianity*, "Preface" 9. Unless otherwise indicated, all English translations of *On Teaching Christianity* are from www.newadvent.org/fathers/1202.htm.
[349] See O'Donnell, "*Doctrina Christiana, De*," *ATTA*, 279.

on preaching in *On the Duties of Ministers*, the former professor of rhetoric would not sacrifice the nourishing content of a message for its flashy form.[350] He wrote, "But we must beware of the man who abounds in eloquent nonsense, and so much the more if the hearer is pleased with what is not worth listening to, and thinks that because the speaker is eloquent what he says must be true."[351] Yet given the pious heart of the interpreter and speaker, Augustine did not prohibit a preacher from using elements of rhetoric:

> Since, then, the faculty of eloquence is available for
> both sides, and is of very great service in the enforcing
> either of wrong or right, why do not good men study
> to engage it on the side of truth, when bad men use it
> to obtain the triumph of wicked and worthless causes,
> and to further injustice and error?[352]

Hence, through *On Teaching Christianity*, Augustine mentored spiritual leaders with some teaching on doctrine, with tools for interpreting the Scriptures for themselves, and with instruction on delivering a message.

Doctrinal apologetic resources. In Augustine's letters we observe that he also sent four works of a theological nature, not originally intended for the clergy, which were included as a resource in the fight against heresy.[353] In *Letters* 24 and 25, Paulinus of Nola thanked Augustine for sending him copies of *On True Religion*, *On Genesis Against the Manichees*, and *On the Catholic and Manichean Ways of Life* to aid him in his struggle against the Manichees.[354] Paulinus remarked that these books were helpful "not for our instruction only, but also for the benefit of the church in many cities."[355] Also,

---

[350] See Ambrose, *On the Duties of Ministers*, 1.101. Augustine referred to Ambrose's example in *On Teaching Christianity*, 4.21.46, 48, 50.

[351] *On Teaching Christianity*, 4.5.7; also 2.36.54; 4.9.23; 4.10.24; 4.11.26; 4.12.28.

[352] *On Teaching Christianity*, 4.2.3; also 4.4.6; 4.13.29; 4.18.37.

[353] We have already noted that Augustine sent *On True Religion* and *On Free Will* to Evodius with *Letter* 162 as a theological resource to satisfy Evodius's speculation. Yet he seems to have sent them to Paulinus to resource him more specifically in the fight against heresy.

[354] *Letters* 24.2; 25.2; 30.2.

[355] *Letter* 25.1.

along with *Letter* 31, Augustine sent Paulinus a copy of *On Free Will* that also seemed intended to resource Paulinus in his theological challenges.[356]

Augustine wrote another seven apologetic works intended to help spiritual leaders who were seeking to uphold orthodoxy. In 414, Paul Orosius, a Spanish presbyter, came to Hippo seeking Augustine's help in the battle against Priscillianism and Origenism that was raging back in his homeland. The following year, as Paul was returning to Spain, Augustine sent with him *Against the Priscillianists*, a thorough refutation of these heresies.[357] In 416 or 417, after receiving the acts of the council of Diospolis from Cyril of Alexandria, Augustine wrote *On the Deeds of Pelagius*, an apologetic against the teachings of Pelagius and sent it to Aurelius as well as Cyril.[358] In 420, Augustine, replying to letters from Julian of Eclanum and some Pelagians in Rome, wrote *Against Two Letters of the Pelagians* to Pope Boniface to inform and influence the pope regarding this heresy.[359] As noted, in 421 Augustine sent his six-volume work, *Against Julian*, along with *Letter* 207 to Bishop Claudius to aid this Italian church leader with a reply to Julian's teaching.[360]

In addition to his letters to Valentinus and the monks of Hadrumetum, Augustine, around 426–427, supplied the men with *On Free Will* and *On Admonition and Grace*.[361] A theological resource on man's nature and will, it also served to persuade Valentinus and the monks to abandon Pelagianism. Finally, in 428 or 429, Augustine wrote *On Heresies*, a catalog of heresies prompted by the repeated requests of Quodvultdeus of Carthage. Because Augustine died in 430, the work was never finished.[362]

Practical church resources. Augustine dedicated another three works to resourcing spiritual leaders in practical church matters. Though they surely enjoyed a broader influence, all three books were initially written to resource church leaders in Carthage. In the early

---

[356] *Letter* 31.7.

[357] See Teske, "*Priscillianistis, Contra,*" *ATTA*, 684.

[358] See Bonner, "*Gestis Pelagii, De,*" *ATTA*, 382–83.

[359] See Bonner, "*Duas Epistulas Pelagianorum, Contra,*" *ATTA*, 288–89.

[360] See Bonner, "*Julianum, Contra,*" *ATTA*, 480.

[361] *Letters* 214–15; 215A; see Bonner, "*Gratia et Libero Arbitrio, De,*" *ATTA*, 400–1.

[362] *Letters* 221; 223; see Teske, "*Haeresibus, De,*" *ATTA*, 412–13.

years of his ministry as bishop in 399, Augustine responded to the deacon Deogratias and his request for help in preparing new believers for baptism with *On the Instruction of Beginners*. Unlike his response to some theological or philosophical questions, Augustine was content to accommodate Deogratias and his needs.[363] He wrote:

> I feel constrained not only by that love and service which is due from me to you on the terms of familiar friendship, but also by that which I owe universally to my mother the church, by no means to refuse the task, but rather to take it up with a prompt and devoted willingness. For the more extensively I desire to see the treasure of the Lord distributed, the more does it become my duty, if I ascertain that the stewards, who are my fellow-servants, find any difficulty in laying it out, to do all that lies in my power to the end that they may be able to accomplish easily and expeditiously what they sedulously and earnestly aim at.[364]

Similar to his thoughts in *On Teaching Christianity*, Augustine taught that the content of instruction should begin with a thorough summary of the Scriptures and that the Scriptures should act as the final authority for spiritual understanding.[365] Believing that the instructor was an agent of God's grace, Augustine emphasized the need to teach from a heart stirred by faith, hope, and love as well as from a contagious, loving communion with Christ.[366] The teacher must be humble and even willing to learn from his catechumen, he must cultivate friendship with his disciple, and he must care for the disciple's personal and physical needs.[367] Further, the instructor should not teach everyone in the same manner but take into account the educational background of the catechumen. Augustine

---

[363] See for example *Letters* 118; 159; 162; 164; 169.

[364] *On the Instruction of Beginners*, 1.2. All English translations are from www.newadvent .org/fathers/1303.htm.

[365] For instance, Augustine argued for the supremacy of the Scriptures over dreams. See *On the Instruction of Beginners*, 3.6; 6.10.

[366] Ibid., 3.6; 4.8; 5.9.

[367] Ibid., 11.16; 12.17; 13.19.

recommended interviewing baptismal candidates before beginning their instruction period: "Although the same charity is due to all, yet the same medicine is not to be administered to all."[368] Finally, in the last half of the work, Augustine practically demonstrated teaching catechumens by furnishing Deogratias with two model discourses.[369]

The two remaining practical works were meant to aid Aurelius in his ministry of overseeing the monasteries in Carthage. Probably between 397 and 399 Augustine wrote the *Rule*—a guide for how monks must live together in community and how superiors should lead.[370] While the Hippo monastery had no such written rule, as it seemed to function around the simple rule of the apostles, it was necessary for Augustine to articulate in writing a set of principles to resource other monastic communities in Africa. Around 400, he further aided Aurelius and the monks at Carthage during a time of crisis with his book *On the Work of Monks*. Essentially the monks wanted to cease from manual labor, spend their time reading, live off the offerings of the church, and adopt the practice of growing long hair.[371] Augustine responded by rebuking the men for their laziness and strange practices, and for twisting the Scriptures to support their proposed lifestyle.[372] While arguing that not everyone in the monastery ought to be set apart to teach the Scriptures, he admonished the men to a work ethic that conformed to the Scriptures.[373] With his exhortation he also shared his own commitment to work:

> We are not binding heavy burdens and laying them upon your shoulders, while we with a finger will not touch them. Seek out, and acknowledge the labor of our occupations, and in some of us the infirmities of our bodies also, and in the churches which we serve, that custom now grown up, that they do not suffer us

---

[368] Ibid., 8.12; 9.13; 15.23.
[369] Ibid., 16–27.
[370] See Lawless, "*Regula*," *ATTA*, 707–8.
[371] *On the Work of Monks*, 17.20; 3.4; 16.19; 33.41; see Bardy, "Les origines," 317.
[372] *On the Work of Monks*, 30.38; 31.39; 33.41.
[373] Ibid., 18.21; 3.4; 8.9; 13.14; 19.22; 22.6, 25.

to have time ourselves for those works to which we exhort you.[374]

In summary, Augustine advocated a balance between a contemplative and an active life.[375] Through the *Rule* and *On the Work of Monks*, Augustine mentored Aurelius as the bishop overseeing the monasteries of Carthage as well as the monks themselves.

Spiritual encouragement. It would be impossible to consider Augustine's mentoring works without acknowledging the importance of his *Confessions*. Though it was read widely in Augustine's day by the laity as well as the clergy, we must remember that the work probably originated at the request of Paulinus of Nola, who wanted to know more about Augustine's spiritual journey. Hence, through *Confessions*, a work that grew out of his letters, Augustine's testimony and example influenced Paulinus and other clergy toward intimacy with God, humility, transparency, and embracing the lifelong journey in the progress of faith.

Church Councils

Following the examples of Cyprian, Basil, and Ambrose, Augustine "took part whenever he could in the councils which the holy bishops held in various provinces."[376] In collaboration with Aurelius, Augustine firmly believed that councils were authoritative and necessary to transform the African church.[377] Two times in *Letter* 22, Augustine wrote to Aurelius of challenges in the church that needed to be "healed . . . by the authority of a council" and "by the heavy sword of councils."[378] The letter also seems to suggest that Augustine was strongly encouraging the bishop of Carthage to use the full mantle of his leadership to convene these gatherings. While Augustine believed that the councils could change the church, he also seemed to enjoy a mentoring influence on the

---

[374] Ibid., 29.37. All English translations of *On the Work of Monks* are from www.newadvent .org/fathers/1314.

[375] Ibid., 17.20.

[376] Possidius, *Life of Augustine*, 21.1.

[377] See Doyle, *The Bishop as Disciplinarian*, 249; and F. L. Cross, "History and Fiction in the African Canons," *JTS* 12 (1961): 229.

[378] *Letter* 22.1.4; 22.1.2; see Cross, "History and Fiction in the African Canons," 229.

bishops of North Africa through his participation in the councils. Between 393 and 427, the evidence suggests that Augustine participated in 22 gatherings of bishops, most of which were convened by Aurelius in Carthage though a handful of others took place locally in Numidia.[379] I will summarize the councils that Augustine attended, considering the issues addressed and the actions taken, followed by a discussion on how Augustine mentored through them.[380]

We have repeatedly mentioned Augustine's presence at the council of Hippo in October 393.[381] Having been a presbyter for a little more than two years, Augustine resourced the clergy in an exegetical manner with his teaching on the Creed that later took the form of the book *On Faith and the Creed*. In a similar vein he probably gave support to canon 38 of the council, which affirmed the books of the canonical Scriptures.[382] Finally, in light of his correspondence with Aurelius and Alypius, Augustine seems to have had an influential role in the council's adoption of a canon prohibiting banquets in the church facility, which effectively reformed the *laetitia* festival.[383]

The following year, in June 394, the African bishops gathered for a council in Carthage. Little is known about this meeting since the acts have not survived, but Augustine seems to have had yet another occasion to instruct the bishops from the Scriptures by responding to their questions on Romans. This later took the form of his *Unfinished Commentary on the Letter to the Romans*. Although Perler argues that this discussion probably did not take place within

---

[379] In the period mentioned Aurelius presided over 25 councils in 393–94, 397 (two meetings), 399, 401 (two meetings), 402–5, 407, 408 (two meetings), 409–10, 411 (two meetings), 416, 418–19, 421, 423–24, 427. Apart from the councils of 393 and 427 (both held in Hippo) as well as 402 (Milevus), the rest convened in Carthage. Augustine was present for every council except those of 408 (both meetings), 409, 411 (second meeting), 416, and possibly 421. The local Numidian councils took place in 412 (Zerta), 416 (Milevus), and 422 (Fussala). See Perler, *Les Voyages,* 430–76.

[380] Due to a lack of evidence, we are unable to discuss the councils of June 397, April 399, and 427 (Hippo). See Hefele, *Histoire des Conciles,* 2.1.99–100.

[381] Cross ("History and Fiction in the African Canons," 229) suggests that the choice of Hippo as a meeting place testified to Augustine's influence to make the gathering happen.

[382] *Letter* 64.3; see commentary in WSA, 2.1.258 and Hefele, *Histoire des Conciles,* 2.1.89.

[383] *Letters* 22; 29; see Bonner, *St. Augustine,* 117; and Hefele, *Histoire des Conciles,* 2.1.88.

the council itself, Augustine was engaged in equipping a group of gathered church leaders in a theological and exegetical manner.[384]

In the second council of 397, which met in August, the bishop of Hippo once again joined with his colleagues in upholding the books of the canonical Scriptures. As noted, Augustine referred to canon 47 of this council and to canon 38 of the 393 council in admonishing the presbyter Quintianus for having read noncanonical books in church.[385]

Two councils were convened in Carthage in 401, the first in June and the second in September. The main issues at the June meeting included the concern over a lack of clergy in the North African church, which prompted a letter being sent to the pope and some Italian bishops seeking their accord to ordain clergy who had come from Donatism. The second issue addressed was the removal of Bishop Equitius of Hippo Diarrhytus. After a three-month break the bishops met again in September. Conforming to the wishes of the Italian bishops, they decided that former Donatists should not be ordained except in extreme cases.[386] Regarding the church at Hippo Diarrhytus, a group of 20 bishops, including Augustine and Alypius, were commissioned to go immediately and restore order in the church and set apart a new bishop.[387] Two significant canons pertaining to church leadership were also drafted in this meeting. Canon 13 allowed an accused clergy up to one year to appeal his charges; although canon 14 forbade a monk from one diocese from being ordained or named the head of a monastery in another diocese. Augustine's *Letter* 60 to Aurelius, which addressed the issue of a monk leaving a monastery in one diocese and then being ordained in another, effectively served as a reminder of canon 14.[388] The final significant resolution of the second council of 401 was its implementation of a missionary strategy to convert the predominantly Donatist countryside.[389]

---

[384] See Peler, *Les Voyages*, 162; and Hefele, *Histoire des Conciles*, 2.1.97.

[385] *Letter* 64.3; see Perler, *Les Voyages*, 222.

[386] *Letters* 61; 245.2.

[387] *Letter* 59.

[388] *Letters* 60; 65.

[389] *To Cresconius, a Donatist Grammarian*, 3.60.66; also Frend, *Donatist Church*, 252; Perler, *Les Voyages*, 233–39; Hefele, *Histoire des Conciles*, 2.1.126–29; and Mandouze,

The council of Milevus met in August 402 and began with a reading of the acts from the councils of 393 and the last council of 401.[390] The key issue facing the council was resolving the power struggle between Xantippus and Victorinus over who should become the senior bishop of Numidia. Augustine certainly had already influenced this process through *Letter* 59, which he wrote to Victorinus before the council. Perler suggests that the case of the deacon Timothy, a thorny issue involving Augustine and Severus of Milevus, was also raised at this council.[391]

Between 403 and 411, Augustine participated in six councils in Carthage that were largely consumed with the Donatist schism. In 403, Augustine's disciple and friend Alypius began to take a more active role by speaking on behalf of the Numidian delegation, of which Augustine was a delegate. The main issue was the drafting of a document, probably prepared by Augustine, inviting the Donatist bishops in every town to a local conference aimed at drawing the Donatists into the unity of the church.[392] Augustine put this decision of the council into practice by reaching out to Proculeianus, his Donatist counterpart in Hippo.[393] Augustine surely influenced the gathering of bishops in this way since he had been initiating toward the Donatists for seven years leading up to the council of 403.[394]

In June 404, the African bishops met again to seek a solution to the Donatist problem. As most were frustrated that the initiative from the previous conference had failed, they decided to appeal to Roman authorities for a forced edict of unity.[395] Augustine and a

---

Prosopographie, 111.

[390] See Perler, *Les Voyages*, 243; and Hefele, *Histoire des Conciles*, 2.1.127.

[391] As previously noted, the issue of Timothy was the subject of Augustine's *Letters* 62–63 to Severus and what prompted his visit (with Alypius) to resolve the matter. See Perler, *Les Voyages*, 243; Hefele, *Histoire des Conciles*, 2.1.135; and Mandouze, *Prosopographie*, 1073.

[392] See Perler, *Les Voyages*, 246; Hefele, *Histoire des Conciles*, 2.1.155; and Frend, *Donatist Church*, 252.

[393] *Letters* 88.7; 76; see Perler, *Les Voyages*, 249.

[394] *Letters* 33; 43–44; 49.

[395] Augustine himself was refused by Proculeianus (*Letter* 88.7) as was Possidius who reached out to his Donatist counterpart Crispinus in Calama and received a rather violent response from Crispinus's followers. See Possidius, *Life of Augustine*, 12.3–8; Mandouze, *Prosopographie*, 890–91, Perler, *Les Voyages*, 251; and Hefele, *Histoire des Conciles*, 2.1.156.

minority of bishops managed to persuade the council to ask simply for protection for the catholics while requesting punishment only for the violent elements of the Donatist party.[396] Finally, Augustine's disciple Evodius as well as Theasis were sent to the Roman court at Ravenna to present the requests of the council of 404.[397]

Before Evodius and Theasis arrived, Maximianus of Bagai, a bishop who had been beaten badly by the Donatists in his church, traveled to Ravenna and appealed directly to the Emperor Honorius.[398] Honorius responded in February 405 with an edict forcing the Donatists to return to unity with the catholic church, effectively rendering Augustine's influence and the decision of the council of 404 null and void. A council of bishops met in 405 and responded to Honorius's decree by sending two clergy from Carthage to thank the emperor in person for his action.[399] Though it was not his preference, Augustine nevertheless actively carried out the order for unity. Yet he chose to appeal to the Donatists as he had before—through persuasion, teaching from the Scriptures, and thoroughly documenting the history of the schism. Many of his sermons in 406 and 407, following the edict, also served as an apologetic against the Donatist cause.[400]

The surviving evidence from the council of 407, which met in June, does not mention the Donatists. Rather, the main item of business was the appointment of seven bishops, including Augustine and Possidius, who were sent following the council to render a judgment in an unspecified issue regarding Bishop Maurentius of Thubursicu Numidarum.[401]

In June 410, Augustine was present at the council of bishops in which the main issue was once again the Donatists.[402] In response to an edict of toleration granting more freedom to religions in the Roman Empire, the bishops decided to send four bishops, including

---

[396] *Letters* 93.5, 17; 185.7.

[397] Perler, *Les Voyages*, 252; see Hefele, *Histoire des Concile*, 2.1.155.

[398] *To Cresconius, a Donatist Grammarian*, 3.43, 47; *Letters* 88.7; 185.7, 27–28; see Perler, *Les Voyages*, 254–56.

[399] See Perler, *Les Voyages*, 256–57.

[400] *Letter* 43; *Reconsiderations*, 2.27; see Perler, *Les Voyages*, 264.

[401] See Perler, *Les Voyages*, 265; and Hefele, *Histoire des Conciles*, 2.1.158.

[402] As noted, Augustine most likely did not participate in the councils of 408–409.

Possidius, to Ravenna to lobby for the decree to be repealed. Not only were the four envoys successful in their mission; Honorius also granted their request for a mandatory face-to-face conference with the Donatists.[403] Surely, Augustine had a significant influence on the decision of this council and on the delegation sent to Honorius as his efforts for some time had been geared toward securing a meeting with the Donatists.

From the outset of the council of 411, it was evident that the Donatist party would be defeated. Though the gathering was called a conference, Marcellinus, the Catholic layman and friend of Augustine who presided over the meeting, announced that the purpose of the council was "to confirm the catholic faith."[404] While the Catholics surely had the advantage, the Donatist leaders proved to be defiant. Though Marcellinus had prescribed that each side would be represented by seven of its leaders, the entire Donatist delegation marched into the meeting place for the opening session.[405] The Donatist Bishop Petilian also demanded a roll call for each catholic and Donatist bishop claiming that the Catholics had conjured up bishops that did not exist.[406] Following the second day of meeting, the Donatists petitioned for a recess to verify the records of the roll call. Further, Petilian attempted to slander Augustine by referring to him as a Manichean. Unlike Alypius and Possidius, who at certain points lost their composure, Augustine refused to fall into Petilian's trap of personal accusation, and he graciously encouraged the Donatists to take their time and verify the record as well as to think about their arguments.[407] When the meeting reconvened five days later, Augustine's prowess as an apologist and rhetor were put on display as he masterfully defeated the Donatist leaders in debate by continually focusing on the core issue, the origins of the schism.[408] Though Marcellinus had clearly favored the Catholics in

---

[403] See Perler, *Les Voyages*, 277–78.

[404] Frend, *Donatist Church*, 275, 280.

[405] The conference met on June 1, 3, and 8; see Brown, *Augustine*, 332–33.

[406] In the end the Catholic bishops (both present and absent) numbered 286, whereas the Donatist contingency numbered 284; see Brown, *Augustine*, 332–33 and Frend, *Donatist Church*, 277.

[407] See Frend, *Donatist Church*, 286; and Brown, *Augustine*, 333–34.

[408] See Frend, *Donatist Church*, 286; and Perler, *Les Voyages*, 291.

the conference, Augustine's keen theological and rhetorical abilities only strengthened the verdict against the Donatists. As a result, the Donatists were ordered to give up their church buildings and to unify with the Catholic Church.

Following the council of 411, Augustine worked to put into effect Marcellinus's decision. Apart from encouraging the seizure of Donatist property and consenting to a modest punishment for the Circumcellions, Augustine's primary aim was to educate the Donatists.[409] Copies of the conference's acts were placed on the walls of the Donatist basilica in Carthage and sent to the capitals of each African province while Augustine had them read in the church at Hippo during Lent and encouraged other leaders to do so as well.[410] To make the proceedings more accessible to the less educated, Augustine wrote a simplified account of the council in his *A Summary of the Meeting with the Donatists*. His other postconciliar writings directed toward the Donatists included *Against the Donatists* as well as *Letters* 141 and 173.[411] In *Letter* 141, in particular, Augustine responded to Donatist charges that Marcellinus had received money from the Catholics in exchange for his verdict by reiterating in writing a clear summary of the origins of the schism. Perler makes the point that Augustine's preaching in the year following the conference also served to instruct the laity on the Catholic position.[412] On at least two occasions, Augustine preached to the former Donatist congregations in Hippo and Cirta.[413]

Between 416 and 418, Augustine took part in two significant councils as well as some other informal gatherings of bishops related to the Pelagian controversy. Although he was not present for the council of Carthage in September 416, a meeting provoked by Paul Orosius's arrival as well as news about Pelagius, the bishops suggested asking Augustine to research the theological issues related to Pelagius's

---

[409] See Frend, *Donatist Church*, 292, 294. The Circumcellions were a violent Donatist faction that actively sought martyrdom.

[410] *Letter* 28*.2; see Frend, *Donatist Church*, 290.

[411] *Letter* 139.3; see Perler, *Les Voyages*, 287, 305.

[412] See Perler, *Les Voyages*, 287–89, 293–98.

[413] Though the acts are lost, Augustine apparently participated in a local Numidian council in Zerta in 412, which met to discuss the Donatist reaction to the council of 411. See *Letters* 139.2; 144; Frend, *Donatist Church*, 290–91; and Perler, *Les Voyages*, 306–7.

teaching toward developing an apologetic.[414] Shortly after the council at Carthage, the Numidian bishops also gathered for a local council in Milevus to discuss Pelagius. Writing on behalf of the council, Augustine addressed *Letter* 176 to Pope Innocent, presenting him with the African position regarding the error of Pelagius's teaching. In addition to the letter, Augustine included a copy of his *On Nature and Grace*, which was a reply to Pelagius's *On Nature*.[415] In the summer of 416, Augustine met with Aurelius, Alypius, Evodius, and Possidius in Carthage to discuss the controversy. He probably drafted *Letter* 177 to Innocent on behalf of this group.

The African councils and meetings of 416 were effective in influencing Innocent as he condemned both Pelagius and his disciple Caelestius.[416] Yet Innocent died shortly thereafter and was replaced by Zosimus, who rather rashly reversed the decision of his predecessor and acquitted Caelestius. The African bishops responded with an informal meeting in 417 in Carthage to discuss their response to Zosimus's decision. This set the stage for the council of Carthage in May 418—a gathering attended by at least 200 bishops.[417] The council produced nine canons dealing with original sin, baptism, and grace that were surely based on the work and thought of Augustine, who had already published books dealing with these issues. The canons were sent to Pope Zosimus along with a letter reminding him of Innocent's decision to condemn Pelagius and Caelestius. The council succeeded in convincing Zosimus, who ultimately reversed his decision on the matter.[418]

The council of 418 also commissioned a group including Augustine, Alypius, and Possidius to keep track of the Donatist movements in North Africa. One task given to the group was traveling to Mauretania Caesarea in 418 to reach out to the Donatist Bishop Emeritus, who had refused to join the Catholic Church. Augustine not only preached to the congregation in Emeritus's basilica but also publicly debated the bishop in hopes of convert-

---

[414] *Letter* 213.5; see Perler, *Les Voyages*, 331.

[415] See Perler, *Les Voyages*, 332; and James McSwain, "*Milevus, Council of*," *ATTA*, 562.

[416] *Letters* 181–83; see Brown, *Augustine*, 282.

[417] See Perler, *Les Voyages*, 339; and Hefele, *Histoire des Conciles*, 2.1.189–91.

[418] See Hefele, *Histoire des Conciles*, 2.1.192–94; see Perler, *Les Voyages*, 342–45.

ing him. Augustine's unsuccessful efforts were recorded in his *Proceedings with Emeritus.*[419]

A final task of the council of 418 was dealing with the Gallic monk Leporius. As mentioned previously, Leporius fled Gaul over his heretical views on the incarnation. Yet, after spending time with Augustine, he recanted his heresy and probably made a public statement of his orthodoxy at this council. With the blessing of this gathering of bishops, Augustine sent him back to Gaul to return to his place in the monastery.[420]

The African bishops met again in May 419 primarily to deal with the case of Apiarus, a presbyter from Sicca who had been excommunicated by Urbanus, one of Augustine's disciples from the clerical monastery in Hippo. Apiarus responded by appealing his excommunication directly to Pope Zosimus, a violation of canon 17 of the council of 418, which prohibited disciplined clergy from taking their grievances overseas. Unfortunately for the African bishops, Zosimus took the side of Apiarus, defending the presbyter's right to appeal on the basis of two canons from the council of Nicea.[421] Augustine and Alypius seemed willing to accept Zosimus's verdict in the affair given that these Nicene canons, absent from their copy in Carthage, could be verified.[422] Hence, Alypius wrote to the bishops of Constantinople, Alexandria, and Antioch, requesting a more faithful copy of the canons, while a follow-up committee that included Alypius, Augustine, and Possidius remained in Carthage awaiting the results of the investigation.[423] Five months later two copies of the canons arrived in Carthage, one from Cyril of Alexandria and the other from Atticus of Constantinople, and neither contained the canons that Zosimus had cited.[424] Hence, through their patient

---

[419] See Mandouze, *Prosopographie*, 62. For more on the region of Mauretania Caesarea, see Map 101 in Richard Talbert, ed., *Barrington Atlas of the Greek and Roman World* (Princeton: Princeton University Press, 2000). Also Perler, *Les Voyages*, 295–96.

[420] *Letter* 219; see Hefele, *Histoire des Conciles*, 2.1.215–16.

[421] See Perler, *Les Voyages*, 351.

[422] We should also note the respect that Augustine, Alypius, and the African bishops had for Zosimus and his office since the pope had passed away in late 418. Thus, their report and findings would be addressed to his successor, Boniface.

[423] Possidius also contributed to the discussion regarding Apiarus. See Perler, *Les Voyages*, 354–55; and Mandouze, *Prosopographie*, 894.

[424] See Perler, *Les Voyages*, 360.

and thorough inquiry, Augustine and two disciples gave direction to this important council and helped influence the policies of how the church in Africa and Rome ought to deal with disciplined leaders and their appeals.[425]

In 422, Augustine and a local council of Numidian bishops met in Fussala to render a judgment in the case of the immoral Bishop Antoninus. As previously noted, Augustine modeled for his colleagues a gracious yet firm approach to disciplining a fallen leader. Yet Augustine also took responsibility for his poor choice in setting apart Antoninus for this ministry while making it a priority to care for the abused flock at Fussala.[426]

Though we know little of the council of Hippo of 427, it was probably Augustine's final church council, and it probably convened in Hippo because of his poor health.[427] This gesture alone demonstrated the great respect that Aurelius and the African bishops had for Augustine.

The African councils that Augustine attended were largely occupied with addressing theological and exegetical questions (393–394, August 397); confronting schism and heresy (403–405, 410–411, 416, 418); reforming church practice (393); and dealing with problems involving church leaders (June/September 401, 402, 418–419, 422, 424). How did Augustine mentor the clergy in the context of the African church councils? First, he served as a theological and exegetical resource for bishops in need of teaching. Augustine most clearly functioned in this role in his first two councils in 393 and 394, in which he taught on the Nicene Creed and responded to questions on Romans.

Second, he served as an effective model for resolving doctrinal controversies. In the council of 403, he led the way in initiating local conferences with Donatist clergy in order to win them to the Catholic Church. Through the council of 410, his influence was felt

---

[425] According to the council of Carthage in 424, Apiarus, who had been transferred to the church of Thabraca, was once again disciplined locally but then appealed to Pope Caelestinus, who supported him. In the end, Apiarus confessed to his misdeeds and the African bishops wrote to Rome expressing once again their concerns about the overseas appeal of disciplined leaders. See Hefele, *Histoire des Conciles*, 2.1.215; and Perler, *Les Voyages*, 379.

[426] See Perler, *Les Voyages*, 372–73.

[427] See ibid., 385.

as the Catholic bishops were granted a compulsory conference with the Donatists. In the council of 411, his superior skills in debate and apologetics were not only the key to defeating the Donatist contingency in the council but also served as a model for his colleagues to do the same. His impact was strongly felt in articulating the canons of the council of 418, which helped defeat the Pelagian movement.

Third, Augustine mentored the North African clergy by conducting himself with wisdom, patience, and focus. At the council of 404, when the frustrated majority of bishops was calling for a forced edict of unity for the Donatists, Augustine prevailed upon the bishops to ask Roman authorities for protection only. Even after Honorius's forceful edict in 405, Augustine still appealed to the Donatists through persuasion and teaching rather than compulsion. When he stood face-to-face with Petilian and his brash delegation in 411, he refused to respond to their accusations or be affected by their maneuvering. Rather, he demonstrated patience and waited for the opportunity to hammer away at the core issues of the schism. In this respect Augustine acted as Ambrose had acted at the council of Aquileia in 381. Augustine also demonstrated focus at the council of 419 as he and Alypius patiently called for a more reliable copy of the canons of Nicea in order to respond effectively to Zosimus's defense of Apiarus. He also modeled grace and kindness for his fellow clergy by affirming the orthodoxy of the reformed heretic Leporius in 418.

Fourth, Augustine influenced the clergy through his letters, books, sermons, and actions that followed up the work or decisions of a council. After the 393 and 394 gatherings, Augustine published *On Faith and the Creed* and the *Unfinished Commentary on the Letter to the Romans* to serve as a lasting resource for the bishops. Following the meeting of 401, Augustine's *Letter* 60 to Aurelius essentially reminded the bishop of Carthage of the decision made about monks being ordained.[428] After the Donatist-focused councils from 403 to 411, Augustine produced a significant number of letters, books, and sermons to support the decisions of the councils.[429] As noted,

---

[428] Augustine also referred to the authoritative decisions of councils in the following mentoring letters: *Letters* 63.2; 64.3; 65.2; 78.4; 215.2; 1*; 26*.1.

[429] *Letters* 88 and 76 were written after 403. *A Summary of the Meeting with the Donatists, Against the Donatists, Letters* 141 and 173 were written after 411.

Augustine had the proceedings of the 411 council placed on the walls of the Donatist basilicas in the provincial capitals of North Africa and also encouraged his colleagues in several cities to read them in their churches during Lent.[430] Augustine's drafting of *Letters* 176 and 177 following the council of Milevus in 416 and the informal gathering of bishops in Carthage later that same year served to articulate the African position against Pelagius and to influence Pope Innocent in this matter.[431] Augustine's efforts to carry out the decisions of the councils also included traveling as a member of a follow-up commission to deal with certain issues. He traveled to Hippo Diarrhytus in 401, to Thubursicu Numidarum in 407, and to Fussala in 422 to deal with church leadership problems. After the council of 418, he traveled with a team of bishops to Mauretania Caesariensis to seek to convert the Donatist Bishop Emeritus.

Finally, Augustine seemed to have a mentoring influence through the church councils by involving his personal disciples in the work of the gatherings. Beginning at the council of 403, Alypius began to have more of a voice. At the council of 411, he was the key orator for the Catholic position next to Augustine.[432] In 418, Alypius traveled with Augustine and the team of bishops to meet Emeritus. In 419, he demonstrated his legal training by requesting more reliable copies of the canons of Nicea. Possidius, as well, accompanied Augustine to Thubursicu Numidarum in 407, was sent to lobby at Ravenna on behalf of the African bishops in 410, participated in the debate with the Donatists in 411, and joined Augustine and Alypius in Mauretania Caesariensis in 418. He also contributed to discussion at the council of 419 and stayed on in Carthage with Augustine and Alypius to finish up the work of that meeting. Evodius was also sent by the African bishops to represent their wishes at Ravenna following the council of 404. The councils of 416, the informal group of bishops that met with Aurelius and Augustine to further discuss the Pelagian issue, included Evodius, Possidius, and Alypius. All three disciples were also listed in the salutation of *Letters* 176 and 177 to Pope Innocent.

[430] *Letters* 139; 185; 28*.2; see Frend, *Donatist Church*, 290; and Mandouze, *Prosopographie*, 496.
[431] Augustine included Pelagius's *On Nature* along with *Letter* 176.
[432] See Mandouze, *Prosopographie*, 56, 59–60.

Though Augustine never became the senior bishop of Carthage or Numidia, he was without a doubt the most influential African bishop of his day. Indeed, Aurelius, unthreatened by Augustine, used his position as bishop of Carthage to convene the African church councils and to provide his friend with a platform to exercise his gifts.[433] Hence, through influence and persuasion more than position, Augustine mentored the African bishops in the context of the councils through his abilities as a brilliant theologian and as a patient and kind apologist. In the follow-up to the councils, his influence continued through writing, teaching, and personal visits. He also seemed to have multiplied his influence by increasingly involving his disciples, who had become church leaders, in the work of the councils.

Personal Visits

Augustine is well-known for his dislike of travel, particularly by sea. He wrote to Paulinus of Nola in 408, "For we do not love the causes and necessities by which one is forced to undertake voyages across the sea; on the contrary, we hate them and try to avoid them as much as we can."[434] After returning to Africa in 388, he never again traveled by sea.[435] Yet the conditions of land travel also left little to be desired. Although the Romans built some excellent roads even in Africa, a traveler in Augustine's day would be fortunate to cover 74 kilometers in a day's time.[436] Even though horses, a horse-drawn carriage, and a type of carriage seat were available, Augustine and other clergy more likely traveled most often by donkey. Land travel was made more difficult by extreme weather conditions, poorly marked routes, and by bandits, thieves, and the Circumcellions.[437]

Yet during his tenure as presbyter and bishop of Hippo, Augustine logged thousands of kilometers across the provinces of North Africa. If he did not enjoy traveling, why did he spend so much

---

[433] See Bardy, "Les origines," 168.

[434] *Letter* 95.1; also *Letters* 122.1; 124.1.

[435] Some of Augustine's trips as bishop to other African provinces could have been accomplished by sea; see Perler, "Les Voyages," 25.

[436] Thus, Augustine's journey from Carthage to Mauretania Caesarea in 418, a distance of nearly 1100 km, probably took at least 15 days; see Perler, "Les Voyages," 31, 347.

[437] Possidius, *Life of Augustine*, 12.1–2; see Perler, "Les Voyages," 32–40; 48–53.

time on the road? Because one aspect of his burden for the ministry was leaving his church in Hippo to help meet the needs of the broader church in North Africa. He not only participated in the African church councils but also traveled to carry out the councils' decisions. Possidius added that Augustine also traveled frequently to resource various churches in North Africa through his preaching.[438] As Perler records, Augustine preached at least 153 sermons in eight other cities outside of Hippo between 393 and 424.[439] While most were preached around the time of a council, others were delivered during trips involving church business and during visits with friends and disciples. Canon 33 of the second council of Carthage of 397 stipulated that when a bishop visited the church of a colleague, he should be invited to preach and preside over the Eucharist.[440] Augustine's colleagues, including Aurelius, Alypius, Florentius, Severus, Antoninus, and possibly Possidius, Paul, Profuturus, Evodius, and Urbanus, took full advantage of this canon by having the visiting bishop of Hippo preach in their churches. While stopping over in Bulla Regia in 399, Augustine began his sermon by recounting how the bishop "retained me, ordered me, pleaded with me, and forced me to speak to you."[441]

While sacrificing his personal preferences by traveling for the needs of the church, Augustine seems to have continued a ministry of mentoring, especially to his Hippo monastery alumni, by traveling with them and stopping over to visit them during trips. Augustine communicated in *Expositions in Psalms* 119 that it was meeting a friend on the other side of a journey that made the hardship of it worthwhile.[442] His comments to Bishop Novatus in *Letter* 84 about the pain of being separated from his friend Severus also suggested that personal visits were an edifying time for Augustine.[443] In order

---

[438] Possidius, *Life of Augustine*, 12.1.

[439] He preached in Bulla Regia (399); Milevus (409); Utica (410, 412, 417); Hippo Diarrhytus (410–411, 419); Fussala (411); Tagaste (414 or 415); and Mauretania Caesarea (418); 134 of his dated sermons were preached in Carthage (397, 399, 401, 403–405, 410–411, 413, 416–419, 423). See Perler, "Les Voyages," 438–77.

[440] See Hefele, *Histoire des Conciles*, 2.1.115.

[441] *Sermon*, 301A.9; see Perler, "Les Voyages," 108.

[442] *Expositions in Psalms*, 119.6; see Perler, "Les Voyages," 35.

[443] *Letter* 84.1; see Perler, "Les Voyages," 14, 55.

to appreciate his contact with his disciples from Hippo, we will briefly summarize the journeys he made with some of these friends as well as his probable visits to their places of ministry.

Alypius and Possidius. In 395, Augustine and Alypius made the journey westward to Cirta for Profuturus's consecration as bishop. The journey must have taken several days and included a stopover in Thuburiscu Numidarum to meet the Donatist Bishop Fortunius.[444] In 400, Augustine and Alypius again traveled to Cirta together on unspecified church business.[445] As previously noted, Augustine and Alypius were among the 20 bishops who went to Hippo Diarrhytus after the council of 401 to restore order and set apart a new bishop.[446] In 402, following a misunderstanding between Augustine and Severus over the deacon Timothy, Augustine and Alypius went to Subsanna, where Timothy had previously been serving, to look into the matter.[447] In 407, Alypius and Possidius traveled with Augustine from Carthage to Thuburiscu Numidarum to investigate the issues surrounding Bishop Maurentius.[448] In 418, the two also made the significant journey with Augustine and others to Mauretania Caesarea.[449] Finally, in 421, Augustine and Alypius traveled to Tubunae to meet the Roman official Boniface.[450]

When Alypius accompanied Augustine to Cirta in 395 and 400, Augustine likely would have stayed over for some time in his native Tagaste with his disciple either on the journey to Cirta or on the return before returning to Hippo.[451] In 402, Augustine visited Alypius to sort out the issue of Honoratus, a monk in Hippo who was from the church in Thiava near Tagaste. Because the issue was delicate, Augustine not only advised Alypius on the issue by letter, but he made a personal visit.[452] In 407 Augustine and Possidius likely stopped over in Tagaste to spend some time with Alypius either

---

[444] *Letter* 44.1; see Perler, "Les Voyages," 208–10.

[445] Mandouze (*Prosopographie*, 57) suggests that it was another encounter with the Donatists. See *Letter* 53; and Perler, "Les Voyages," 231.

[446] Perler, "Les Voyages," 86.

[447] *Letters* 62–63; see Perler, "Les Voyages," 242–43; and Mandouze, *Prosopographie*, 58.

[448] See Perler, "Les Voyages," 265.

[449] Possidius, *Life of Augustine*, 14.3; see Perler, "Les Voyages," 86, 346.

[450] *Letters* 44.3.6; 220.3; see Perler, "Les Voyages," 86, 472.

[451] See Perler, "Les Voyages," 231.

[452] *Letter* 83; see Perler, "Les Voyages," 241–42; and Mandouze, *Prosopographie*, 58.

before or after the three had traveled to Thubursicu Numidarum.[453] In 414 Augustine also journeyed to Tagaste to participate in a local Numidian church council, where he surely stayed with Alypius while also preaching at least four sermons in the Tagaste church.[454]

As Augustine likely stopped in Tagaste in 400 on the way to Cirta, it also seems likely that Alypius and Augustine would have stopped and spent some time with Possidius in Calama, either before continuing on to Cirta or on their return.[455] Augustine's most significant visit to Possidius in Calama was in 408 following the violent attack that Possidius suffered in the church at the hands of the pagans in his city.[456] Because the local authorities did not defend Possidius in the attack, Augustine advised him to travel to Ravenna and appeal to the emperor.[457] Though Augustine did provide Possidius with advice, it seems that his trip to Calama was primarily to encourage his friend and disciple through this time. Augustine gave such priority to this visit with Possidius that this was probably the reason he was absent from the councils of Carthage in 408 and 409.

Severus. While attending the council of 402 in Milevus, Augustine probably stayed with Severus. A few months prior Augustine had been to Subsanna to deal with the issue of the deacon Timothy, which was a sensitive issue with Severus as Augustine's *Letters* 62 and 63 attest. The timing of the council of Milevus and Augustine's opportunity to visit his friend seem to have been crucial to their ongoing relationship.[458] The evidence suggests that Augustine and Severus did remain close, for Augustine visited Milevus again in 408 or 409 and delivered two sermons to that congregation.[459] He probably stayed with Severus during the council of 416, which met in Milevus.

Profuturus and Fortunatus. As noted, Augustine and Alypius traveled to be with Profuturus in Cirta in 395 when he was ordained bishop.[460] The following year Augustine and Profuturus traveled together

---

[453] See Perler, "Les Voyages," 265.

[454] See ibid., 325–26, 462–63.

[455] See ibid., 232.

[456] *Letter* 91; see Perler, "Les Voyages," 266–69; and Bonner, *St. Augustine*, 125.

[457] See Mandouze, *Prosopographie*, 891.

[458] See Perler, "Les Voyages," 242–43.

[459] See ibid., 272–73.

[460] *Letter* 53; see Perler, "Les Voyages," 210, 231.

through Numidia, possibly meeting with Donatist leaders, though the reason is ultimately unclear. During this journey the two discussed the issue of anger, which Augustine brought up again in his letter to Profuturus in 397.[461] In 400, probably shortly before Profuturus's premature passing, Augustine and Alypius once again visited their friend from Hippo. In 402, probably on his return from Thiava, Augustine visited Fortunatus, another disciple from Hippo, who was ordained bishop of Cirta after Profuturus's death.[462] Augustine probably stopped at Cirta to visit Fortunatus on the way home from Milevus in 409 as well as on the return from the council of Zerta in 412.[463]

Evodius, Boniface, and Antoninus. In 410, Augustine may have stopped over in Uzalis to spend some time with Evodius while traveling between Hippo and Hippo Diarrhytus.[464] Around 424 Augustine spent time with Evodius while investigating miracle claims involving the relics of the martyr Stephen.[465] Though the reason for the visit is unclear, Augustine visited Boniface in Cataqua in 414 or 415.[466] In 422, Augustine traveled to Fussala in order to remove his Hippo disciple Antoninus from his place of ministry while seeking to minister to the wounded congregation at Fussala.[467]

Conclusions

For nearly 40 years, Augustine was actively involved in mentoring spiritual leaders in Hippo, throughout Africa, and at times beyond. As we have shown in this chapter, his primary mentoring strategies included the monastery, letters, books, participation in church councils, and personal visits. What conclusions can be drawn from Augustine's mentoring forms? First, regardless of whether he had personal contact with a spiritual leader, his mentoring was warm and personal. The tone of his books and letters seems consistent with how he was portrayed in the monastery, in a church council, or

---

[461] *Letter* 38.2; see Perler, "Les Voyages," 86; and Mandouze, *Prosopographie*, 930.
[462] *Letter* 78; see Perler, "Les Voyages," 245.
[463] *Letter* 144; see Perler, "Les Voyages," 273–74, 309.
[464] See Perler, "Les Voyages," 280.
[465] *City of God*, 22.8; see Perler, "Les Voyages," 380.
[466] *Letter* 149; see Perler, "Les Voyages," 326–28; and Mandouze, *Prosopographie*, 150.
[467] *Letters* 209; 20*; see Perler, "Les Voyages," 369–73.

on a personal visit. Letters, as noted, merely facilitated a conversation that could not take place face-to-face. Second, we observed Augustine making use of all six mentoring strategies from the earliest stages of his ministry until his death.

Augustine combined multiple mentoring approaches within the same context. We have noted how Augustine sent several letters accompanied by books intended to resource the clergy.[468] We have also shown how he wrote letters to spiritual leaders prior to church councils, giving his thoughts on a pending subject while also following up councils with letters affirming or putting into practice the council's decisions.[469] In treating his involvement in the church councils, we mentioned how he traveled and made personal visits carrying out the will of the council. Often these visits were in the company of disciples or included a stopover to visit a disciple. We also showed that in the two delicate cases of church business involving Alypius and Severus, Augustine not only wrote a letter about the matter but also made a personal visit to these disciples.[470] After his visit to Profuturus in 396, he wrote a letter the next year reminding him of their discussion.[471] Augustine also resourced those who had personally come to spend time with him in the Hippo monastery with books and letters upon their departure. This was the case with two monks from Hadrumetum as well as Paul Orosius.[472]

Through Augustine's multifaceted approach to mentoring, he provided spiritual direction and encouragement, rebuke and discipline, practical advice for dealing with church matters, exhortation toward maintaining sound doctrine, as well as theological and exegetical help to teach the Scriptures and fight heresy. In many cases, he was personally available and worked alongside leaders of every rank of clerical office, resourcing them toward fulfilling their ministries to the church.

---

[468] *Letters* 24–25; 31; 162; 169; 173A; 174; 207; 214–15; 215A; 16*; 23*; 29*.

[469] *Letters* 22; 59; 60; 139; 141; 173; 176–77; 185; 219; 28*.

[470] *Letters* 83; 62–63.

[471] *Letter* 38.2.

[472] Augustine sent the monks off with *Letters* 214–15; 215A as well as *On Grace and Free Will* and *On Admonition and Grace* while Paul left Hippo with *Against the Priscillianists* in his possession.

Chapter Five

AUGUSTINE'S THOUGHTS
ON MENTORING

uilding on Augustine's approach to mentoring spiritual leaders outlined in the previous chapter, we will move toward
articulating his thoughts on mentoring. In keeping with our
practice, these principles will first be drawn from clearly observable and repeated behavior evident in his mentoring forms. In addition, his convictions on mentoring, articulated in his writings and
sermons, will serve to complement his behavior and enable us to
make an argument for a set of mentoring principles. In considering
Augustine's thoughts on mentoring in light of the New Testament
model presented in the first chapter, it will become apparent that
his principles were largely consistent, though to varying degrees,
with this model. Hence, his mentoring principles also included the
group context, the mentor as disciple, selection, the mentor-disciple
relationship, sound teaching, modeling and involving in ministry,
releasing leaders, and resourcing leaders. As a result, I will assert
that Augustine left a legacy that impacted the church in the period
following his death and even to the present.

The Group

Augustine's entire life was characterized by the need for friendship and the constant presence of companions. Friends like Alypius, Nebridius, and Evodius played a key role in his spiritual journey, but in addition his experience as a Christian and a leader in the church included a community of brothers pursuing spiritual progress together. As Augustine mentored spiritual leaders, he was undoubtedly committed to the group context.

Augustine's Model in the Group

Chapter 4 showed how Augustine went about mentoring men in a group context—the most evident form being, of course, the monastery. We gave consideration to the progress of Augustine's monastic itinerary from being more philosophical and contemplative at Cassiciacum and Tagaste to being church focused and concerned with the burden of ministry at Hippo. At each stage he was the prime mover in bringing men together to pursue spiritual growth through disciplines such as prayer, psalm singing, reading, dialogue, work, and service. For more than 40 years he lived daily in a community of spiritually like-minded men. From 395 to 430 he served as a bishop-monk, mentoring other spiritual leaders in the context of an ongoing ministry to the church.

We also showed how Augustine mentored in a group manner through his participation and influence in the African church councils between 393 and 427. He influenced the gathered church leaders by articulating sound teaching, by winsome arguments delivered to the church's enemies with patience and wisdom, and by serving on task forces following several councils.

Augustine also mentored during his travels. Whether traveling to or from a church council, serving on a follow-up task force for a council, or visiting one of his Hippo alumni, he was at each recorded instance in the company of at least a small group of disciples or church leaders.

Augustine's mentoring epistles also provide evidence for mentoring in a group context. No fewer than 25 of his letters to clergy were addressed to two or more recipients.[1] His encouragement, exhortations, and resourcing were intended for groups of spiritual leaders. In addition to the named recipients, his letters were copied, so they probably enjoyed a wider influence on other clergy and groups of clergy. He also coauthored at least 23 letters with fellow clergy. With addressees including the clergy, the pope, Donatist leaders, and secular authorities, Augustine penned 10 letters with Alypius, one with Possidius, five with the "brothers with him," and seven with other clergy.[2] Through involving these groups of spiritual leaders in his ministry of letter writing, he was indirectly mentoring them. Finally, Augustine indicated in his correspondence with Paulinus of Nola that he shared Paulinus's letters with the clergy and monks that lived with him.[3]

Augustine also mentored in a group context through his books. The theological and philosophical dialogues at table in Tagaste and Hippo helped him clarify his thought toward writing such works as *On Eighty-three Varied Questions* and *On the Trinity*.[4] While his fellow clergy and monks aided Augustine in developing his thoughts on these subjects, they surely benefited greatly from his input in these discussions as well. Alypius apparently contributed to the writing of Augustine's monastic *Rule*—an appropriate project for two brothers who had journeyed together for many years in the common life.

Augustine's Teaching on the Group

Given Augustine's observed commitment to spiritual growth through community, what did he believe about the group as it

---

[1] *Letters* 31; 42; 45; 80; 95 (Paulinus and Theresia); *Letter* 48 (Eudoxius and monks of Capararia); *Letter* 62 (Severus and brothers); *Letters* 78; 122 (clergy and faithful at Hippo); *Letters* 83; 15*; 22* (Alypius and others); *Letters* 84; 28* (Novatus and brothers); *Letters* 115 (Fortunatus and brothers); *Letter* 142 (Saturninus and Efrata); *Letters* 159; 162 (Evodius and brothers); *Letters* 173A; 25* (Deogratias, Theodore, and others); *Letters* 214–15 (Valentinus and monks of Hadrumetum); *Letters* 219 (Proculus and Cillenius); *Letters* 253–54 (Benenatus and brothers).

[2] *Letters* 41; 53; 62–63; 69–70; 170–71; 186; 188 (with Alypius); *Letter* 137 (with Possidius); *Letter* 110 (with "brothers"); also *Letters* 125; 159; 162; 254; *Letters* 88; 128–29; 141; 176–77; 219 (with various other clergy); Possidius and Alypius were among the clergy listed in the greeting of *Letters* 176–77 to Pope Innocent.

[3] *Letters* 31.2; 42.2.2.

[4] See Gustave Bardy, *Saint Augustin: L'homme el l'oeuvre,* 7ème èd. (Paris: Bibliothèque Augustinenne, 1948), 196.

pertained to mentoring spiritual leaders? From his sermons, *Expositions in Psalms*, and other writings, four key themes emerge: the group must live together in unity; the community itself is a means of spiritual growth; growth is facilitated by Christian friendship; and the group is a model for the church. Although much of what Augustine taught about growth in community relates to the monastery, my goal is to highlight those monastic principles relevant to mentoring leaders.[5]

Living together. In establishing the clerical monastery, Augustine made the conscious choice to live among the people of the church, its clergy, as well as the monks. In *Letter* 95, he wrote to Paulinus of his desire to live among citizens of the heavenly Jerusalem for their benefit.[6] In *Expositions in Psalms*, he referred to the monastery as a "common life" (*uita communis*), adding, "You cannot be separated from the human kind, as long as you live among men."[7] Ladner asserts that Augustine's commitment to living with a community of men in the context of serving the church defined his monastic stance. He writes, "For Augustine true monasticism is cenobitical, not hermitical, and also that it is apostolic or, in modern terminology, mixed rather than purely contemplative."[8]

Augustine's inspiration for such a common life was the example of the early apostles. As noted, before there was an articulated monastic rule, Augustine and his companions simply lived accord-

---

[5] For more on Augustine's monastic theology, see Charles Brockwell, "Augustine's Ideal of Monastic Community: A Paradigm for His Doctrine of the Church," *Augustinian Studies* 8 (1977); Adele Fiske, "St. Augustine and Friendship," *Monastic Studies* 2 (1964): 127–35; George Lawless, "Augustine's First Monastery: Thagaste or Hippo?"; Brian Patrick McGuire, *Friendship and Community*; M. Mellet, *L'Itinéraire et L'Ideale Monastique de Saint Augustin* (Paris: Desclée De Brouwer, 1934); A. Sage, *La Regle de Saint Augustin Commenté par ses Ecrits* (Paris: La Vie Augustienne, 1961); A. Sage, "La Contemplation dans les Communautés de Vie Fraternelle," *Recherches Augustiniennes* 8 (1971): 245–302; Tarsicius Van Bavel, *La Communauté Selon Augustin: Une Grâce Pour Notre Temps*, trad., M. J. Schuind (Bruxelles: Éditions Lessius, 2003); Luc Verheijen, "Saint Augustin: Un Moine Devenu Prêtre et Evêque," and Zumkeller, *Augustine's Ideal of the Religious Life.*

[6] *Letter* 95.5–6; see *Sermon*, 355.1; see Andre Mandouze, in Bouësse, 138.

[7] *Expositions in Psalms*, 99.12; 54.9, English translation from G. B. Ladner, *Idea of Reform,* 340.

[8] Ladner, *Idea of Reform*, 340.

ing to the precepts of Acts 4:31–35.[9] An important aspect of the apostolic model was that brothers dwell together in unity. In his sermon on Psalm 132 and this notion of unity, Augustine wrote, "And what does 'in unity' mean? He says 'and they had one soul and one heart toward God.'"[10] In the same teaching, he attempted to clarify the meaning of a monk living in a community. He wrote:

> For *monos* means "one," and not just "one" in any sense. . . . They therefore live in unity so as to make up one man, so that they really have what has been written "one soul and one heart." . . . They have many bodies, but not many souls; they have many bodies, but not many hearts. They are rightly called *monos*, that is, "one alone."[11]

Augustine further illustrated this oneness of mind and heart by referring to the group as the temple of God. In *City of God* he wrote, "We are all together his temple, as each one is by himself, for God deigns to dwell in the community of all men as he does in us one by one."[12]

The group as a means of growth. As Augustine lived with his disciples, he, like Basil, believed that the group itself was a vital means of spiritual growth, for the only vow prescribed in his *Rule* was a commitment to communal living.[13] How did Augustine conceive of the community as a means of growth? First, he believed that ascetic disciplines were essential for the Christian, and especially a monk, to make spiritual progress and that the best environment for such a commitment was the monastery.[14] The individual was strengthened in prayer, fasting, reading, study, work, and service because of the

---

[9] Possidius, *Life of Augustine*, 5; *On the Works of Monks*, 17.20, 25, 32, 38; *Expositions in Psalms*, 132.2; *Sermon*, 356.1; also Zumkeller, *Augustine's Ideal*, 131.

[10] *Expositions in Psalms*, 132.2; English translation from Zumkeller, *Augustine's Ideal*, 398; also Mary Clark, *Augustine* (Washington, DC: Georgetown University Press, 1994), 88.

[11] *Expositions in Psalms*, 132.6; English translation from Zumkeller, *Augustine's Ideal*, 400.

[12] *City of God*, 10.3.2; English translation from Zumkeller, *Augustine's Ideal*, 130; also *Letter* 187.13.38; *Sermons*, 336.1.1; 337.1.1; and *Rule*, 1.8.

[13] *Rule*, 1.2–4, 8; also Clark, *Augustine*, 89.

[14] See Mandouze, *L'aventure*, 167–68.

support and accountability of the group. Members of the community did not simply pray, for example, near one another or ask one another if they had prayed that day; rather, they were in the habit of performing this and other spiritual disciplines corporately. Hence, the group provided strength to do what the individual member was too weak to do on his own. For this reason Augustine pleaded with the monks to bear with those who were younger and weaker in their faith and not to abandon them:

> Will he who makes good progress retreat so that he permits no human company at all? What if before he made progress no one wished to suffer him at all? . . . Let your love then pay attention. The apostle says "bearing with each other in love, eager to preserve the unity of the Spirit in the bond of peace."[15]

Second, the group nurtured its members in pursuing intimacy with God. Clark asserts that the monastic enterprise was founded on the individual's yearning for connection with God. Hence, the community became a collective, contemplative soul, hungering for God while sharing the joys and sorrows of the experience with one another.[16]

Finally, the group enabled each of its members to be sharpened not only spiritually but also intellectually, especially toward a solid grasp of theology. Augustine was the catalyst in their theological formation through his regular teaching in the monastery. The spiritual leaders and monks in the community were even further developed through dialogue and mealtime discussions. While Augustine's lectures were certainly important and imparted much to the community, members were challenged to reason, articulate, and debate through dialogue, rendering them more capable thinkers and theologians.

The role of Christian friendship. A third aspect of Augustine's thought on spiritual growth in the group was the role of Christian friendship. In *Sermon* 299D, he declared that two things in life

---

[15] *Expositions in Psalms,* 99.9; English translation from Zumkeller, *Augustine's Ideal,* 388.
[16] *Expositions in Psalms,* 99.5; also Clark, *Augustine,* 88–89.

were essential—health and friendship—with the latter being the more important.[17] Although Augustine was personally motivated by friendship, his thoughts on the subject were certainly influenced by the preoccupation with friendship in the Roman world of the fourth and fifth century.[18] Though a thorough body of scholarship has been dedicated to Augustine and friendship, my interest is to focus on his views on friendship related specifically to spiritual growth.[19]

Before his conversion and during his initial years as a Christian, Augustine largely held to the classical Roman idea of friendship (*amicitia*), which was based on common interest and experience and often included some pursuit of wisdom or a shared understanding of virtue. Augustine's involvement as a hearer in the Manichean sect and his attempted communal experiment with friends seeking the "happy life" (*uita beata*) reveal his initial leanings toward *amicitia*.[20] While also characterized by affection and human sympathy, classical friendship was initiated by the individual choosing a like-minded companion.[21]

As Augustine matured as a Christian and spiritual leader, his later writings reveal a break with the notion of *amicitia* as he began to describe friendship as *caritas*, a love for God and neighbor as

---

[17] *Sermon*, 299D.1; also Donald Burt, *Friendship and Society: An Introduction to Augustine's Practical Philosophy* (Grand Rapids: Eerdmans, 1999), 57.

[18] See Lawless, *Monastic Rule*, 5.

[19] See Brockwell, "Augustine's Ideal of Monastic Community"; Burt, *Friendship and Society*; William J. Collinge, "The Role of Christian Community Life in Augustine's Apologetics," *Augustinian Studies* 14 (1983): 63–73; Eoin Cassidy, "The Recovery of the Classical Ideal of Friendship in Augustine's Portrayal of *Caritas*," in Thomas Finan and Vincent Twomey, eds., *The Relationship Between NeoPlatonism and Christianity* (Dublin: Four Courts, 1992), 127–40; Fiske, "St. Augustine and Friendship"; Lawless, *His Monastic Rule*; Joseph T. Lienhard, "Friendship in Paulinus of Nola and Augustine," *Augustiniana* 1 (1990): 279–96; McGuire, *Friendship and Community*; Mary A. McNamara, *Friendship in St. Augustine* (Staten Island, NY: St. Paul, 1964); John Monagle, "Friendship in St. Augustine's Biography: Classical Notion of Friendship," *Augustinian Studies* 2 (1971): 81–92; Tarsicius Van Bavel, *La Communauté Selon Augustin: Une Grâce pour Notre Temps*, trad. trans. M. J. Schuind, Bruxelles: Éditions Lessius, 2003; Carolinne White, *Christian Friendship in the Fourth Century* (Cambridge: CUP, 1992); Zumkeller, *Augustine's Ideal*.

[20] See Cassidy in Finan and Twomey, 129; Lienhard, "Friendship in Paulinus of Nola and Augustine," 291; and Lawless, *Augustine of Hippo and His Monastic Rule*, 5.

[21] See Cassidy, "Recovery," 129; Lienhard, "Friendship in Paulinus of Nola and Augustine," 290–91; and Lawless, *Monastic Rule*, 5.

modeled by the Trinity.[22] Brockwell asserts that as it related to Augustine's common life among monks and spiritual leaders, *caritas* was the "motivational core of monastic community."[23]

Given this brief definition, how was Christian friendship distinct from classical friendship? First, for Augustine *caritas* was like the Greek concept of *agapē* in which a friend was loved for his own sake and because Christ dwelt in him.[24] Second, instead of human sympathy or common interest providing the basis for friendship, *caritas* was a bond that was a gift of the Holy Spirit.[25] Hence, as God gave this level of relationship to Christians, their individual choice played less of a role in initiating friendship. Third, *caritas* was completely focused on God and was therefore not a goal in and of itself. Further, it was also a love that longed for others to find God and experience salvation.[26] Fourth, while *amicitia* was driven by common interest, *caritas* was characterized by a common faith and an agreement between believers on divine things. Finally, some observed characteristics of Christian friendship included trust, service, carrying one another's burdens, and spurring one another on toward good deeds.[27]

What were the outcomes of Christian friendship? First, *caritas* resulted in unity, the "one heart in God" (*cor unum in Deum*), which was the primary goal of the common life in the monastery.[28] Second, Christian friendship was in general a wonderful experience and had a blessed outcome for believers. In his sermon on Psalm 132, Augustine said, "There He has ordered his blessing; there those

---

[22] See Cassidy, "Recovery," 132, 134; *On the Catholic and Manichean Ways of Life*, 1.33.73; *On Eighty-three Varied Questions*, 83.71.1; also Zumkeller, *Augustine's Ideal*, 104, 127.

[23] See Brockwell, "Augustine's Ideal," 97.

[24] *Confessions*, 6.16.26; *Sermons*, 336; 349; *On the Trinity*, 8.10; Burt, *Friendship and Society*, 57; Cassidy, "Recovery," 138; and Lienhard, "Friendship," 292.

[25] See Lienhard, "Friendship," 291, 293; *City of God*, 19.8; and Cassidy, "Recovery," 129.

[26] *Confessions*, 4.9.14; *On Teaching Christianity*, 1.27.28; Burt, *Friendship and Society*, 62; and Cassidy, "Recovery," 130, 133, 137.

[27] See *Letter* 258; Lienhard, "Friendship," 292; *City of God*, 10.3.2; *Sermons*, 34.4; 358.4; *On the Trinity*, 9.4.6; Burt, *Friendship and Society*, 62–63, 66; and Cassidy, "Recovery," 132, 137, 139.

[28] *Rule*, 1.1; also *Letter* 258.1; Zumkeller, "Augustine's Ideal," 124; and Cassidy, "Recovery," 139.

who live in harmony praise the Lord."[29] Finally, *caritas* resulted in spiritual growth for the members of the community. Brockwell writes, "The more one placed the good of the community before his personal interests, the more rapidly he would progress in the spiritual life."[30]

Though Augustine did not fully abandon the classical notion of friendship that characterized his earlier life, the notion of *caritas* nevertheless transformed his reasons and purpose for friendship.[31] With the relationship of the members of the Trinity as his model, Augustine believed that *caritas* brought unity and oneness of mind and heart to the group, which facilitated the pursuit of spiritual perfection. Brown is correct in asserting that Augustine enjoyed more personal fellowship with his friends and disciples in the initial years of his ministry in Hippo, since later many were set apart to serve the church in Africa.[32] Nevertheless, Augustine continued to cultivate Christian friendship with these men through letters and visits as well as with new monks who were joining him in Hippo.

The group as a model for the church. As the Trinity modeled Christian friendship for the monastic community, Augustine also believed that the group in the monastery should be a model for the church. Though the monks chose a rather secluded lifestyle in order to be protected from the sinful influences of the world, they were still very much integrated into the life of the church, which meant they were not sheltered from its problems.[33] Regarding the church as the monastery's "mother," Augustine believed that the monastery ultimately existed to serve the church.[34]

What did the monastic community model for the church? Though regarded as a more consecrated group, in one sense they

---

[29] *Expositions in Psalms*, 132.13; English translation from Zumkeller, *Augustine's Ideal*, 404; also *City of God*, 19.13.1; Cassidy, "Recovery," 138.

[30] See Brockwell, "Augustine's Ideal," 100.

[31] See Lienhard, "Friendship," 293.

[32] See Peter Brown, *Augustine of Hippo: a Biography* (Berkeley: University of California Press, 1967, 2000), 467.

[33] See Brockwell, "Augustine's Ideal of Monastic Community" 108; and L. Johann van der Lof, "The Threefold Meaning of *Servi Dei* in the Writings of Saint Augustine," *Augustinian Studies* 12 (1981): 58.

[34] *Tractates on the Gospel of John*, 13.12; see van der Lof, "Threefold Meaning, 57.

were simply modeling the common life of a believer—a citizen of the New Jerusalem.[35] As they lived and served in plain view of the church, Augustine wanted to impress upon the laity that this life was not reserved for the "superspiritual" but was accessible to the average church member. Hence, the church could also be a community built on Christian friendship, having one heart and one mind. Cassidy comments, "The realization of true friendship is nothing other than the bringing to fruition the body of Christ."[36]

The Mentor as Disciple

Augustine demonstrated a personal commitment to growing spiritually from the time of his conversion to the end of his life. Hence, he mentored other spiritual leaders by inspiring them from his own example and by providing a model for them to imitate. Augustine once told his congregation in Hippo, "For you I am a bishop, with you I am a Christian."[37] In arguing for this second principle of mentoring in Augustine, we will consider how Augustine demonstrated a continual desire to grow spiritually as well as what he believed and taught about a mentor being a disciple.

Augustine's Example of a Mentor as a Disciple

The first way we observed Augustine as a disciple was in his commitment to ascetic living in the context of a community. He believed that an ascetic lifestyle was the most strategic approach to achieving perfection and that the community of monks provided the needed accountability and support.[38] Even though his books were widely circulated, he was in great demand as a preacher, and he was the most influential African bishop of his day, Augustine never outgrew his need for a group of men living under the rule of the apostles. In this sense his posture as a continual disciple resembled that of Pachomius.

Second, like Simplicianus, Augustine continued to grow by being humble about what he did not know or understand and by actively

---

[35] *Sermon*, 355.1; 356.1; also van der Lof, "Threefold Meaning," 58.

[36] Cassidy, "Recovery," 140; also Mandouze, *L'aventure*, 238.

[37] *Sermon*, 340.1; also *Expositions in Psalms*, 126.3.44.

[38] *Letter* 211.12; see Mandouze, *L'aventure*, 167–68.

inviting others' input. We noted in his famous correspondence with Jerome that Augustine invited Jerome's input on his arguments while acknowledging the benefit he received from Jerome's books.[39] Even during times of significant disagreement, Augustine maintained the humble posture of a learner toward his contemporary in Bethlehem.[40] He even sent a disciple to study under Jerome and then return to Hippo to share what had been learned.[41] Though the younger Augustine outranked the presbyter Jerome in the clerical hierarchy, he did not let pride of position block his learning and growth.[42]

In his correspondence with Paulinus of Nola, Augustine also requested books, posed numerous theological questions, and generally communicated with the posture of a learner.[43] Though responding to Simplicianus's theological questions, Augustine also asked for his former mentor's input on what he had written. He even requested Aurelius's feedback on an initial draft of *On Teaching Christianity*.[44]

Augustine's commitment to learning was not limited to interaction with other spiritual leaders. In his letters to the layman Januarius, which dealt with various subjects, Augustine confessed his limited understanding.[45] In *On the Instruction of Beginners*, Augustine advised Deogratias that a spiritual leader need not have an answer for every question to be able effectively to teach a catechumen. In fact, he urged the teacher to be open to learn from his students.[46] He also showed great humility as a learner by drawing from the hermeneutical rules of the Donatist Bishop Tyconius in articulating his ideas for scriptural interpretation in *On Teaching Christianity*.[47]

---

[39] *Letters* 28.4.6; 40.2.2; 71.

[40] *Letters* 67.2; 82.2.15; 82.5.34.

[41] *Letter* 73.2.2.

[42] *Letter* 82.33.

[43] *Letters* 31.7–8; 80; 95; 149.3.34.

[44] *Letters* 37.3; 41.2.

[45] *Letter* 55.35; also Lee Bacchi, *The Theology of the Ordained Ministry in the Letters of Augustine of Hippo* (San Francisco: International Scholars, 1998), 103–5.

[46] *On the Instruction of Beginners*, 11.16; also Frederick van der Meer, *Augustine the Bishop. Church and Society at the Dawn of the Middle Ages*, trans. B. Battershaw and G. R. Lamb (London: Sheed and Ward, 1961), 8.

[47] *On Teaching Christianity*, 3.1.30.42–37.56; also Daniel Doyle, "The Bishop as Teacher," in Kim Paffenroth and Kevin Hughes, *Augustine and Liberal Education* (Aldershot, UK: Ashgate, 2000), 91.

Though he spent much of his ministry battling with the Donatists, there was still something to be learned from their scholars.

A third observable way in which Augustine was a growing disciple was in his theological development. Within the course of his book *To Simplicianus*, he changed his views on grace, moving from favoring man's free will to assigning more importance to God's sovereignty.[48] He humbly related this theological journey to the Gallic clergy Prosper and Hilary in *On the Predestination of the Saints*.[49] Toward the end of his life, Augustine seems to have developed in his views on miracles and on the role of relics in Christian worship.[50]

A fourth way Augustine grew spiritually was through writing. In *Letter* 143, he declared to Marcellinus: "I freely confess, accordingly, that I endeavor to be one of those who write because they have made some progress, and who, by means of writing, make further progress."[51] In *On the Trinity* he added, "I myself confess that I have by writing learned many things which I did not know."[52] As a growing disciple putting the fruits of his study into published form, he regarded a finished work as a stage of the ongoing conversation toward understanding divine things. As he had invited feedback from Jerome, Simplicianus, and Aurelius, he also appealed to all of his readers, "Assuredly, as in all my writings I desire not only a pious reader, but also a free corrector."[53] According to Possidius, Augustine continued to grow spiritually through writing even to the end of his life: "Not long before his death, he reviewed the books he had dictated and published whether in the early days of his conversion when he was still a layman or in his years as a priest and then bishop. He revised and corrected anything he found to be at odds with the church's rule."[54] While taking time to edit his books and

---

[48] *Reconsiderations*, 2.1; also James Wetzel, "*Simplicanum, Ad*," *ATTA*, 798.

[49] *On the Predestination of the Saints*, 3.7; 4.8.

[50] *City of God*, 22.8; *Letter* 227; 29*; *Reconsiderations*, 1.13.7; also Brown, *Augustine*, 418–19; and van der Meer, *Augustine the Bishop*, 544.

[51] *Letter* 143.2; English translation from www.newadvent.org/fathers/1102.htm; also Brown, *Augustine*, 354.

[52] *On the Trinity*, 3.1.1, All English translations of *On the Trinity* are from www.newadvent.org/fathers/1301.htm.

[53] *On the Trinity*, 3.1.2; Brown, *Augustine*, 270.

[54] Possidius, *Life of Augustine*, 28.1.

categorize them for the library at Hippo, Augustine published his *Reconsiderations*, a book that carefully reconsidered and clarified his positions on an array of subjects.

Finally, Augustine showed a lifelong commitment to growing as a disciple through demonstrating humility and transparency. This humility was evident in his correspondence as well as in his conduct during church councils. Though a highly revered bishop, his transparency as one continuing to struggle with sin was a resounding theme of the *Confessions*. During the last 10 days of his life, he "had the very few Davidic Psalms on repentance written out and the sheets attached to the wall opposite his bed; then, while he lay ill, he looked at them, read them, and wept continually and copiously."[55] Breaking with his normal practice of receiving visitors, he spent his final days in prayer.

Augustine's Teaching on the Mentor as Disciple

In addition to his observed behavior, Augustine upheld these mentoring principles in his writings. In his reply to the questions of Dulcitis, written in 424, he expressed his preference for learning over teaching: "I for my part . . . like it better to learn than to teach . . . the sweetness of truth then should invite us to learn, the necessities of charity should force us to teach."[56] Content to remain a learner, as Cyprian and Ambrose had also been, Augustine was motivated to teach out of love for the church. As he grew in stature as a bishop and preacher, he asserted that a minister should always be a student in the school of Christ.[57] Around 415, he wrote to Jerome, "Although it is more fitting that old men should be teachers than learners, it is nevertheless more fitting for them to learn than to continue ignorant of that which they should teach to others."[58] He insisted that the effective

---

[55] Ibid., 31.2.

[56] *On Eight Questions, from Dulcitus*, 2.6; English translation from Ladner, *Idea of Reform*, 338.

[57] *Sermons*, 49.2; 91.5; 101.4; 137.13–14; 179.7; 270.1; 340.1; 355.2; *Expositions in Psalms*, 66.10; 126.3; *City of God*, 19.19; Rémi Crespin, *Ministère et Sainteté* (Paris: Études Augustiniennes, 1965), 183–84; George Howie, *Educational Theory and Practice in Saint Augustine* (New York: Teachers College Press, 1969), 221; and Luc Verheijen, "Saint Augustin: Un Moine devenu Prêtre et Evêque," 307.

[58] *Letter* 166.1.1.

A view from within the remains of the basilica of peace including the apse and seat from which Augustine preached.

preacher must be experiencing the reality of the faith that he is advocating: "For if the minister [of God] is not on fire when he preaches he does not set afire him to whom he preaches."[59]

"Making progress" (proficere). Zumkeller writes, "The inner life of the Christian consists, according to Augustine, in the ever-progressing renewal of God's image in man," resulting in "perfection in love . . . that is, love of God, and in God, of one's neighbor."[60] In his *On the Creed, to the Catechumens*, Augustine emphasized man's need for spiritual growth by comparing him to the perfect example of Christ.[61] Yet in another work he exhorts the Christian to make progress because Jesus Himself had grown in wisdom and favor with God during his life in the body.[62] In *On the Perfection of Human Righteousness*, he even argued that in light of man's imperfection

---

[59] *Expositions in Psalms*, 103.2.4; English translation from Ladner, *Idea of Reform*, 338.
[60] Zumkeller, *Augustine's Ideal*, 103–4.
[61] *On the Creed, to the Catechumens*, 3.8.
[62] *On Eighty-three Varied Questions*, 75.2; Luke 2:40.

and ongoing struggle with sin, the purpose of this life was to strive continually toward perfection.[63] To support his argument, Augustine referred to Phil 3:12–15, the same passage referenced in the New Testament model in chapter 1 to show that a mentor is a disciple.[64] Hence, when he wrote of the need for himself, spiritual leaders, and Christians in general to grow continually as disciples, he often described this by using the term "making progress" (*proficere*).

In *Confessions* Augustine remarked that believers needed to continue to grow spiritually after their baptism: "For even though people have been baptized and initiated, and have submitted to these material sacraments, they would proceed no further, did their souls not rise to a new level of spiritual life, and move on from elementary doctrine toward maturity."[65] His preaching also challenged the faithful to daily progress in their faith.[66] He recounted in *Sermon* 82 that it delighted his heart as a minister to see people experiencing life change as a result of his preaching.[67] In *On the Instruction of Beginners*, he wrote that a new convert's desire to grow gave the minister hope, which outweighed the disappointment of others who turned away from the faith.[68]

How did Christians make spiritual progress? First, Augustine argued that they advanced in their faith by observing bad and evil examples. In *On the Literal Interpretation of Genesis*, Augustine wrote that God sovereignly used bad examples to encourage believers to pursue spiritual growth. Sometimes wicked examples were even present within the church![69]

Second, Augustine affirmed that progress happened as a result of God's work and grace in the believer's life.[70] In one of his homilies on 1 John, he argued that because man naturally cannot love his

---

[63] See Zumkeller, *Augustine's Ideal*, 105.

[64] See *On the Perfection of Human Righteousness*, 8.19.

[65] *Confessions*, 13.20.28; also Heb 6:1–3.

[66] *Sermons*, 16A.1; 22.8; 169.15.18.

[67] *Sermon*, 82.12.15; also *On Teaching Christianity*, 4.6.9; 4.53; Doyle, "Bishop as Teacher," 85.

[68] *On the Instruction of Beginners*, 14.21.

[69] *On the Literal Interpretation of Genesis*, 11.14; also *Sermon*, 5.8.

[70] *On the Spirit and the Letter* 2.4; *Sermon*, 156.12.13; 227.1; *On Nature and Grace*, 58.68.

neighbor, the believer must depend on God to realize this love in his life.[71] Similarly, the monk, cleric, or servants of God must also rely on God for strength to maintain an ascetic lifestyle.[72] Though progress was ultimately dependant on God's grace and work, Augustine urged them to respond actively by placing their confidence in God's power to see spiritual growth happen.[73]

Third, Augustine believed that spiritual growth happened through obedience to the Scriptures taught in the community of faith.[74] As noted, Augustine was happy to see members of the church abandoning sinful practices because of their obedience to the Scriptures. In *Letter* 36, Augustine affirmed the presbyter Casulanus for his growth in the Scriptures, which enabled him to teach and be a blessing to the church: "For I am very pleased by your studies and by your words themselves, and I desire that you make progress at this young age and abound in the word of God in order to build up the church, and I exhort you in this."[75] Though Augustine did not enjoy his role as a judge, Possidius indicated that he faithfully carried out this ministry in order to influence the involved parties from the Scriptures, which would help them to achieve spiritual progress.[76]

Fourth, Augustine, like Pachomius, taught that spiritual progress occurred through an ascetic lifestyle pursued in community. While individual spiritual disciplines were important, the group itself, as we have argued, was also a significant means of growth. Augustine also commended celibacy, particularly in the case of virgins and widows, and manual labor as acetic disciplines that aided progress.[77]

Fifth, as Augustine believed that suffering led to the best of all possible worlds, spiritual progress was realized through pain, suffering, and difficulty. In a sermon on Psalm 29, he reminded his

---

[71] *Tractates on the First Letter of John*, 9.2.
[72] *Confessions*, 10.31.45.
[73] *Expositions in Psalms*, 45.12; *Letter* 214.7; *Tractates on the First Letter of John*, 9.2; *Sermon*, 34.8; *On Teaching Christianity*, 3.10.14.
[74] *Sermon*, 82.12.15; 227.1; *Letter* 36.1.1; *Expositions in Psalms*, 69.6; *Tractates on the First Letter of John*, 3.1; *On Instructing Beginners*, 7.11; Possidius, *Life of Augustine*, 19.3–4; *On Teaching Christianity*, 4.6.9; 4.53.
[75] *Letter* 36.1.1.
[76] Possidius, *Life of Augustine*, 19.3–4.
[77] *Expositions in Psalms*, 99.9, 12; *On the Predestination of the Saints*, 4.8; *On the Good of Widowhood*, 18.22; *On Holy Virginity*, 22.22; *On the Work of Monks*, 17.20.

listeners of Paul's promise to Timothy that "all who desire to live godly in Christ Jesus will be persecuted."[78] Suffering and hardship indeed came through atrocities such as the Vandal invasion, but they also came on a personal level as the growing believer was scorned or even discounted for his spiritual progress.[79]

Finally, a believer made progress in the faith by maintaining a future hope. The promise of the resurrection, heaven, and eternal life encouraged the sojourner in the earthly city to deal with life's hardships and to persevere in the walk of faith. Progress was further realized by renouncing the things of this world and meditating on heavenly and eternal things.[80]

Imitation. Because Augustine believed and advocated by example that a mentor should be a disciple, others considered him a model for Christian living and ministry. In this sense he joined Jesus, Paul, Pachomius, Cyprian, Basil, and Ambrose as leaders who mentored their disciples through imitation.

Possidius stated that even though Augustine was wonderfully gifted in preaching, teaching, and defending the faith, his greatest impact was on those who saw his life up close: "I believe, however, that they profited even more who were able to hear him speaking in church and see him there present, especially if they were familiar with his manner of life among his fellow human beings."[81] Possidius concluded his work with a vow to "emulate and imitate him in the present world and enjoy the promises of almighty God with him in the world to come."[82] Paulinus too referred to Augustine's disciples at Hippo as his "imitators in faith and virtue."[83] Though Augustine resourced his friend with letters, on one occasion Paulinus sent some of his disciples to Hippo to receive another kind of letter, the opportunity to observe firsthand Augustine's faith and example.[84] And Severus wrote that Augustine had taught him how to love God

---

[78] *Expositions in Psalms*, 29.2.8; 2 Tim 3:12.
[79] *Expositions in Psalms*, 118.20.1; 123.6; and *Letter* 167.3.12.
[80] *Sermon*, 170.11; *Letter* 2*.6; *On Holy Virginity*, 22.22; and *Expositions in Psalms*, 119.3; 122.3.
[81] Possidius, *Life of Augustine*, 31.9.
[82] Ibid., 31.11.
[83] *Letter* 24.2.
[84] *Letter* 31.2; see Brown, *Augustine*, 152.

and neighbor through his example: "I have already made some progress by imitating you, so that I desire to be that sort of man you are . . . you bring us to a love of our neighbor, which for us is the first step toward the love of God."[85]

In addition to these testimonies of Augustine's colaborers and disciples, how did Augustine mentor by example? First, he practiced what he preached. In *On the Work of Monks,* he exhorted the monks to work and reminded them of his own work: "We are not binding heavy burdens and laying them upon your shoulders, while we with a finger will not touch them."[86] Second, he was a model of service to the clergy. In the greeting of *Letter* 217, written toward the end of his life, Augustine referred to himself as a "servant of the servants of Christ."[87] Third, he left a mentoring example through his *Rule.* Though articulated well into his monastic itinerary in 399, Augustine's monastic rule, like that of Pachomius, encapsulated much of who he was as a monk and spiritual leader. As Monceaux puts it, "Justly, Augustine's *Rule* has been called his legacy to those who would imitate him in that life."[88] Finally, Augustine modeled transparency, humility, and the lifelong walk of faith of a spiritual leader through his *Confessions.*

Aside from his own example, Augustine believed that imitating holy examples resulted in spiritual growth. He preached that the foundation of the Christian life was imitating Christ—that is, loving, following, and becoming like Christ. In *Sermon* 304, he declared, "If we truly love him, let us imitate him. For we can yield no better fruit of love than the example of our imitation."[89] This imitation did not exclude the possibility of suffering and even martyrdom.[90] In

---

[85] *Letter* 109.2.

[86] *On the Work of Monks,* 29.37.

[87] *Letter* 217; also *Sermon,* 340.1; Maurice Jourjon, "L'évêque et le Peuple de Dieu Selon Saint Augustin," 157–58.

[88] See Paul Monceaux, "Saint Augustin et Saint Antoine: Contribution à l'histoire du monachisme," in *Miscellanea Agostiniano,* 2.61–89 in Zumkeller, *Augustine's Ideal,* 94.

[89] *Sermon,* 304.2.2; English translation from Zumkeller, *Augustine's Ideal,* 114; also *Sermon,* 96.7.9.

[90] *Letter* 228; *Tractates in the Gospel of John,* 123.3; also Michelle Pellegrino, *The True Priest: The Priesthood as Preached and Practiced by St. Augustine,* trans. Arthur Gibson (Langley, UK: St. Paul, 1968), 168.

encouraging the monks and nuns to maintain monastic discipline, including the vow of celibacy, Augustine urged them to imitate the examples of Christ and Mary.[91]

Through his preaching Augustine also held up the examples of saints and martyrs as models for imitation. As noted, Augustine refused Paulinus of Milan's request that he write a *Life* of the martyrs because he had already preached more than 100 sermons commemorating the testimony of many who had suffered and died for their faith.[92]

We have previously argued that Augustine viewed the monastic community as a model for the church. It is clear from *Sermon* 355 that he wanted the church to imitate members of the monastery at Hippo: "I think our way of life is plain for you to see; so that I too may perhaps make bold to say what the apostle said, though I can't of course be compared with him: 'Be imitators of me as I too am of Christ.'"[93] In *Letter* 41, Augustine also indicated to Aurelius that it was good for the members of the church to imitate the clergy, particularly those who preached.[94] Although Augustine desired that the church imitate the clergy who were imitating Christ, he also said that the monastic community at Hippo began with "brothers of good will, my companions in poverty, having nothing just like me, and imitating me."[95] While responding to Augustine's initiative as a teacher and spiritual leader at the outset of the Hippo experiment, there is no indication that the members of the garden monastery or clerical monastery ever ceased imitating Augustine. Leading with humility and transparency, Augustine wanted his men to imitate him; and as the church at Hippo imitated the monastic community, they were also imitating Augustine.[96]

---

[91] *On Holy Virginity*, 26–27; see Zumkeller, *Augustine's Ideal*, 114.

[92] *Letter* 29*.1; *Sermon*, 46.9; *Expositions in Psalms*, 36.3.20; *Tractates in the Gospel of John*, 123.5; *Against Faustus, a Manichee*, 20.21; also Louis Hamilton, "Possidius' Augustine and Post-Augustinian Africa," *JECS*, 12 (2004): 92.

[93] *Sermon*, 355.1; also Rémi Crespin, *Ministère et Sainteté* (Paris: Études Augustiniennes, 1965), 187.

[94] *Letter* 41.1; also Rousseau, "Augustine and Ambrose: The Loyalty and Single-Mindedness of a Disciple," 159.

[95] *Sermon*, 355.2.

[96] See Verheijen, "Saint Augustin," 315; and Rousseau, "Augustine and Ambrose: The Loyalty and Single-Mindedness of a Disciple," 159.

Like Pachomius, Antony, Basil, and Ambrose, Augustine's example was preserved through a *Life*. Though departing from the "holy man" genre that characterized the depictions of Antony and Ambrose, Possidius's work seems to have been a deliberate mentoring tool for the clergy. It was set in Augustine's daily ministry context of dealing with heretics, participating in church councils, living in a monastery, and carrying out the duties of church ministry. In addition, Possidius chose to include the full text of Augustine's letter to Bishop Honoratus, a practical resource for leading the church during persecution, which is significant because the letter made up one-fifth of the entire work. Hamilton writes, "The uniqueness of the [*Life*] stems from its intended clerical and African audience and from its practical (as distinct from devotional or liturgical) purpose."[97] As Possidius had lived with Augustine, observed the quality of his life, and desired to imitate his example, he offered the same opportunity to the clergy of Africa and beyond through his *Life of Augustine*.

Selection of Disciples

Though scores of spiritual leaders joined Augustine in the monastery and church during his 40 years in Hippo, evidence for how he selected men as well as his thoughts on selection is rather limited. It seems, however, that his manner of selecting disciples paralleled the development of his thought on Christian friendship.

Before his conversion Augustine's charisma and personality attracted like-minded friends to join him in the Manichean sect, to consider pursuing a "happy life" community, and to join him for a retreat in the country on Verecundus's estate. Augustine, who was inclined to friendship (*amicitia*), rallied friends who shared the same interests.

Upon his conversion Possidius wrote that Augustine "resolved with his companions, to serve God."[98] At this point his natural charisma coupled with the zeal of newfound faith continued to attract others. Lawless writes, "Meanwhile, this monastic impulse in the young Augustine manifested itself in his indefatigable desire for God and the intensely personal character of his experiences to

---

[97] Louis Hamilton, "Possidius' Augustine and Post-Augustinian Africa," 92–97.
[98] Possidius, *Life of Augustine*, 2.1.

such a pitch that his proselytizing temperament attracted others to share their lives with him."[99] Later the decision to return to Africa and establish a "servants of God" community at Tagaste was one that Augustine made with friends.[100] The selection of disciples at Cassiciacum and Tagaste was in many respects nothing more than Augustine inspiring a group of like-minded friends to pursue a common interest.

Although the garden monastery at Hippo initially reflected the values of classical friendship present at Cassiciacum and Tagaste, Augustine's manner of selecting men seemed to change upon his ordination as bishop and the establishment of the clerical monastery.[101] Once many of his friends who had followed him to Cassiciacum, Tagaste, or Hippo were being sent out to serve other churches in Africa, Augustine seemed willing to receive new monks and clergy who initiated toward him. Certainly within this group were men with whom Augustine did not naturally bond, which made Christian friendship (*caritas*) an even greater value in Augustine's selection. As Augustine received the likes of Paulinus of Nola's disciples, monks from Hadrumetum, Paul Orosius, bishops Paul and Eutropius, as well as others who joined the monastery indefinitely, his manner of selection resembles the precedent established by Pachomius.

Indeed Augustine had high standards of holiness for his disciples, as *Sermons* 355 and 356 indicate. Yet the only outward condition that he required for a potential monk or clergy was the renunciation of property and the vow to live a common life. Unable to predict how the disciple would turn out, Augustine, like Valerius, preferred to believe the best and give the potential disciple the benefit of doubt. In his teaching on Psalm 99, he related, "To recognize a man as evil, you must first test him within the monastery. So how do you shut out the man who is about to enter and who is to be tested afterward, but cannot be tested unless he has entered? Will you send all the wicked men away?"[102]

---

[99] See Lawless, *Monastic Rule*, 34.

[100] Possidius, *Life of Augustine*, 3.1.

[101] *Sermon*, 355.1.

[102] *Expositions in Psalms*, 99.11; English translation from Zumkeller, *Augustine's Ideal*, 389.

The Mentor-Disciple Relationship

Because friendship was paramount for Augustine, it logically follows that the relationship between mentor and disciple was an important aspect of his mentoring. Augustine's relationships were characterized by his demonstration of discipline and spiritual authority, through his posture as a shepherd, and through peer mentoring.

Discipline and Authority

As we have shown, Augustine cultivated an atmosphere of discipline and holiness in the clerical monastery. He demanded that the men renounce personal property and commit to common living. Women were not allowed near the monastery, nor were the monks allowed to venture out into places of temptation. Gossip was not tolerated, especially at meals, and the daily schedule was characterized by a rigorous program of spiritual disciplines and ascetic living. For Augustine, the superior gave spiritual direction to the monks on the basis of his spiritual authority.[103] He wrote:

> The superior should be obeyed as a father with the respect due him so as not to offend God in his person, and, even more so, the priest who bears responsibility for you all. But it shall pertain chiefly to the superior to see that these precepts are all observed and, if any point has been neglected, to take care that the transgression is not carelessly overlooked but is punished and corrected.[104]

Though his letters were generally kind in their tone, Augustine regularly used letters to encourage leaders toward a position of sound doctrine, to exhort them to spiritual growth, or to admonish them to be faithful in their ministries. Hence, Augustine wrote from a posture of spiritual authority with the intent to influence or persuade.

---

[103] Possidius, *Life of Augustine*, 5.1; 26:1–3; 22.6; *Sermon*, 355.2; *Rule*, 1.2–4, 8; 4.4–5; 2–4.

[104] *Rule*, 7.1–2; English trans. http://ccat.sas.upenn.edu/jod/augustine/ruleaug.html.

Augustine believed that a bishop should have spiritual authority over the church, its clergy, and its monks. As one who would give a greater account on the Day of Judgment than other clergy, the bishop needed to exercise his authority to aid those in need of spiritual healing while also protecting the church from evil influences.[105] Augustine used this authority to deal with spiritual leaders, especially leaders who had failed morally. During his ministry as bishop, he dealt with such issues with his own clergy in Hippo as well as with leaders in his sphere of influence in Numidia. Following a thorough investigation in which the accused were presumed innocent until proven guilty, Augustine exposed the sin to the entire church, invited the offending parties to repent, and excommunicated those clergy who refused.[106]

A Shepherd

While relating to his disciples from the authority of his position as bishop, his true effectiveness as a leader came through his example, which Possidius testified was a model for imitation.[107] Thus, he also related to spiritual leaders from the posture of a shepherd or pastor. In his letters to the clergy that dealt with practical church matters, exhortation to spiritual growth, and general encouragement, Augustine's tone reflected the care of a shepherd. This was also evident in his references to Paul Orosius and Quodvultdeus as "my dear son" and as "my holy son" respectively in the introduction of works that resourced these disciples against heresy.[108] In *Letter* 213, he indicated that he had been a father figure to Eraclius as well.[109]

Augustine also shepherded leaders by serving them. As a servant to the church and Christ, he ministered by being a "servant to the

---

[105] *On the Catholic and Manichean Ways of Life*, 1.32.69; also Brown, *Augustine*, 200; and Bacchi, *Augustine's Ideal*, 80–82.

[106] *Sermons*, 355.6; 356.14–15; *Against the Letters of Petilianus*, 3.43–44; *Letters* 65; 78; 82–83; 85; 209; 236; 248; 251; 267; also Roy W. Battenhouse, *A Companion to the Study of St. Augustine* (New York: Oxford University Press, 1955), 75; Crespin, *Ministère*, 190–95; and Doyle, *Bishop as Disciplinarian*, 277, 310.

[107] Possidius, *Life of Augustine*, 24.2.

[108] *Against the Priscillianists*, 1.1; *On Heresies*, preface, 1; also *Letter* 222.

[109] *Letter* 213.6.

servants of Christ."[110] Though Augustine's superior had spiritual authority within the monastic context, personal happiness and the need to be served by others did not figure into this authority. Rather, the superior used his position to serve the brothers as Augustine communicated in the *Rule*:

> The superior, for his part, must not think himself fortunate in his exercise of authority but in his role as one serving you in love. In your eyes he shall hold the first place among you by the dignity of his office, but in fear before God he shall be as the least among you. He must show himself as an example of good works toward all . . . he should strive to be loved by you rather than feared.[111]

We have shown that Augustine mentored the monks and clergy through teaching and through facilitating dialogue. Yet because he thought of a teacher as an aid to the "inner teacher" at work inside the disciple, Augustine regarded the mentor as a servant to the process of learning and discipleship.[112] Paffenroth writes that for Augustine "a teacher is there only as an occasion, not a condition."[113]

Augustine also demonstrated the posture of a shepherd by extending grace to the clergy. In some instances this grace was almost shocking in the case of immoral church leaders and heretics. We have noted the leniency and compassion shown to Antoninus in the aftermath of his abusive treatment of the flock at Fussala.[114] As the Pelagian controversy heated up, Augustine's convictions on grace and free will did not keep him from loving his theological adversary. In *Letter* 146 he wrote to Pelagius: "May the Lord recompense you with those blessings by the possession of which you may be good for ever, and may live eternally with Him who is eternal, my

---

[110] *Letter* 134.1; *Against Faustus, a Manichee*, 22.56; *Sermons*, 3.9.63; 46.2; 339; 340.1; *On the Work of Monks*, 29.37; see *Letter* 217; and Mandouze, "L'aventure," 139.

[111] *Rule*, 7.3; also *Confessions*, 10.4.6; *On the Work of Monks*, 29.37; *Letter* 23.1; also Verheijen, "Saint Augustin," 315.

[112] *On the Teacher*, 14.45.

[113] Paffenroth and Hughes, *Liberal Education*, 10.

[114] *Letter* 209.5, 9.

lord greatly beloved, and brother greatly longed for."[115] We learn from *Letter* 219 and from the acts of the council of Carthage in 418 that Augustine was gracious to the reformed heretic Leporius. By encouraging the church leaders in Gaul to receive him back into fellowship, he modeled restorative grace for these clergy.[116] Also, when he wrote to the young Bishop Auxilius, Augustine kindly confronted his colleague over his harsh excommunication of a family. His gracious and humble intervention also taught Auxilius about grace in articulating his principles for excommunication.[117]

A final way in which Augustine mentored as a shepherd was through patiently teaching his disciples. In *Sermon* 47, he advocated that a pastor should patiently instruct his flock from the Scriptures.[118] Yet Augustine's books and letters, which thoroughly treated the questions of spiritual leaders, also testified that Augustine was committed to this principle in his relationships with spiritual leaders. At the clerical monastery, a place of hospitality with an open door to visitors, Augustine generously gave of his time to instruct Paul Orosius, Leporius, and the monks of Hadrumetum, and others who came to study with him.

Peer Mentoring

Augustine's commitment to peer mentoring was evident as he collaborated with men like Aurelius during the African church councils. We have also noted Augustine's letters exchanged with peers like Paulinus, Simplicianus, Aurelius, and Jerome. We have shown how Augustine facilitated mealtime dialogue in the monastery in which he was challenged by the men to develop his thoughts on various theological subjects while also imparting much to them.

Even though he was clearly the authority figure or a shepherd, Augustine's language in communicating with other spiritual leaders was still fraternal. This was evident in the greetings of his letters

---

[115] *Letter* 146; English trans. from www.newadvent.org/fathers/1102.htm; also *Letter* 43.1; and Doyle, *The Bishop as Disciplinarian*, 277.

[116] See Charles J. Hefele, *Histoire des Conciles d'apres les Documents Originaux, Vol. II* (Paris: Letouzey et Ané, 1908), 2.1.215–16.

[117] *Letter* 250.1–3; 1*.

[118] *Sermon*, 47.9; also Howie, *Educational Theory*, 145.

and in the dedications of certain works. While it is not surprising that Augustine addressed peers like Paulinus, Jerome, and Aurelius as "brother" (*frater*), it is remarkable that he would greet a host of other clergy in the same manner.[119] In one letter he greeted Saturninus and Eufrates as "brother priests" (*fratribus presbyteris*), which is remarkable because they were former Donatists who had joined the Catholic Church and had been set apart as leaders.[120] He addressed Jerome, Aurelius, and a large number of other clergy as "fellow priests" (*compresbytero/consacerdoti*); Alypius and others were addressed as "fellow bishop" (*coepiscopo*); and a handful of leaders were called "fellow deacon" (*condiacono*).[121]

Sound Teaching

When Augustine was ordained to the priesthood in 391, his first request of Valerius was a sabbatical to study the Scriptures, which ultimately served to prepare him for his primary role of ministry—preaching.[122] Augustine also expected that other bishops and presbyters should be thoroughly trained for preaching.[123] Possidius depicted Augustine as a Bible teacher who carried out his ministry amid an ongoing battle with the likes of pagans, Manicheans, Donatists, Pelagians, and Arians.[124] Certainly Augustine regarded

---

[119] *Letters* 27; 31; 42; 45; 95 (to Paulinus). Augustine actually addressed Paulinus and his wife as "brothers" (*fratribus*). In *Letter* 95, he also calls them "fellow disciples" (*condiscipulis*). *Letters* 28; 40; 67; 71; 73; 82; 19* (to Jerome). *Letters* 41; 60; 174; 16*; *On the Trinity* (prologue); *On the Work of Monks*, 1.1 (to Aurelius). *Letters* 36; 38; 48; 61–64; 74; 78; 80; 83–85; 92A; 101–2; 110–11; 115; 122; 125; 142; 148–49; 159; 162; 164; 171; 173A; 177–79; 186; 190–2; 194; 196; 202A; 207; 212; 214–15; 215A; 219; 224; 228; 236–37; 245; 249; 250; 252–54; 269; 3*–6*; 8*–10*; 15*; 22*–23*; 25*; 26*; 28*–29*; *On the Instruction of Beginners*, 1.1; *On Admonition and Grace*, 1.1 (to other clergy).
[120] *Letter* 142.
[121] See *Letters* 28; 40; 67; 71; 73; 82; 19* (Jerome); *Letters* 36; 38; 64; 92A; 102; 111; 173A; 191; 194; 25* (other clergy); *Letters* 41; 60; 174; 16*; *On the Trinity*, prologue (Aurelius); *Letters* 59; 62–63; 65; 74; 84–85; 110; 115; 125; 159; 178; 219; 245; 250; 254; 269; 4*; 6*; 28* (other clergy) *Letters* 83; 98; 101; 149; 162; 164; 171; 179; 186; 190; 196; 202A; 207; 212; 228; 236–37; 5*; 26* (Alypius and other clergy); *Letters* 192; 222; 224; 249; 3*; 29* (fellow deacons).
[122] *Letter* 21; *Confessions*, 11.2.2.
[123] *On Teaching Christianity*, 4.4.6; also Eugene Kevane, *Augustine the Educator* (Westminster, MD: Newman, 1964), 117, 212; and van der Meer, *Augustine the Bishop*, 405.
[124] Possidius, *Life of Augustine*, 1–18; see Hamilton, "Possidius' Augustine," 88.

the Scriptures as authoritative for Christian belief and practice, and he firmly believed that teaching them was his most important contribution as a minister. This resolve for sound teaching was only quickened with the challenges brought on by heresy.

Augustine's Example with Sound Teaching

How did Augustine demonstrate the value of maintaining sound teaching as a mentor to spiritual leaders? First, we noted his involvement in the African church councils between 393 and 427 in which he mentored the clergy by providing much-needed teaching from the Scriptures, by modeling how to deal shrewdly yet graciously with heretics and by carrying out the decisions of councils through follow-up visits, letters, and books. Second, he wrote 31 letters resourcing spiritual leaders on theological issues and another 18 encouraging other leaders to maintain sound doctrine. Third, Augustine wrote eight theologically oriented books specifically intended for certain clergy, annexing another eight already completed books with letters in reply to the questions of other clergy. He also authored seven apologetic and doctrinal works specifically for spiritual leaders and sent four other completed works along with letters. Fourth, through his public debates and correspondence with heretics, he modeled defending sound doctrine for his colleagues in ministry.[125] Finally, his sermons, whether preached in Hippo or in another city, were often directed against the Manicheans, Donatists, or Pelagians, and thus provided a model to other spiritual leaders for how to uphold sound doctrine in their preaching.[126]

Augustine's Thought on Sound Teaching

Augustine's writings mention "sound teaching" (*sana doctrina*) nearly 30 times, mostly in his communication with Manicheans, Pelagians, and those affected by such heresies. What did Augustine believe about sound teaching? First, it exposed mere opinions and wrong ideas about God while at the same time making the attributes of God clear. In *Letter* 188, Augustine and Alypius urged Juliana to

---

[125] Possidius, *Life of Augustine*, 6; 7.1; 9; 12–14; 16–18.
[126] Ibid., 9.2; also Bardy, *Saint Augustin*, 252.

avoid opinions contrary to the grace of God or sound doctrine.[127] In his commentary on John's Gospel, Augustine asserted that spiritual lust and an unhealthy fascination with words and ideas carried men off into unsound teaching.[128] His personal journey as a rhetor who spent nine years among the Manicheans made him extra sensitive to eloquent words that lacked the substance of spiritual truth. In debating Faustus the Manichean, he argued that sound teaching affirmed and supported the existence of the Son of God and the Son's divine partnership in the Trinity.[129]

Second, Augustine believed there was a necessary and natural link between sound teaching and holy living. In *On Faith and Works*, he asserted that because of sound teaching, a believer can live out the holiness associated with his baptism, for sound teaching calls the Christian to conform his thoughts and actions to the teachings of Scripture.[130] In his replies to questions on Matthew's Gospel, Augustine affirmed that the Word of God transmitted through sound teaching transforms the heart and conduct of a hypocrite.[131] And in *Letter* 208 Augustine wrote of the good shepherd's integrity in leading his flock with sound doctrine and holy living worthy of imitation.[132]

Third, Augustine taught that sound teaching provided a guide for proper practice in the Christian life. In *Letter* 262 he wrote to a certain woman who had chosen to adopt a celibate lifestyle without the consent of her husband. Augustine pointed out that she had ignored sound teaching on the matter by not consulting what the Scripture taught on celibacy.[133] In *On the Good of Widowhood*, he similarly urged that decisions about perpetual virginity and widowhood be guided by an understanding of sound doctrine.[134] And he replied to Faustus's allegation that Christians sacrificed to martyrs

---

[127] *Letter* 188.1.1; also *Letter* 92.4.
[128] *Tractates on the Gospel of John*, 97.3; also *Against Faustus, a Manichee*, 21.16; and *Against Secundinus, a Manichee*, 26.2.
[129] *Against Faustus, a Manichee*, 5.6. For more on how *sana doctrina* clarifies the attributes of God, see *Against Faustus, a Manichee*, 15.5; *On the Nature of the Good*, 40; *Against Julian, an Unfinished Book*, 2.217; *On Genesis, Against the Manichees*, 2.8.11.
[130] *On Faith and Works*, 26.48; 5.7.
[131] *Questions on the Gospels*, 1.8.
[132] *Letter* 208.5.
[133] *Letter* 262.2; 1 Cor 8:1–5.
[134] *On the Good of Widowhood*, 6.9; 15.19.

by asserting that such a practice was not Christian at all because it contradicted sound teaching.[135]

Finally, Augustine affirmed that sound teaching was the teaching of Scripture itself. *Sana doctrina* follows the *hugiainousē didaskalia* discussed in the New Testament model in chapter 1. In *On Heresies*, Augustine rejected a group called the Severiani as heretics in part because they denied the Old Testament.[136] Augustine also communicated to Faustus that what made his teaching unsound was his rejection of the Scriptures:

> Hence you leave sound doctrine, and turn to impious fables; and in your perversity and estrangement from the society of saints, you reject the instruction of the New Testament, which, as we have shown, contains statements similar to those which you condemn in the Old Testament.[137]

In the same debate, Augustine affirmed that sound teaching was based on the Scriptures as opposed to Faustus's fables.

Augustine's View of the Scriptures

Augustine considered sound teaching to be essentially the teachings of Scripture, but Augustine accepted only the canonical Scriptures (*Scripturas canonicas*)—the "authoritative list of books belonging to the Old Testament or New Testament" that were affirmed at the council of Hippo in 393 and the second council of Carthage in 397.[138] In *On Teaching Christianity* he made a point of listing the canonical books before proceeding to the primary teaching on interpreting Scripture.[139]

---

[135] *Against Faustus, a Manichee*, 20.21.

[136] *On Heresies*, 24.

[137] *Against Faustus, a Manichee*, 22.21; English translation from www.newadvent.org/fathers/140622.htm; also *Against Faustus*, 12.27; 15.5; *On Adulterous Marriages*, 4.4; *Against Julian, an Unfinished Book*, 2.217; *On Genesis, Against the Manichees*, 2.8.11.

[138] R. T. Beckwith, "Canon of the Old Testament," *NBD*, 166; and Hefele, *Histoire des Conciles*, 2.1.89; also *Letter* 64.3.

[139] *On Teaching Christianity*, 2.8.12–13; also *To Catholic Members of the Church*, 19.51.

Implicit in their distinction as canonical, the Scriptures had authority over all other expressions of truth. First, they were superior to the writings of the philosophers. In *Letter* 82, Augustine compared the works of the philosophers to the Scriptures: "They are worthless, not because everything they say is false, but because they have put their trust in many false theories and, when they are found to speak the truth, they are strangers to the grace of Christ, who is the truth itself."[140]

Second, Augustine affirmed that the canonical Scriptures held precedence over the writings of even the most upright Christian leaders. Despite making positive reference to the works of Ambrose, Jerome, Athanasius, and Gregory of Nazianzus in *Letter* 148, Augustine wrote to Fortunatianus, "After all, we ought not to regard the writings of any people, though catholic and highly praised, as being on a par with the canonical Scriptures."[141] In *On Baptism* Augustine warned the Donatist leaders against looking to the writings of Cyprian of Carthage as an authoritative basis for their schism. Though holding Cyprian in high regard, Augustine wrote, "But who can fail to be aware that the sacred canon of Scripture, both of the Old and New Testament, is confined within its own limits, and that it stands so absolutely in a superior position to all later letters of the bishops."[142]

Third, Augustine believed that the Scriptures had authority over the words of any Christian leader or the actions of any council. In *To the Members of the Catholic Church*, he quickly dismissed the schismatic teaching of the Donatist bishops by comparing their teaching to Scripture.[143] This principle was also at work in his famous exegetical dispute with Jerome over whether Paul lied in Galatians about Peter's actions. He wrote, "For I regard it as absolutely disastrous to believe that there is a lie in the holy books, that is, that those men who gave us and put into writing that Scripture lied in their books."[144] In response to Jerome's assertion that there was a lie in the Scriptures, Augustine charged him with elevating Peter's

---

[140] *Letter* 82.2.13; also *Letter* 101.2; *City of God*, 19.19; and Brown, *Augustine*, 265.
[141] *Letter* 148.4.15.
[142] *On Baptism*, 2.3.4; English translation www.newadvent.org/fathers/14082.htm.
[143] *To the Members of the Catholic Church*, 11.28.
[144] *Letter* 28.3.3.

authority over that of the Scriptures.[145] In *On Baptism* Augustine argued that the Scriptures had authority over the decisions of church councils, while in *Against Two Letters of the Pelagians*, he wrote that the Scriptures clarified the erroneous decisions made by a council of bishops that supported Pelagius.[146]

The Scriptures were authoritative in that they settled doctrinal disputes, especially in the face of heretical ideas. Augustine urged the Donatists that a proper understanding of the nature of the church as well as a basis for why rebaptism was unnecessary could be found in the Scriptures.[147] He also communicated to the Pelagians that the question of original sin could be resolved through the Scriptures.[148] Finally, in his treatise to Maximinus, Augustine related to his Arian counterpart that a proper understanding of the nature of God could also be found in the Scriptures.[149]

As Augustine viewed the canonical Scriptures as the highest authority for Christian teaching and practice, he demonstrated that conviction by using them as his primary source for his writings and preaching. Possidius wrote of Augustine's "books and sermons, which flowed from the marvelous grace of God who inspired him, were filled with abundant arguments and based on the authority of the sacred Scriptures."[150] Just as Augustine warned Christians against assigning too much importance to the words of a bishop, he urged his own congregation to consider the Scriptures as superior to his own words. In *Sermon* 356 he illustrated this conviction by beginning the sermon by rereading a passage already read by a deacon. He explained, "It gives me more pleasure, you see, to be reading these words than to be arguing my case with my own words."[151] Indeed, Augustine's sermons and writings were saturated with the words of Scripture. Hamman notes that in Augustine works, some 40,000 references to Scripture have been counted representing every chapter

---

[145] Doyle, "Augustine as Teacher," 85.

[146] *On Baptism*, 2.3.4; *Against Two Letters of the Pelagians*, 4.8.20.

[147] *To the Members of the Catholic Church*, 3.6; 18.47; 20.56; 24.69.

[148] *On the Merits and Forgiveness of Sins and on Infant Baptism*, 3.6.12.

[149] *Against Maximinus, an Arian*, 2.22.2.

[150] Possidius, *Life of Augustine*, 7.3.

[151] *Sermon*, 356.1; see Brown, *Augustine*, 451.

and book from the Old and New Testaments. Hamman concludes, "The Scripture had become his thought, his life, and his teaching."[152]

Like Ambrose, Augustine did not attribute authority to the canonical books alone; rather, they needed to be interpreted properly by a bishop or presbyter walking in the way of holiness. Both Ambrose and Augustine were drawn into theological battles in their day because of heretical groups that misused or ignored the Scriptures. He labored greatly in providing his fellow clergy with *On Teaching Christianity*, a resource largely concerned with principles and tools for interpreting Scripture. As we learn from Augustine's heated exchange with Jerome, the task of interpreting the canonical books was "not like someone playing on the field of the Scriptures, but like someone gasping for air in the mountains."[153] In short, understanding and teaching the truth of Scripture was a serious matter for Augustine, and it was very much a part of his ministry burden.

Augustine at first asked Valerius for a period of time to study the Scriptures, but his hunger to grow in his knowledge of the Scriptures never ceased.[154] The Scriptures were authoritative for his own spiritual growth and for the spiritual leaders he mentored. The Scriptures were the main course of study in the monasteries at Hippo for spiritual leaders. Augustine wrote that Possidius "was nourished through our ministry, not in that literature that those enslaved to various desires call liberal, but with the bread of the Lord."[155] This training program formed "venerable men of continence and learning" whose "zeal for the spread of God's word increased,"[156] and they were sent to serve the churches of North Africa.

---

[152] Andre Hamman, *"Etudes Patristiques: Méthodologie, Liturgie, Histoire, Théologie"* (Paris: Beachesne, 1991), 274 (translation my own); also van der Meer, *Augustine the Bishop*, 343; and Kevane, *Augustine the Educator*, 117, 233.

[153] *Letter* 82.1.2.

[154] See *On Eight Questions, from Dulcitius*, 2.6; *Sermons*, 49.2; 91.5; 101.4; 137.13–14; 179.7; 270.1; 340.1; 355.2; *Expositions in Psalms*, 66.10; 126.3; *City of God*, 19.19; and *Letter* 166.1.

[155] *Letter* 101.1; See Brown, *Augustine*, 129–30; and Rousseau, "Augustine and Ambrose," 156–58.

[156] Possidius, *Life of Augustine*, 11.3–4; also Martin, *"Clericatus sarcina (ep. 126.3)*," 2.

Modeling and Involving in Ministry

Augustine performed his duties as a presbyter and bishop while living in community in the monastery at Hippo. There he ministered alongside his clergy and with other African bishops during periods of travel. Although Possidius argued that the quality of his life as a Christian was worthy of imitation, Augustine also modeled to other clergy how to be effective Christian leaders. His colleagues in ministry observed him in the roles of preacher, ecclesiastical leader, liturgist, judge, and property administrator; and they saw him administering in church councils, writing, debating with the church's theological enemies, and traveling on behalf of the church.

Augustine's Example of Involving in Ministry

How did Augustine involve men in ministry? First, he used every rank of the clergy in leading the worship assembly. Like Valerius he set apart presbyters to preach as well as to preside over the sacraments. At times Augustine sent his presbyters to other churches to minister as the needs of the diocese were constantly increasing. Deacons also assisted during the Eucharist and instructed the catechumens. Readers read the Scriptures and led in the singing of psalms. Like Cyprian and Ambrose, many of Augustine's readers were young men who were promoted to higher ranks of clergy given time and faithfulness on their part.[157]

Second, Augustine involved leaders in the work of the clerical monastery. As we noted in the previous chapter, each year Augustine set apart a provost who had administrative and financial authority over the monastery.[158] Other monks were entrusted with tasks such as dispersing gifts made to the monastery; looking after the community's clothes, shoes, and books; overseeing the kitchen; and caring for the sick.[159] Like the church the work of the monastery became so

---

[157] See Zumkeller, *Augustine's Ideal*, 44, 193; Crespin, *Ministère*, 180; and Bardy, *Saint Augustin*, 196.

[158] Possidius, *Life of Augustine*, 24.1.

[159] *Rule*, 5.3–11.

demanding that Augustine purposefully involved more monks in lead-ing it so that he would not neglect other aspects of his ministry.[160]

Third, Augustine involved many clergy in his ministry of writ-ing. As we have noted, 23 of Augustine's letters were coauthored by members of the clergy. More significant, however, was the large number of clergy employed to deliver letters. Acolytes, subdeacons, deacons, presbyters, and even bishops were among those who served as couriers.[161] Through identifying and often commending the letter carrier within the body of the letter, Augustine, like Cyprian, not only showed how much he valued having his correspondence safely deliv-ered but also how he appreciated the ministry of these colleagues.[162] Surely his appreciation for this ministry increased after his relation-ship with Jerome had suffered because letters arrived late.[163]

Fourth, Augustine involved his disciples, particularly Alypius, Possidius, and Evodius, in the African church councils. By partici-pating in conciliar debates, traveling to carry out the will of the council, or appealing to the pope or secular authorities on behalf of the African church, these leaders became increasingly influential in the North African church.

Finally, Augustine involved his men in some of his travels related to church business. This business—unrelated to the African coun-cils—at times included consecrating bishops, meeting with Donatist leaders, restoring order in churches plagued by leadership problems, and encouraging discouraged leaders.

Augustine's Thought on Involving in Ministry

In light of Augustine's example of involving disciples in the work of ministry, what did he believe or prescribe about this mentoring principle? Continuing to demonstrate the posture of a servant leader, the bishop of Hippo communicated in *Sermon* 49, "I am a worker

---

[160] *On Eighty-Three Varied Questions*, 71.

[161] *Letters* 191.1; 192.1; 194.1 (acolytes); 68; 73.1.1; 82.1.1; 222.3 (subdeacons); 71.1.1; 73.1.1; 82.4.30; 110.1; 164; 174; 10*.1; 19*.1; 23*.5 (deacons); 80.1; 194.1; 197.1; 198.1; 202A.1; 224.1; 6*.1; 19*.1; 25*.1 (presbyters); and 10*.1; 19*.1 (bishops).

[162] In *Letters* 82.1.1; 82.4.30, Augustine referred to the subdeacon Austerius and the deacon Cyprian as "my colleague" (*collegam meum*).

[163] *Letters* 40.3.3–4.7; 71.1.2.

like you and with you; according to the strength that God has given me, I work in this vineyard."[164]

Augustine also believed that a spiritual leader should be apprenticed through practical involvement in ministry. Convinced that a preacher must learn to interpret Scripture, Augustine not only modeled this through hundreds of sermons; but also, like Valerius, he deliberately involved Eraclius and perhaps others in preaching.[165] In *On the Instruction of Beginners*, Augustine shared with the clergy his principles for preparing believers for baptism together with a set of model lessons to be used with catechumens. After resourcing deacons like Deogratias with this work, the task of teaching new believers remained the work of deacons.[166]

Augustine was aware of his own strengths in ministry, and he knew which aspects of ministry most motivated him. We know that he was especially driven by studying, teaching, writing, and debating; but he was also aware of his weaknesses and disdain for ministries such as administration, traveling, and serving as a judge.[167] Like Valerius, Augustine humbly involved other clergy in areas that compensated for his weaknesses. Eraclius, his eventual successor in Hippo, was initially challenged to relieve him of the burdens of administration and serving as a judge, allowing Augustine more time to study and write. Surely Augustine was pleased that disciples like Alypius, Evodius, and Possidius were willing to travel overseas to appeal to church or secular leaders on behalf of the African church. While relieving Augustine of such undesired ministries, these disciples were increasingly involved in the work of ministry and developing as leaders in their own right.

While Augustine allowed men to serve in areas of ministry where he was weak, he also seemed motivated, like Ambrose and Valerius, to encourage spiritual leaders to pursue ministries that corresponded with their gifts and abilities.[168] Punic speakers like Lucillus, who

---

[164] *Sermon*, 49.2; also Mandouze, *L'aventure,* 139.

[165] *On Teaching Christianity*, prologue,1–9.

[166] *On the Instruction of Beginners*, 16–27; see Lienhard, "Ministry," *ATTA*, 569.

[167] Possidius, *Life of Augustine*, 19.6; *Letters* 33.5; 95.1; 122.1; 124.1; 213.5–6; 24*.1; also Bacchi, *Ordained Ministry*, 32, 39.

[168] *On the Duties of Ministers*, 1.215.

served as a deacon in Hippo, and Antoninus, the infamous bishop of Fussala, were set apart for their respective ministries largely because of their linguistic abilities.[169] Because of his background and training in law, Alypius seemed especially qualified to serve as judge in his ministry at Tagaste. Augustine's skills in communication and debate were put to use, particularly during the councils of Carthage in 403, 411, and 419. His legal mind must have proved useful during various trips on church business in Africa and during appeals made to the Roman court and church leadership between 419 and 421.

Finally, Augustine demonstrated the value of involving spiritual leaders in ministry at increasing levels of responsibility over time. We have noted the clergy who lived with Augustine in the garden monastery or clerical monastery at Hippo, who were later sent out to serve as bishops and clergy in the churches of North Africa. He involved many monks in the work of the monastery, even as he involved every rank of the clergy in the various ministries of the church. He probably increased the responsibilities of promising leaders before setting them apart as leaders in other churches. This was certainly the case with Eraclius—a presbyter and member of the clerical monastery who was entrusted with administration, serving as a judge, and preaching, before assuming the role of bishop upon Augustine's death.

This value of increasingly involving disciples in ministry was also evident in the African church councils. Though Augustine was the predominant figure in the councils, we have noted the increased role played by Alypius, Possidius, and Evodius after 403. At the 411 council of Carthage, four of the seven speakers defending the Catholic position included Augustine and the Hippo alumni of Alypius, Possidius, and Fortunatus.[170] Following the councils of Milevus and Carthage in 416, the small group of bishops that met to discuss further the Pelagian heresy included Augustine, Evodius, Possidius, and Alypius. All four were listed in the salutations of *Letters* 176 and 177, which explained to Pope Innocent the conclusions of the councils and meetings of 416.

---

[169] *Letters* 84; 209; 20*.

[170] See Othmer Perler, "Les Voyages de Saint Augustin," *Recherches Augustiniennes* 1 (Paris: Etudes Augustiniennes, 1958), 289–90.

Releasing to Ministry

A logical outcome of Augustine's involving men in ministry with increasing responsibility was to release them to be consecrated as bishops and leaders in other churches where they assumed responsibility and authority for that ministry. Having trained men in the garden monastery, clerical monastery, and the church at Hippo, Augustine was willing to deploy his disciples and friends to serve the needs of the church in Africa.[171] He was also committed to releasing leaders to ministry by participating in the ordination of bishops in Numidia. As noted, he played the definitive role in setting apart his own successor, Eraclius.

Through his actions and writings, what did Augustine believe and prescribe about releasing spiritual leaders to ministry? First, in breaking with the practice of Valerius and other fourth- and fifth-century bishops, he refused to ordain anyone by force. This was most evident in the case of Pinian as well as Augustine's first choice of bishop for Fussala.[172]

Second, Augustine valued ordaining men in a manner that honored both the universal and local church. As an active participant in the African church councils, he highly regarded their authority and worked to uphold the decisions of these councils as well as those of plenary councils. Because he was aware of the canons of the council of Nicea of 325 that forbade two bishops serving from in the same church, Augustine did not allow Eraclius to be ordained bishop of Hippo until after his death. While Possidius wrote that Valerius was unaware of these canons, Augustine essentially showed disapproval for his own ordination through the manner that he ordained Eraclius. Also, it seemed important to Augustine that the congregation be involved in the decision and give their approval for a new bishop.[173] Having observed the consequences of failing to do this in the churches of Milevus and Fussala, Augustine was

---

[171] Possidius, *Life of Augustine*, 11.2–3; 31.8.

[172] *Letters* 124; 126.

[173] Hefele records that canon 1 of the fourth council of Carthage indicated that the clergy and laity's consent ought to be sought before a bishop was consecrated; see Charles J. Hefele, *A History of the Councils of the Church: From the Original Documents, Vol. II* (Edinburgh: T&T Clark, 1896), 410–11.

careful to secure the blessing of the people of Hippo for his appointment of Eraclius.[174]

Third, despite the great needs in the African church for spiritual leadership, Augustine maintained high standards for holiness, sound doctrine, and competence in the clergy he ordained.[175] He was also committed to following the canons of the council of Carthage in 397, which imposed stringent standards upon all candidates for the clergy. For instance, they were to be prudent and gentle in their conduct, at least 25 years of age, and their entire household needed to be Catholic Christians. It was also imperative that they affirmed sound doctrine—especially regarding the Trinity, the Scriptures, and salvation.[176] Along with being a man of upright character and sound doctrine, the candidate for ordination needed to be competent in his abilities to perform the required tasks.[177]

Fourth, before ordaining a spiritual leader, Augustine valued personally knowing the candidate and his quality of life or at least having a credible reference to commend the candidate. Residing in the monastery allowed him to know the character of his men and determine who was suitable for ordination.[178] Men like Alypius, Severus, Profuturus, Possidius, Evodius, and Urabanus—bishops, who from all accounts served the African church in an exemplary manner—testified to Augustine's ability to discern leadership ability. Yet it would be incorrect to assume that Augustine was able to judge perfectly the character of even the most devoted monk. Setting apart leaders had its risks, as the accounts of Paul of Cataqua and Antoninus of Fussala illustrate. Augustine had known Antoninus since he had entered the monastery as a youth. Augustine had appointed him as a reader. Though Antoninus had been in some sort of trouble in the monastery, Augustine apparently relied heavily on the opinion of the provost Urbanus, who recommended Antoninus

---

[174] *Letter* 213.1–6; Possidius, *Life of Augustine*, 8; also Paul Zmire, "Recherches sur la Collégialité Épiscopale dans l'église d'Afrique," *Recherches Augustiniennes* 7 (1971): 14; and van der Meer, *Augustine the Bishop*, 271.

[175] *Letter* 167.18; 18*; also Doyle, *The Bishop as Disciplinarian*, 305.

[176] See Hefele, *History of the Councils*, 2.410–11; Doyle (*Bishop as Disciplinarian*, 181, 305) cites canons 11–19 of the 397 council of Carthage.

[177] *Letter* 26*.1–2.

[178] See Crespin, *Ministère*, 180.

for the vacancy in Fussala.[179] Despite his personal contact with Antoninus and despite Urbanus's recommendation, Antoninus's true character went undetected.

Although we may firmly assert that it was impossible for Augustine or anyone else to discern a potential leader's character, it seems that in the case of Antoninus, other factors distracted Augustine and impaired his judgment. As Fussala was dominated by the Donatists, Augustine wanted to install a Catholic bishop to engage in that doctrinal battle. Also, as noted, Fussala was largely Punic speaking, and Augustine desperately needed someone to serve there with those linguistic abilities, which few seemed to have had. So when his initial choice for bishop withdrew, Augustine must have been embarrassed by his inability to supply a bishop in the face of a mocking Donatist opposition. Also, as the primate of Numidia was already en route to ordain the new bishop in Fussala, Augustine probably felt great pressure to find a replacement.[180] The pressure and circumstances in Fussala caused him to make a hasty and poor decision that he later regretted.

Finally, Augustine, like Valerius, believed in allowing his released clergy to become their own type of minister. Possidius recorded that though Augustine did not accept property to be held in trust by the church, he did not forbid other clergy from doing so. Also, though Augustine cared little for constructing buildings for the church, he allowed other bishops the freedom to make their own decisions in such matters.[181] He encouraged other bishops to exercise their own gifts in the context of their ministry. Hence, he seemed content that Alypius's ministry in Tagaste would include traveling on behalf of the church and serving as an advocate for the church before secular authorities. Thus, as Augustine released spiritual leaders to ministry, he released them with authority and responsibility. As a continual mentor who maintained an influence, he did not use that influence to give heavy-handed direction to the ministries of other bishops.

---

[179] *Letter* 20*.2; also Henry Chadwick, 'New Letters of St. Augustine,' *Journal of Theological Studies* 34.2 (1983): 441.

[180] *Letter* 20*.3; also Chadwick, "New Letters of St. Augustine," *JTS* 34 (1983): 441.

[181] Possidius, *Life of Augustine*, 24.9, 13.

Resourcing

Having involved men in ministry and released them to their own ministries, Augustine continued to be available as a resource to spiritual leaders. Upon setting apart Eraclius as a bishop-elect, he assured his successor as well as the congregation:

> In any case in which he may think my advice necessary, I will not refuse it; far be it from me to withdraw this: nevertheless, let everything be brought to him which used to be brought to me. Let Eraclius himself, if in any case, perchance, he be at a loss as to what should be done, either consult me, or claim an assistant in me, whom he has known as a father.[182]

Augustine's availability extended to those spiritual leaders from Hippo and Numidia that he had personally released, as well as to other leaders from Africa and beyond who sought him out as a mentor.

As we have shown, Augustine's primary form of resourcing spiritual leaders was through his letters. He wrote 31 letters in reply to theological or exegetical questions from the clergy, 18 influencing leaders to maintain sound teaching, while 35 letters contained instruction and advice related to practical church matters. Hence, Augustine, like Paul, Cyprian, Pachomius, Basil, and Ambrose, valued letters as a significant means of continually discipling and resourcing clergy in the course of their ministries.

In chapter 4, we also showed that Augustine resourced clergy through books. In all he wrote 19 books to the clergy in Africa, Italy, Gaul, and Egypt while sending another 10 already completed works along with letters. Like his letters his books resourced the clergy in theology and exegesis, in apologetics toward maintaining sound teaching, and in practical church matters. The key recipient of his books was Aurelius, whom he also resourced with sermons.[183] Though Aurelius did not exhibit strengths as a preacher or theologian, he was not threatened by Augustine but welcomed his input. More than that, he used his position as the primate of Africa and

---

[182] *Letter* 213.6.
[183] *Letters* 16.*1; 23A*.3.

primary convener of the councils of the African church to provide Augustine with a platform to resource the church leaders in theology, exegesis, and sound teaching. Hence, Augustine was able to put his strengths as a thinker, writer, and teacher to the work of resourcing clergy like Aurelius and others.

We also noted that Augustine resourced his Hippo alumni by visiting them. At times he stopped through while traveling to or from a church council or to another city on church business. At other times the visit was for the express purpose of encouragement. During visits Augustine resourced his friends with spiritual encouragement, with practical help and problem solving related to church issues while likely engaging in spiritual or theological dialogue.

Finally, Augustine demonstrated humility in resourcing his own disciples at Hippo by encouraging them to visit and be resourced by other spiritual leaders. We know that Augustine encouraged Evodius and Possidius to visit Paulinus of Nola during their trips to Italy.[184] Before being consecrated as bishop of Tagaste in 394, Alypius visited Jerome in Bethlehem.[185] Augustine wrote to Jerome that he was sending Profuturus to Bethlehem not only to deliver a letter but also to "be exposed to and nourished with your sweet and profitable conversations."[186] Even in the midst of their disputes, Augustine wanted to send a disciple from Hippo to learn from Jerome.[187] After receiving Paul Orosius for a season of study and mentoring at Hippo and resourcing him with *Against the Priscillianists*, Augustine encouraged him to visit Jerome in Bethlehem. He wrote to Jerome, "I have taught him all that I could, and, as for the things in which I could not teach him, I have told him from whom he may learn them, and have exhorted him to go on to you."[188] By exposing his men to other spiritual leaders, Augustine humbly acknowledged his limitations as a teacher. Regarding himself as a servant to both

---

[184] *Letters* 80.1; 94–5.
[185] *Letter* 28.1.
[186] *Letter* 28.4.6.
[187] *Letter* 73.2.5; also Pellegrino, *True Priest*, 54.
[188] *Letter* 166.1.2; also *Letter* 169.4.13; Bardy, *Saint Augustin*, 295; Perler, *Les Voyages*, 329–30; and Hefele, *Histoire des Conciles*, 2.1.176.

the disciple and the disciple's inner teacher, he was not threatened by the contribution of other servants like Paulinus and Jerome.

Augustine's Legacy

Brown writes that with the Vandal invasion, "Augustine lived to see his life's work destroyed in Africa."[189] Indeed, the horrific destruction that characterized the fall of Roman Africa dealt a severe blow to the church movement as church buildings were burned, nuns and consecrated virgins were violated, and church leaders were displaced. Yet what was Augustine's life's work? Contrary to Brown's assertion, Augustine did leave a legacy to the African church in the period following his death, including some aspects that continue to have an impact on the present day.

First, according to Possidius, "his legacy to the church was a very numerous clergy."[190] In the previous chapter we listed the bishops and church leaders who left Hippo to serve the African church. Though five of the 10 leaders served only briefly because of moral failure or untimely death, Alypius, Possidius, Evodius, Severus, and Urbanus had a significant role in the church during Augustine's lifetime. Possidius was probably the only Hippo alumni to survive Augustine and continue in the ministry after 430, and it is significant to note the continuing presence of Catholic leaders in Africa amidst the Arian Vandal presence. In 484, when Catholic worship was suppressed in Africa, 500 clergy in Carthage alone were sent into exile.[191] Despite a hundred years of Vandal domination, a Catholic bishop could still be found leading the church at Hippo when the Byzantines arrived in 533. Finally, 220 Catholic bishops gathered for a church council in Carthage in 534.[192]

Though Augustine probably had a personal influence on many Catholic clergy who endured the Vandal period, his legacy was probably felt more in the transformation of the priestly office itself. As a bishop-monk who had monasticized the clergy in Hippo, he

---

[189] See Brown, *Augustine*, 429.
[190] Possidius, *Life of Augustine*, 31.8.
[191] This decision was largely reversed by 496; see François Decret, *Le Christianisme en Afrique du Nord Ancienne* (Paris: Seuil, 1996), 278.
[192] See van der Meer, *Augustine the Bishop*, 16; and Decret, *Le Christianisme*, 279.

certainly helped to solidify the prevailing value that priests should be celibate. Finally, his devotion to philosophy, exegesis, and theology inspired scholarship among future bishops and church leaders who were gifted in these areas.[193] As Ambrose and Simplicianus had shown Augustine that he could be a thinker, a Christian, and a church leader, Augustine surely passed along this value to future generations of church leaders far beyond Africa.

Second, Augustine left a legacy of monasteries that existed to serve the church. Possidius recorded that as Augustine's disciples founded monasteries, "they prepared brothers for the priesthood and then advanced them to other churches."[194] That is, they held to the Augustinian value that a monastery was an excellent training center for clergy. Though it was not necessary or recommended that every monk be ordained to the ministry, the monasteries nevertheless existed to serve the church.

As noted, Zumkeller claims that by the end of the fifth century, 38 monasteries existed in North Africa, most of which were begun by Augustine or his disciples or were at least influenced by him.[195] Both Quodvultdeus, Augustine's correspondent who probably became bishop of Carthage in 437, and Bishop Fulgentius of Ruspe (467–533), who adopted a monastic lifestyle after reading Augustine's writings, oversaw monasteries in their diocese. Yet during the Vandal oppression both men were expelled from Africa and effectively continued Augustine's legacy by establishing monastic communities in Italy and Sardinia.[196] Augustine's monastic influence continued to be felt 800 years after his death when Pope Innocent IV organized the monks of Tuscany (Italy) in 1244 into a monastic order patterned after his life and values.[197] Even to the present day,

---

[193] For a summary of such leaders in the period after his death, see O'Loughlin, "Fifth Century," *ATTA*, 362. For a summary of Augustine's long-term influence as a thinker, see Howie, *Educational Theory*, 277–317.

[194] Possidius, *Life of Augustine*, 11.3.

[195] Zumkeller, *Augustine's Ideal*, 84.

[196] Quodvultdeus set up a monastery near Naples while Fulgentius did the same in Sardinia; see Thomas Smith, "Fulgentius of Ruspe," *ATTA*, 373–74; and Michael P. McHugh, "Quodvultdeus," *ATTA*, 693–94.

[197] See Kenneth S. Latourette, *A History of Christianity Vol. I: Beginnings to 1500* (Peabody, MA: Prince, 1997), 426–27.

monasteries belonging to the Order of Saint Augustine can be found throughout the world.[198]

Finally, after investing much of his adult life writing works that in many cases resourced the clergy, Augustine left a lasting legacy through his books. Possidius recorded that during Augustine's lifetime,

> the church's teaching on saving faith, hope, and love thus became known through many and among many, not only in all parts of Africa but also in regions overseas. By means of published books, which were translated into Greek, all this teaching was able with God's help to make its way from one man and through him to many.[199]

While influencing the church of his day, Augustine continued to be read by church leaders and theologians in the century following his death, while his works impacted medieval thinkers like Thomas Aquinas (1224–1274) as well as the Protestant reformers Luther (1483–1540) and Calvin (1509–1564).[200] The curiosity of modern scholars continues to be aroused by Augustine's philosophical and theological works in particular, as the steady stream of scholarship testifies.

As Augustine invested much of his life writing, he helped his own legacy by undertaking a project toward the end of his life to index, recopy, and preserve his books in the library at Hippo.[201] Though Augustine left no will, Possidius wrote that "he always intended that the library of the church and all the books in it should be carefully preserved for posterity."[202] This was strategic in light of the imminent Vandal invasion, for history has proven that literature was often lost or destroyed during such conquests. His books served to strengthen the church in his day, and they continue to be read and analyzed in the present day.

While Augustine left a legacy of spiritual leaders, monasteries, and books, in what ways did he fail to have a lasting impact?

---

[198] For information on the OSA see www.osanet.org.

[199] Possidius, *Life of Augustine*, 11.5.

[200] See O'Loughlin, "Fifth Century," *ATTA*, 362.

[201] See Bardy, *Saint Augustin*, 450.

[202] Possidius, *Life of Augustine*, 31.6–8; Possidius noted that the library contained Augustine's works as well as those of other men.

First, though he involved presbyters in the work of preaching and resourced spiritual leaders with *On Teaching Christianity*, none of his disciples from Hippo seemed to have come close to being the preacher that he was. In fact, the sermons of Possidius and Eraclius reveal that both men were rather weak in the ministry of preaching.[203] It seems especially surprising that Augustine would set apart someone for his own church whose abilities were lacking in the area that was clearly Augustine's primary ministry as bishop.

Second, despite the fine literary contribution of men like Fulgentius, Prosper (c. 390–455), Eugippius (c. 455–c. 535), and Isidore (560–636) in the period after Augustine's death, as well as the modest efforts of Quodvultdeus and Possidius, none of Augustine's Hippo disciples took up a pen to defend the church against heresy or to resource it with theological or exegetical works.[204] The most likely candidate to succeed Augustine in this manner would have been Evodius, especially after Augustine had resourced him with several letters and a small library in Uzalis. Though he may have written one anti-Manichean work, Evodius failed to emerge as a writer.[205]

Despite these apparent problems with Augustine's legacy, the outcomes of Augustine's mentoring was still significant. In the generation after his death, Fulgentius could pick up his commentary on Psalm 36 and decide to become a monk-bishop.[206] Spiritual leaders in Africa and beyond continued to be inspired by *Confessions* and Possidius's *Life of Augustine*, as well as to contemplate the theological issues that Augustine had raised.[207] Monasteries that Augustine initiated or influenced would remain and even expand. Finally, ordained Catholic clergy would carry on in a priesthood that Augustine had forever influenced.

---

[203] See Brown, *Augustine*, 266; Henri-Irenee Marrou, *Saint Augustin et la Fin de la Culture Antique* (Paris: Boccard, 1948), 528; and van der Meer, *Augustine the Bishop*, 413.

[204] See Smith, "Fulgentius of Ruspe," *ATTA*, 373–74; McHugh, "Prosper of Aquitaine," *ATTA*, 685–86; O'Donnell, "Eugippius," *ATTA*, 338–39; O'Loughlin, "Isidore of Seville," *ATTA*, 457–58; and McHugh, "Quodvultdeus," *ATTA*, 693–94.

[205] *Letter* 159; 162; 164; 169; also Brown, *Augustine*, 270, 355; Fitzgerald ("Evodius of Uzalis," *ATTA*, 344) credits Evodius with the work *On the Faith, Against the Manichees*.

[206] See Smith, "Fulgentius of Ruspe," *ATTA*, 373.

[207] See O'Loughlin, "Fifth Century," *ATTA*, 362.

SHEPHERDING
SHEPHERDS TODAY

wenty-first-century Christian leaders ought to consider seriously Augustine's thoughts on mentoring in a trinitarian community of Christian friends. The peoples of the Western world are largely in a hurry to accomplish and pack more into their schedules. This race, aided by the speed of increasing technology, tends to squelch human relationships. The church, particularly evangelical Protestants, seems to be in a similar hurry; and discipleship ministries, though well programmed and efficient, are often entirely lacking Augustine's notion of community. Though his monasticism should not necessarily be imposed on the modern church, the church would do well to slow down and place more emphasis on quality relationships in which there is spiritual depth. Would it be too radical for mentors and disciples to eat an unrushed meal together and talk about their spiritual lives? Could two peers shut off their cell phones and pursue theological dialogue over coffee? What about pausing at some point in the day and praying with a fellow disciple?

A resounding theme of this book has been that a mentor must still be a disciple. Nothing is more attractive or inspiring to a student or disciple than to see his teacher continually learning. What is the ongoing plan for spiritual growth for modern pastors and spiritual leaders? Will these leaders accept a "brother at heart" as Augustine did Alypius, or will the busyness of church business push them into unnecessary isolation resulting in burnout or moral failure?

Augustine and the church fathers were deeply committed to sound doctrine based on the proper interpretation of the Scriptures. In America in particular, with the emphasis on marketing the church, we are in the midst of a Bibleless Christianity. Will we allow an ever-changing culture and the uncertain foundations of its values determine how we lead the church and disciple believers? What about a revival of biblical and theological study among pastors and the laity? Could we envision training new believers as Augustine encouraged Deogratias to do in *On the Instruction of Beginners*— with passion, joy, and theological soundness?

In the context of the "burden" of ministry, Augustine, like Valerius, was aware of his shortcomings but committed to putting capable leaders to work where he was weak. He deliberately involved men in ministry on an increasingly difficult level and happily released them to their own ministries. Will today's church leaders intentionally look at the leadership potential around them and search for able people to outshine them? Will they recognize potential in others and encourage them to step out in faith despite their hesitation? Will they happily entrust others with ministry responsibility or possessively retain it, believing they are the only ones able to carry it out?

As Augustine wrote mentoring letters and visited disciples, he deliberately stayed in contact with these friends. As encouragement was a key value in his mentoring approach, it was not without verbal communication. Putting a pen to paper is now rare, but spiritual leaders might well follow Augustine's example with e-mail, voice mail, or text messaging. Or they might invest time in an encouraging phone call or a personal visit. Again, resourcing and encouraging requires a sacrifice of time, which will surely take one away from other tasks and accomplishments. Yet, since the church is a body of people, this Augustinian value of friendship and community should take priority over all other work.

INDEX

A

acolytes   *132–33*
agapē   *220*
allegorical interpretation   *129*
Ambrose of Milan   *71–89, 103–9, 190*
  books by   *79–81*
  letters of   *76–78*
  mentoring ideas   *82–89*
amicitia   *219–20, 232*
Arianism   *62, 64, 72, 74–75, 80, 87, 98, 146, 189, 238, 243*
ascetic living   *222, 228, 234*
Athanasius   *42, 51, 53, 59, 61, 66, 69*
Augustine
  as bishop   *127–32*
  as judge   *131*
  as mentor   *2, 138, 144, 147–48, 151, 154–56, 179, 183, 184, 186, 191, 195–96, 204, 206, 208, 211–12*
  baptism of   *107–8, 136*
  books of   *185–95*
  conversion of   *1, 98–99, 101*
  death of   *180*
  end of life   *225*
  friendships of   *2–3, 100*
  humility of   *127, 222–24, 253*
  influence of   *2*
  legacy of   *157, 254–57*
  letters of   *3, 157–85*
  mentors of   *101–6, 109–13, 115–20, 187*
  ministry responsibilities   *119–23*
  mother's influence   *93–100*
  ordination of   *113–14, 126–28*
  overseeing the church   *129–30*
  preaching of   *128–29*
  travels   *207–11, 246–47*
authority, spiritual   *234–36*

B

Basil of Caesarea   *52–71*
  letters of   *58–63*
  mentoring strategies   *55–58*
bishop   *24–29, 34, 37, 39, 54–55, 65, 82, 91, 126–27, 130–31, 132–33, 148–49*
bishop, metropolitan   *26, 64, 70, 72, 132*

C

Cappadocian fathers   *53*
caritas   *219–21, 233*

261